Islamic Law & Wisdom – 2
SHARIAH (THE LAW)

Building on the foundation created in Level 7, this level will focus on the laws given by Allah SWT for Muslims to lead their lives in this world. This level covers Islamic law in detail, including examples of its implementation in societies, their history, and the wisdom behind it.

Ghamidi Center of Islamic Learning
www.ghamidi.org   AN INITIATIVE OF AL-MAWRID US.

Publisher: Ghamidi Center of Islamic Learning - Al-Mawrid US
ISBN: 978-1-966600-32-9

Address: 3620 N Josey Ln, Suite 230 Carrollton, TX 75007
Website: www.ghamidicenter.com
Email: info@ghamidi.org

Chapter 1

Introduction to the Course

Introduction

- Our beloved Prophet Muhammad (peace be upon him) emphasized that seeking religious knowledge is obligatory for every Muslim, regardless of gender.
- Following the assertion of our Prophet, the purpose of this course is to provide its students with the necessary knowledge and offer fresh insight into Islam, its beliefs, its practices, and the wisdom behind them.
- In this two-part course, students will learn about Islam, its core beliefs and teachings, and appreciate the true essence of the directives given by Allah SWT: the purification of oneself.
- Every lecture or discussion will be a sincere effort to understand how these beliefs and directives play a significant role in self-development and personal growth.
- Students will be asked to evaluate the subject matter rationally. The first part of the course will focus on articles of faith and their relationship to our social lives, with a brief introduction to rituals.
- The second part (this course) will focus on the laws given by Allah SWT for Muslims to lead their lives in this world.

Objectives:

- The main objective of the second part of this course is to discover the rationale for Islamic rituals and laws, understand their wisdom, and learn how to practice them in our daily lives with that wisdom in mind. The effort is to recognize that it is OK to rationalize God's commandments and the reasons for the success criteria in God's eyes. At the end of this course, the students will be able to:
    - Understand why worship rituals and certain laws (also known as *Shariah*) are precisely prescribed by God and not left to human beings
    - Identify matters in which God has provided His guidance and matters in which He has allowed individuals or collective wisdom to decide according to the norms of the society
    - Explore every worship ritual and law in detail and understand the principles on which they are based
    - Rationally evaluate the wisdom behind the laws given by the Almighty
    - Understand how the objective of Islam, purification, is at the center of every commandment given by God
    - Learn how ethics and morality are related to the rituals and laws

Structure of the course

- The course is structured into two main modules:
  - The first module covers faith (beliefs) and morality, which have not changed since the time of Adam.
  - The second module deals with religious laws and the rationales behind them, which vary across time and place.

Faith and Morality
Part 1

- A deeper look into **Faith & Morality** in Islam.
- Rationally evaluate the reasoning behind the Articles of Faith and moral commandments.
- Understand how purification is at the center of every commandment.
- How to achieve success in the Hereafter.

Islamic Law and Wisdom
Part 2

- A deeper look into the Laws given in Islam.
- Academically and rationally evaluate the laws.
- Significance of the directives of Islam, their objectives, and Western interpretation.
- Understand how laws achieve the target of purification and success in the Hereafter.

Why are you a Muslim?

Why revisit Islamic rituals and laws?

- The QURAN declares:

ثُمَّ جَعَلْنَاكَ عَلَى شَرِيعَةٍ مِّنَ الْأَمْرِ فَاتَّبِعْهَا وَ لَا تَتَّبِعْ اَهْوَآءَ الَّذِينَ لَا يَعْلَمُوْنَ

After this, O Prophet, We have made you adhere to a clear *Shariah* of Our Religion. So, follow it, and do not follow the desires of men who know not. (Quran 45:18)

This journey is <u>unavoidable</u> to fully understand the Shariah prescribed by God

- Islam is the most misunderstood religion on Earth, not only by non-Muslims but also by Muslims themselves. And most of these misunderstandings fall within the realm of Shariah (Islamic Law).
- Some Muslim scholars argue that Islamic law has nothing to do with the human intellect.
- There is a common misunderstanding that Islam provides a complete code of life or a complete system.
- Shariah and Fiqh are often conflated, and it is necessary to distinguish between them.
- The sources of Islamic law are the Quran (sacred text) and Sunnah (sacred acts), but their interpretation has always remained a human effort.
- It is the arguments and reasoning grounded in the original sacred sources that should form the basis for accepting or rejecting an interpretation.

Why should you learn about Islamic Shariah?

- Before telling anyone about Islam, it is your responsibility to learn about Islam and its laws for your own sake. You should comprehend what you believe and practice.
- To know exactly what Allah wants from you when you are acting on rituals.
- To counter Islamophobia around us at the personal level, especially related to Islamic Shariah.
- To be aware of the innovations introduced into Islam. Anyone can say "this is Islam".
- To be the ambassador of Islam with confidence wherever you live and work.
- It will help you connect with your heritage and feel part of the global Muslim community.
- To teach true religion to your children.

If you had to explain Islamic laws to a non-Muslim friend in 2 minutes, what would you tell them?

Few things to know

- Muslims always say "Peace and blessings of Allah be upon him," with the name of Prophet Muhammad. In the slides, it is omitted for editing purposes, but we should say that we mention his name.
- Allah (The Most-High) is the only True God. In this course, God and Allah are used interchangeably and mean the same.
- Islam is the message for all Muslims, regardless of their gender. In this course, you may find references in the Quran and the Hadith that use the masculine gender only. As in many other languages, in Arabic, when both genders are addressed, masculine pronouns are used.

Islamic Resources

Join Ask Ghamidi
A community-driven discussion portal to ask, answer, share, and learn
https://www.ghamidi.org/app/

Meezan Lectures – English
By Dr. Shehzad Saleem
https://www.youtube.com/playlist?list=PL3yXG2ufxd6USiyYQVHtzpXAnMvXC4-C9

Annotated linguistic resource on Quran with Arabic grammar, syntax, and morphology for each word
https://corpus.quran.com/

Islam – A Comprehensive Introduction
Meezan translation by Dr. Shehzad Saleem
https://archive.org/details/mizan-english-ghamidi/Islam%20A%20comprehensive%20introduction%20-%20Javaid%20Ahmed%20Ghamidi%20%28English%20translation%20of%20Mizan%29/page/n5/mode/1up

Quran Translation and Commentary by Javed Ahmed Ghamidi
https://www.javedahmedghamidi.org/#!/quran-home

Hadith Resources
https://ahadith.co.uk/
https://sunnah.com/

Important Notes

- You are required to attend all classes unless you have a valid reason to skip.
- Please send a note (or ask your parents) to your teacher on Google Classroom if you will skip a session.
- Attendance will be taken at the beginning of every class. Arriving in class 5 minutes after the start will be considered tardy.
- Three (3) tardies will be counted as one absence.
- Attendance will be counted toward your final assessment.
- Every student will be assessed via:
    - Participation in the class
    - Multiple Quizzes
    - Assignments
    - Semester Exam
    - End-of-Year Exam

Chapter 2

True Religion (Revision)

This chapter is a short summary of what we studied in Level 7: the introduction to Islam, its essence, content, main objective, and what God demands of us.

Islam and its essence

Definition of Islam

The word Islam comes from the root *Salama*. It means submitting yourself to God, which in essence means submitting your free will to God with humility and servility.

The essence of Islam

- In a word, the essence of religion in Quranic terms is "*ibadah*" (worship) of God.
- It is "worship" that the Creator of this world desires from His "servants."
- God said in the Quran:

And I created jinn and mankind <u>only</u> to 'worship' Me. (51:56)

- The word 'worship' is used in Islam in two aspects:
  - It is specifically used for rituals we perform as part of religion, such as prayers and fasting (Ibadaat).
  - In a broader sense, it describes an attitude that is the opposite of arrogance and rebellious behavior. An attitude that shows humility and servility in front of God as His creation and acts according to that.
- In this verse, the word *Ibadah* is used in its broader sense and does not simply mean rituals like prayers, etc.
- This expands a believer's scope of worship.

Examples of Worship

- Studying to earn pure living.
- Spending time with family because Allah said so.
- Changing opinion after knowing the truth.
- Helping less fortunate people.
- Playing sports to remain healthy.
- Earning Halal to take care of the family.
- Gaining the knowledge of your religion.

The worship rituals

- Muslims generally think of Islam as a collection of rituals and practices.
- What we just understood about the concept of *Ibadah* changes how we should view worship rituals.
- Worship rituals are just symbolic expressions of the actual "worship," which is the inner sense of humility and servility before God in every matter of life.
- The inner sense of humility and servility should result in the following:
  - Humbleness with no sign of arrogance, pride, or vanity
  - God consciousness with no element of disobedience
  - Trust in God with no ungratefulness
  - Development of goodness and no sign of oppression against anyone
- The symbolic expressions of the above behavior must be reflected in our worship rituals.
- For example, prayers or salah embody humility, and fasting embodies obedience.

- When God reminded us in the Quran, He means the total submission that He requires from us:

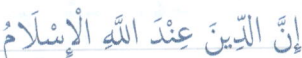

The only true religion in God's sight is Islam (3:19)

.... and he who chooses a religion other than Islam, it will not be accepted by him, and in the hereafter, he will surely be among the losers. (3:85)

History and Sources of Islam

History of Islam

- When talking to non-Muslims or even Muslims, you may get a sense as if Islam, as a religion, was started by Prophet Muhammad in the 6th century in the Arabian Peninsula. That is completely against the picture that the Quran paints for us about Islam and its origin.

شَرَعَ لَكُم مِنَ الدِّينِ مَا وَصَّى بِهِ نُوحًا وَالَّذِي أَوْحَيْنَا إِلَيْكَ وَمَا وَصَّيْنَا بِهِ إِبْرَاهِيمَ وَمُوسَى وَعِيسَى أَنْ أَقِيمُوا الدِّينَ وَلاَ تَتَفَرَّقُوا فِيهِ

He has prescribed for you (O Muhammad) the same religion which He prescribed for Noah, and which We have now revealed to you and which We enjoined on Abraham, Moses, and Jesus, with the assertion: "Adhere to this religion [in your lives] and do not create any divisions in it. (42:13)

- In light of this information from God, one can easily conclude that Judaism and Christianity are offshoots of Islam. These nations formed their own religion after rejecting the Messenger sent to them. For example, Jews rejected Jesus as their messenger and formed Judaism; Prophet Musa taught them the same Islam as Prophet Muhammad.

Sources of Islam

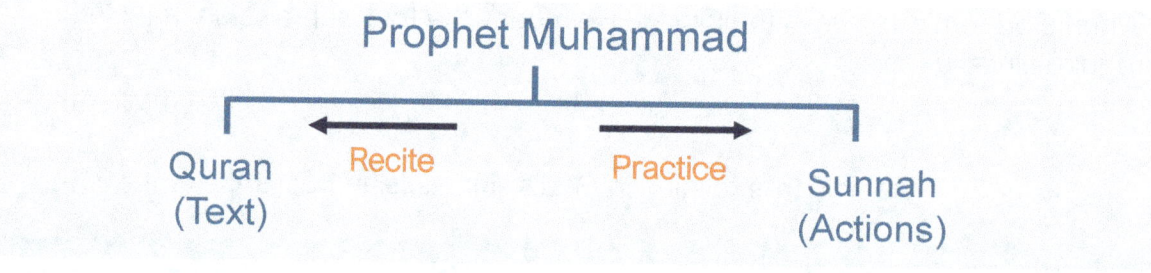

Quran	Sunnah
<ul><li>The last book of Islam revealed to Prophet Muhammad by God.</li><li>Preserved in its original language and continuously transmitted first orally and then in written form through generations without any gaps.</li><li>Verbatim words of God.</li><li>Source for beliefs, morality guidelines, and some laws.</li></ul>	<ul><li>The tradition and practices of Prophet Ibrahim.</li><li>Prophet Muhammad instituted it after reviving and reforming it, adding certain practices, and now he is its source for us.</li><li>Transmitted through perpetual practice through generations without any gaps.</li><li>Source for rituals and most of the laws.</li></ul>

Hadith and its relationship with the sources

- The historical record of Prophetic sayings, actions, and approvals reported by a few people.
- It further explains and demonstrates what is already present in the primary sources of Islam: the Quran and Sunnah.
- Naturally, companions began writing down their interactions with the Prophet Muhammad for their own benefit.
- They naturally transmitted that knowledge through generations, sometimes verbally and sometimes in writing (in their personal notes).
- Practically turned into a body of knowledge after a couple of hundred years of the prophet's death.
- The great scholars of Islam spent decades researching and sifting through hundreds of thousands of reports, grading them into different categories so we can be a little more certain whether a narration was actually said by the Prophet.
- It's a treasure because his divinely guided wisdom and understanding of religion are preserved in the hadith.
- Through hadith, we learn about his life, personality, daily activities, exemplary practice of Islam, character, morals, and wise statements.

An Example Chain

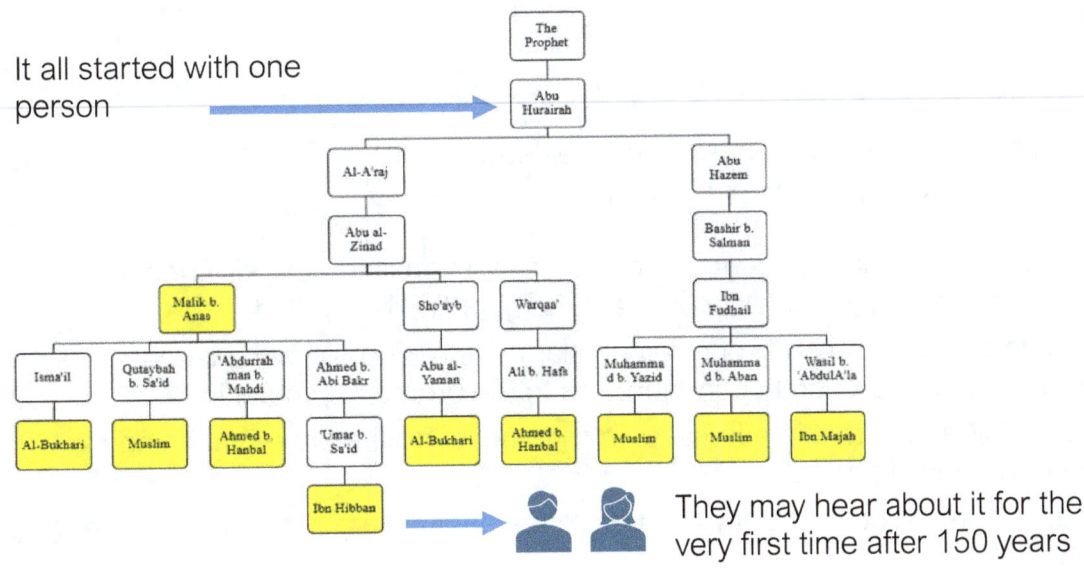

Difference between Sunnah and Hadith

- Hadith is often misunderstood to be a synonym for the word Sunnah.
- In classical Islamic scholarship, the distinction is well understood and used accordingly.
- The science of hadith decides its relative authenticity. It can be relatively more authentic, a little less authentic, not reach the prophet, or even fabricated.
- Sunnah gives us the religion through perpetual practice of the generations after Prophet Muhammad, while Hadith provides us with the record of the exemplary way our Prophet practiced that religion.

Sunnah (the actual religion)	What does hadith provide? *Exemplary way*
Prayers	How did Prophet pray?
Fasting	What did he eat in the morning, and what were his daily activities during the fast?
Sacrifice animal	What animal he sacrificed and how did he do it?
Perform Hajj	How many times did he do it, and how did he perform the steps already mentioned in Sunnah?

Why can't hadith be an independent source?

O Messenger, deliver what has been revealed to you from your Lord; if you do not, you have not conveyed His message. (5:67)

- Prophet Muhammad was entrusted with the responsibility of delivering and explaining the religion to all people around him, and he fulfilled it.
- Anything in the main body of religion (Islam) cannot be given to just one person and left to his/her discretion to communicate to the broader community.
- Prophet Muhammad did not make arrangements for the preservation and dissemination of hadith.
- People were practicing Islam way before the hadith was recorded, scrutinized, and compiled.
- Hadith can only clarify or dispel misunderstandings within the main body of Islam, as already received through the Quran and the Sunnah.

The content of Islam

- When understanding any religion, it is important to distinguish what is within its scope and what is not.
- It is important to note that Islam is also sometimes used to imply the outer aspect of religion. A person who does certain acts is called a Muslim.
- However, the entire content of Islam has a scope, and it is comprised of two main content types:

Al-Hikmah

- The metaphysical and ethical basis of the worship prescribed by religion – matters of faith (beliefs) and morality.
- Remains the same for all prophets and their nations.
- It reminds us of the wisdom behind the law.

Al-Kitab (Law)

- Contains the laws (Shariah) suitable for the time, including rituals and limits.
- Changes due to evolution in human civilizations and societies.
- Current laws are based on the laws given to Prophet Ibrahim, and then sanctioned by Prophet Muhammad, which have been shaped into the Sunnah since then.

Al-Hikmah	Al-Kitab (Law)
Worship Allah SWT alone	Daily prayers and its procedure
Don't consume other people's wealth unjustly	Interest/Riba is outlawed
Spend on the poor and in the path of Allah	Pay your Zakah at the rate of X%
Do not go near obscenity or adultery, it is an act of Satan	100 lashes for someone who commits adultery
Do not follow Satan and consider him your open enemy	Perform Hajj and its practices including stoning Satan

Why is understanding the wisdom behind any given law so important?

Al-Kitaab and Al-Hikmah

- Whenever Al-Kitaab and Al-Kitaab appeared together in the Quran, they encompassed the entire content of the religion.
- Some of the verses are presented below:

هُوَ الَّذِي بَعَثَ فِي الْأُمِّيِّينَ رَسُولًا مِنْهُمْ يَتْلُو عَلَيْهِمْ آيَاتِهِ وَيُزَكِّيهِمْ وَيُعَلِّمُهُمُ الْكِتَابَ وَالْحِكْمَةَ

It is He who has sent among the unlettered a Messenger from amongst themselves who recites to them His verses and purifies them, and [for this purpose] he instructs them in Shariah (the law) and in Hikmah (Faith and Morality). (62:2)

وَأَنْزَلَ اللَّهُ عَلَيْكَ الْكِتَابَ وَالْحِكْمَةَ وَعَلَّمَكَ مَا لَمْ تَكُنْ تَعْلَمُ ۚ وَكَانَ فَضْلُ اللَّهِ عَلَيْكَ عَظِيمًا

And God has revealed to you al-Kitab and al-Hikmah and in this manner taught you what you did not know before, and great is God's favor upon you. (4:113)

وَاذْكُرُوا نِعْمَتَ اللَّهِ عَلَيْكُمْ وَمَا أَنْزَلَ عَلَيْكُمْ مِنَ الْكِتَابِ وَالْحِكْمَةِ يَعِظُكُمْ بِهِ ۚ وَاتَّقُوا اللَّهَ وَاعْلَمُوا أَنَّ اللَّهَ بِكُلِّ شَيْءٍ عَلِيمٌ

And remember the favors He has bestowed upon you, and the al-Kitab and al-Hikmah which He has revealed to you, of which He instructs you, and keep fearing Allah, and know that He has knowledge of all things.(2:231)

- The word Al-Kitaab is used in many places in the Quran to refer to the law.
- In Surah Bani Israel (17), verses 22-39, God listed all matters of belief (in the one true God) and morality, and, in the end, called them the matters of *Al-Hikmah*.

ذَٰلِكَ مِمَّا أَوْحَىٰ إِلَيْكَ رَبُّكَ مِنَ الْحِكْمَةِ

..... these are from the counsels of wisdom which your Lord has revealed to you. (17:39)

> Over time, people tend to overlook aspects of *Al-Hikmah* (wisdom) and pay more attention to *Al-Kitab* (the law). This reduces religion to mere rules, and the essence of those laws is lost.

The Moral Guidance (Al-Hikmah)

10 Commandments of Islam

Do not associate partners with God

- Worship God alone
- Be good with parents and relatives
- Be moderate in spending
- Be chaste and modest
- Do not kill a human life
- Do not devour the orphan's wealth
- Keep your promises
- Be honest in your business
- Do not follow speculations about others
- Avoid arrogance, pride, and vanity

Do not associate partners with God

The Law (Al-Kitaab)

- Islam provides guidance on various aspects of life. The laws are given for the following:

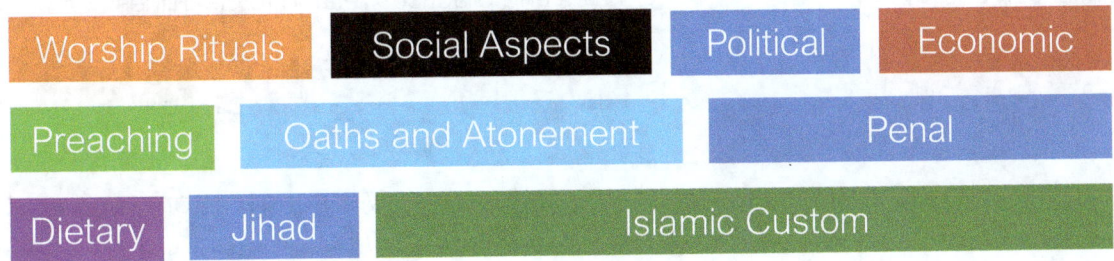

| Worship Rituals | Social Aspects | Political | Economic |

| Preaching | Oaths and Atonement | Penal |

| Dietary | Jihad | Islamic Custom |

Objective of Islam

- The content of Islam is very closely related to its objective.
- Every instruction given in the Quran and Sunnah is for one objective: *Tazkiyah* (**purification** of the self).
- It demands that our beliefs and deeds be developed in the right direction that helps us attain **purification**.
- Our objective should be entering paradise, and according to the Quran, paradise is prepared for 'purified souls'.
- There is no instruction, teaching, practice, or law within Islam that is not targeted to achieve the objective of purification. If an instruction does not meet this criterion, it cannot be part of Islam.
- The picture below depicts that relationship.

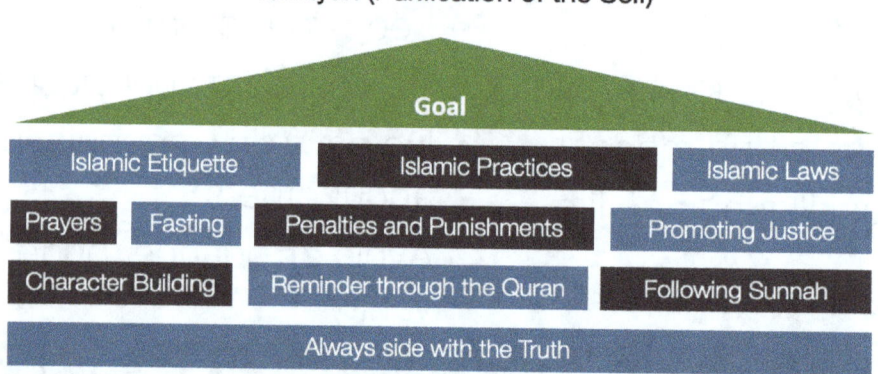

Target	Instructions
Purification of Soul	Beliefs and worship rituals
Purification of Food	Dietary laws and nature's guidance
Purification of Morals	Guidance on morality and laws
Purification of Body	Laws and practices related to cleanliness

It is He who has sent among the unlettered a Messenger from amongst themselves who recites to them His verses and purifies them, and [for this purpose] he instructs them in Shariah (the law) and in Hikmah (Faith and Morality). (62:2)

Compare the following religions with Islam in the following concepts:

1. God or A Supreme Being
2. Main rituals
3. Laws

A – Christianity
B – Judaism
C - Hinduism

Chapter 3

Sunnah

This chapter provides the foundation for the term Sunnah and what is considered Sunnah in Islam.

Sunnah of Prophet Muhammad

The Sunnah refers to the tradition of Prophet Ibrahim's religion (practices), which Prophet Muhammad instituted for his followers as the religion after **reviving** and **reforming** it and after making certain **additions** to it.

- Literally, it means a path that is followed. It is an independent source of religion.
- The Quran directed Prophet Muhammad to follow the practices of Ibrahim.
- It is transmitted through the consensus of the Prophet Muhammad's companions and practiced perpetually, from generation to generation.
- Most Islamic rituals and laws have originated from Sunnah.
- Historically, it predates the Quran, dating back to Prophet Ibrahim (or earlier). However, for us, it is now the Sunnah of Prophet Muhammad.
- It is distinct from Hadith, which sometimes transmits various records of Sunnah.

ثُمَّ اَوْحَيْنَآ اِلَيْكَ اَنِ اتَّبِعْ مِلَّةَ اِبْرٰهِيْمَ حَنِيْفًا ۚ وَ مَا كَانَ مِنَ الْمُشْرِكِيْنَ

Then We revealed to you to follow the ways of Abraham, who was true in faith and was not among the polytheists. (16:123)

قُلْ اِنَّنِيْ هَدٰىنِيْ رَبِّيْ اِلٰى صِرَاطٍ مُّسْتَقِيْمٍ ۚ دِيْنًا قِيَمًا مِّلَّةَ اِبْرٰهِيْمَ حَنِيْفًا ۚ وَ مَا كَانَ مِنَ الْمُشْرِكِيْنَ

Tell them, O Muhammad, my Lord has guided me to a straight path, a correct religion which is the way of Ibrahim, who was focused on the truth and was not among the polytheists. (6:161)

- Prophet Muhammad has been reported to have said:

تَرَكْتُ فِيْكُمْ أَمْرَيْنِ لَنْ تَضِلُّوا مَا تَمَسَّكْتُمْ بِهِمَا كِتَابَ اللَّهِ وَسُنَّةَ نَبِيِّهِ

I have left two matters with you. If you hold on to them, you will never go astray. They are the Book of Allah and the Sunnah of His Prophet. (Muwatta, Imam Malik, Book of Decree)

Some practices go back to the time of Adam.

The scope of Sunnah
- Sunnah contains the practical aspects of the religion, both for individual and collective (societal) purposes.
- It is the body of rituals and laws given to Prophet Ibrahim as the leader of the believing nations to come; all prophets who came after him followed it.

- Being the last prophet of Islam, Prophet Muhammad sanctioned (or added) all those practical aspects of religion (including the relevant details) that will remain with us until the day of judgment.
- It is now the authority of Prophet Muhammad who can declare something as part of religion.
- It contains practices that are independent of the Quran – the Quran may or may not talk about them; for example, circumcising male children is not mentioned in the Quran, but is an authentic Sunnah of all prophets.

The principles of determining the Sunnah

- It is important to understand that not everything that Prophet Muhammad did was Sunnah. There are some principles to be used when determining the Sunnah of the Prophet that is part of Islamic Shariah.
- Also, as with other parts of Shariah, some Sunnah are mandatory, and some are optional.

I am also a human being. When I direct you about something which relates to your religion, take it from me, and when I express my own opinion [about something which is outside this sphere], then my status in this regard is nothing more than that of a human being … I had suggested to you about something (referring to an incident about pollination of palm-trees). Do not hold me accountable for such things based on opinions and suggestions. However, if I say something on behalf of God, take it because I will never lie about God … You very well know about your worldly affairs. (Sahih Muslim 6127, 6126, 6128)

1. Religious in nature

- Something can be called Sunnah only when it is religious by nature. The Prophet was appointed to deliver religion (Deen) and nothing else.
- Fighting with swords and arrows, traveling on a camel, building a mosque with palm trees, eating dates, wearing white clothes, etc. CANNOT be religion.

2. Deals with practical affairs

- It entirely relates to practical matters of life. Because the word Sunnah can only be applied to practical matters.
- Beliefs, ideology, faith, history, and similar things do not fall in the sphere of Sunnah.
- Praying, brushing teeth, cleaning the mouth, and trimming mustaches are all practical aspects of religion.

3. Must be initiated or sanctioned by the Prophet

- Sunnah is the practice initiated by the Prophet or at least sanctioned it if it existed in the Sunnah of Prophet Ibrahim.
- The practical aspects of religion that are related to certain laws and initiated by the Quran cannot be regarded as Sunnah.
- Implementing punishments for some crimes and fighting a war with disbelievers are all initiated by the Quran.
- The language and context in the Quran determine whether it is initiating something or merely referring to something already in the Sunnah.

4. Must be original and unique

- Acting on an existing Sunnah voluntarily does not make it a new Sunnah.
- E.g., Prayers are part of the Sunnah, but performing extra prayers with Isha prayers does not make it a new Sunnah. Or, e.g., Hajj is also Sunnah, and Prophet Muhammad did only one Hajj. In this case, performing one Hajj only cannot be a Sunnah.

5. Some aspects of human nature are part of religion

- There are many things stated within Islam that are merely a description of human nature. These things cannot be called Sunnah unless the Prophet makes them Sunnah.
- E.g., avoiding lions and tigers for eating cannot be termed as-Sunnah. Or taking a bath without any religious reason cannot be called Sunnah.
- However, all acts related to keeping yourself clean, like brushing teeth, making Wudu, etc., are more natural, but the Prophet made them part of the Sunnah.

6. The Prophet must have emphasized them

- The Prophet always emphasized the Sunnah when acting on it and made sure it was known to everyone.
- Some practices are told by the Prophet only when people ask for them. These cannot be termed as Sunnah also. E.g., some Azkar during Salah that the Prophet taught to different people when they asked for it.
- The simple rule is that if it is part of religion, it must be known to everyone around the Prophet because he has been sent to deliver the religion.

7. Must be transmitted through perpetuity

- All acts of Sunnah were known to Muslims at that time, and they passed them on to the next generation with due care.
- Prophet was given the responsibility to deliver the religion. He cannot give it to one or two people separately and then leave it at their discretion to pass it on.

شَرَعَ لَكُمْ مِّنَ الدِّيْنِ مَا وَصّٰى بِهٖ نُوْحًا وَّ الَّذِىٓ اَوْحَيْنَآ اِلَيْكَ وَ مَا وَصَّيْنَا بِهٖٓ اِبْرٰهِيْمَ وَ مُوْسٰى وَ عِيْسٰىٓ اَنْ اَقِيْمُوا الدِّيْنَ وَ لَا تَتَفَرَّقُوْا فِيْهِ ۚ

He has enjoined on you the same religion which He enjoined on Noah, and which We have now revealed to you, which We enjoined on Abraham, Moses, and Jesus, with the assertion: "Adhere to this religion [in your lives] and do not create any divisions in it." (42:13)

List of Sunan (the plural of Sunnah)

- This is the comprehensive list of Sunan categories. Each category has multiple Sunnah, and details of those Sunnah are also considered Sunnah.

Worship Rituals

- The Prayer and its details.
- Zakah and Sadaqah of Eid al-Fitr and its details.
- Fasting and Eitikaf and its details.
- Hajj and Umrah and their details.
- Animal Sacrifice and its details.
- Takbirs during the days of Tashriq (11-13 Dhul Hijjah).

Social Sphere

- Marriage and Divorce and their relevant details.
- Abstention from sexual intercourse during the menstrual period and the period immediately after childbirth.

Dietary Sphere

- Prohibition of pork, blood, the meat of dead animals, and animals slaughtered in the name of someone other than God.
- Slaughtering in the prescribed manner of Tadhkiyah by pronouncing God's name and draining all the blood.

Customs and Etiquette

- Remembering Allah's name before eating or drinking.
- Using the right hand for eating and drinking.
- Greeting one another and responding with Salam.
- Saying Alhamdulillah after sneezing and responding to it by saying Yarhamukallah.
- Keeping mustaches trimmed.
- Removing pubic hair.
- Removing hair under the armpits.
- Clipping fingernails.
- Circumcising the male children.
- Cleaning the nose, mouth, and teeth.
- Cleaning the body after excretion and urination.
- Bathing after the menstrual and the puerperal periods.
- Taking a bath after sexual intercourse.
- Bathing the dead before burial.
- Enshrouding a dead body and preparing it for burial.
- Burying the dead.
- Eid al-Fitr.
- Eid al-Adha.

The difference between Sunnah and Hadith

- Hadith is often misunderstood to be a synonym for the word Sunnah.
- In classical Islamic scholarship, the difference is well understood and used as such.
- Hadith does not offer certain knowledge and hence cannot add anything to the Sunnah practices of the religion.
- The science of hadith decides its relative authenticity. It can be relatively more authentic, a little less authentic, not reaching to the prophet, or even fabricated – Sunnah has no chain .
- Sunnah gives us the practices of the religion, and Hadith provides us with the record of the exemplary way our Prophet practiced those practices.

Hadith only describes an event or record of a Sunnah act that is already transmitted through Sunnah independently.

Sunnah - *Religion*	What does hadith provide? *Exemplary way*
Prayers	How did Prophet pray?
Fasting	What did he eat in the morning and what were his daily activities during the fast?
Sacrificing animal	What animal he sacrificed and how did he do it?
Performing Hajj	How many times he did it and how did he perform the steps already mentioned in Sunnah?

How do we determine Sunnah today?

- Sunnah is determined today by identifying the practices of Prophet Muhammad that have been transmitted through the perpetual consensus of the Muslim Ummah (Ijma') and their continuous, practical adherence across generations.
- Today, the scholars of Islam determine if something is a Sunnah or not by applying the following method:
  - The practice must be adopted by most Muslims (a large majority) worldwide today. If it is adopted by a particular group of Muslims, especially in a specific region, it is not considered an authentic Sunnah.
  - Muslims must have been practicing it the same way a few hundred years ago, also throughout the world. These things are usually documented in the books of scholars and writers of those times, especially the books of Fiqh.
  - The early Muslims (companions and their children) must have been practicing it after the death of Prophet Muhammad. Similarly, these things are usually documented in the books of scholars and writers of those times, especially the books of Fiqh.
  - There are reports that Prophet Muhammad and his companions practiced it during the time when Prophet Muhammad was alive.
- Any practice that qualifies all these checks is considered a Sunnah in Islam.
- There are many practices people claim are Sunnah but are not, for one reason or another.
- For example:
  - Eating date for Iftaar – Prophet never emphasized it as a Sunnah
  - Celebrating the birthday of Prophet Muhammad – a practice that began a few hundred years after the Prophet's death.

Applying the principles of Sunnah

Practice	Sunnah? (Yes/No)
Praying 2 Rakah of Eid al-Fitr in a big ground	
Folding up your pants to uncover ankles before praying	
Breaking your fast with dates	
Praying 12 voluntary rakah during the day with your 5 daily prayers	
Slaughtering an animal by taking the name of God	
Covering your mouth while sneezing	
Wearing long clothes like people wear in Arab countries	
Cleaning mouth and teeth	
Eating certain food that Prophet Muhammad loved to eat	
Celebrating the birthday of Prophet Muhammad	
Taking the name of God when start eating	
Wearing a cap before praying	

- Some Ahadith also describe sunnah practices; why are they not the source of this knowledge?
- What should be the way to distinguish between must-have and good-to-have Sunnah?

Chapter 4

Al-Kitaab

This chapter discusses the concept of Al-Kitaab, a term used in the Quran to refer to the laws of Shariah.

Sunnah of Prophet Muhammad

The Sunnah refers to the tradition of Prophet Ibrahim's religion (practices), which Prophet Muhammad instituted for his followers as the religion after **reviving** and **reforming** it and after making certain **additions** to it.

- Literally, it means a path that is followed. It is an independent source of religion.
- The Quran directed Prophet Muhammad to follow the practices of Ibrahim.
- It is transmitted through the consensus of the Prophet Muhammad's companions and practiced perpetually, from generation to generation.
- Most Islamic rituals and laws have originated from Sunnah.
- Historically, it predates the Quran, dating back to Prophet Ibrahim (or earlier). However, for us, it is now the Sunnah of Prophet Muhammad.
- It is distinct from Hadith, which sometimes transmits various records of Sunnah.

ثُمَّ اَوْحَيْنَا اِلَيْكَ اَنِ اتَّبِعْ مِلَّةَ اِبْرٰهِيْمَ حَنِيْفًا ۗ وَ مَا كَانَ مِنَ الْمُشْرِكِيْنَ

Then We revealed to you to follow the ways of Abraham, who was true in faith and was not among the polytheists. (16:123)

قُلْ اِنَّنِيْ هَدٰنِيْ رَبِّيْ اِلٰى صِرَاطٍ مُّسْتَقِيْمٍ ۚ دِيْنًا قِيَمًا مِّلَّةَ اِبْرٰهِيْمَ حَنِيْفًا ۚ وَ مَا كَانَ مِنَ الْمُشْرِكِيْنَ

Tell them, O Muhammad, my Lord has guided me to a straight path, a correct religion which is the way of Ibrahim, who was focused on the truth and was not among the polytheists. (6:161)

- Prophet Muhammad has been reported to have said:

تَرَكْتُ فِيْكُمْ أَمْرَيْنِ لَنْ تَضِلُّوْا مَا تَمَسَّكْتُمْ بِهِمَا كِتَابَ اللهِ وَسُنَّةَ نَبِيِّهِ

I have left two matters with you. If you hold on to them, you will never go astray. They are the Book of Allah and the Sunnah of His Prophet. (Muwatta, Imam Malik, Book of Decree)

Some practices go back to the time of Adam.

The scope of Sunnah

- Sunnah contains the practical aspects of the religion, both for individual and collective (societal) purposes.
- It is the body of rituals and laws given to Prophet Ibrahim as the leader of the believing nations to come; all prophets who came after him followed it.

Shariah or Al-Kitab

Shariah, or Shariah Law, is the Islamic legal system derived from the two main religious sources of Islam: the Quran and the Sunnah.

- It is a body of moral and religious principles derived from divine sources as opposed to human legislation.
- In the Quran, the term Al-Kitab is used for Shariah – the general meaning of Al-Kitab is the book, but the Quran uses it as a term (as compared to Al-Hikmah) to describe the divine law.
- Shariah covers laws related to worship, personal affairs, and societal affairs.
- There is a misconception that Shariah only relates to criminal law, but that is just one aspect of it.
- All moral instructions and prohibitions in Islamic Shariah are based on the concepts of good and evil inherent in human nature.

ثُمَّ جَعَلْنَاكَ عَلَى شَرِيعَةٍ مِّنَ الْأَمْرِ فَاتَّبِعْهَا وَ لَا تَتَّبِعْ اَهْوَآءَ الَّذِيْنَ لَا يَعْلَمُوْنَ

Then We set you on a clear *Shariah* regarding religion. So, follow it, and do not follow the desires of men who know not. (45:18)

لِكُلٍّ جَعَلْنَا مِنْكُمْ شِرْعَةً وَّ مِنْهَاجًا

For each of you, We have ordained a Shariah and assigned a path. (5:48)

وَ اَنْزَلَ اللهُ عَلَيْكَ الْكِتٰبَ وَ الْحِكْمَةَ وَ عَلَّمَكَ مَا لَمْ تَكُنْ تَعْلَمُ ۖ وَ كَانَ فَضْلُ اللهِ عَلَيْكَ عَظِيْمًا

And God has revealed to you al-Kitab and al-Hikmah, hence taught you what you did not know before, and great is God's favor upon you. (4:113)

What is Shariah for?

- Every believer has an unwritten covenant with their Lord.
- God gives Shariah to regulate the relationship, or covenant, between God and the believer.
- Shariah guides a believer in various capacities and roles that they manage in this life (for example, as a servant of God, husband/wife, merchant, factory owner, leader of a nation, Prime Minister or President, etc.).

- The laws given in Shariah aim to purify that relationship/covenant. That's why the rules of Shariah apply only to Muslims in society.
- Even criminal laws are given as a chastisement for breaking the covenant and polluting that relationship, which must remain pure at all times.
- For example, the law of inheritance is given so that believers do not commit injustice to their relatives. God gave them guidance on how to distribute the inheritance. It is not befitting for a believer, then, not to distribute their inheritance according to the law given by God, if they firmly believe that their God is All-Wise and must have given them the best guidance for distributing inheritance.

In the West, non-Muslims are afraid of introducing Shariah-based personal laws for the Muslims living in this part of the world. What is the reason for this fear?

The scope and limits of Shariah

- It is a common misunderstanding that Islam provides a complete system in every domain of life (like financial, political, social, judicial, etc.).
- Contrary to that, only the fundamental guiding principles related to the laws in Shariah are given without any details – For example, it is not correct to say that Islam provides a "financial system".
- We can say Islam provides the principal guidance related to moral behavior that Muslims should manifest when they develop their financial system or deal in economic matters. That financial or monetary system can be anything, but the principal guidance should be followed when establishing it.
- The details of implementation are left to the human faculty of jurisprudence, so that different societies can apply the guiding principles of Shariah to different situations in life, according to time and place.
- Similarly, for example, Islam commands Muslims living in a society to form a state or government through mutual consultation. This principle can be applied in tribal communities as well as in modern democracies, though the implementation details differ.
- Also, Shariah only covers a few critical circles of life where human beings, if left alone, can err and take extreme positions if not guided by God, as can be seen in some societies.
- For example, Shariah provides no guidance on how to develop a country's educational system. Only moral guidance will guide it.

The Temperament of Shariah

- The temperament of the Shariah is that if a directive cannot be followed in its original form or becomes too tough to follow, then lesser forms should be adopted to serve as its reminder. An advantage is that once circumstances return to normal, one becomes inclined to follow the directive in its original form.

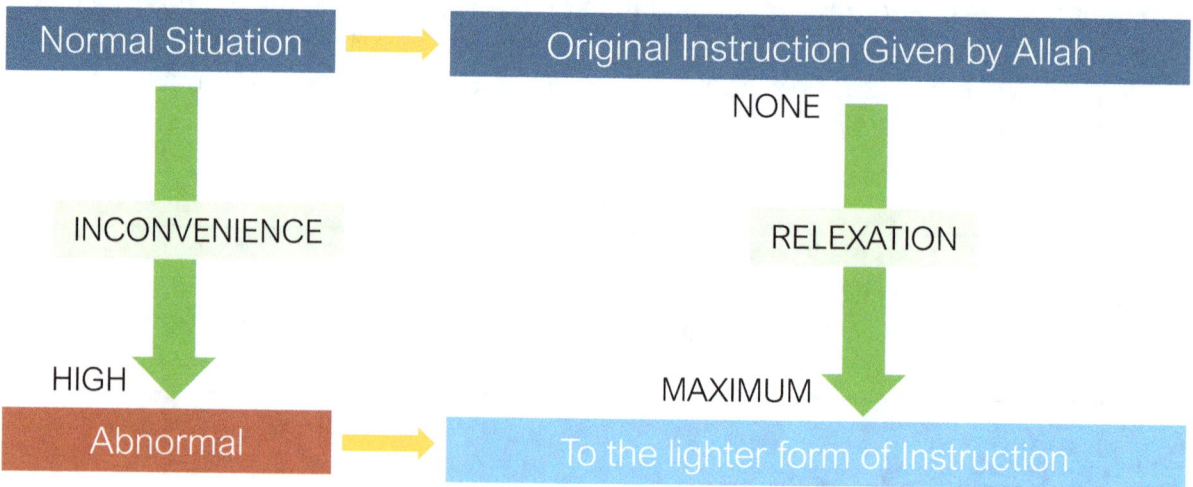

- Allah wants to maintain the instruction even in its symbolic form. For example, when performing dry Tayammum, there is no apparent cleanliness one can achieve, but it's more symbolic, bringing a person into a state of mind in which he or she is about to stand before God.

- When a person should benefit from this relaxation is entirely a matter of ijtihad, because only that person is fully aware of the situation and what they can afford at that time. A scholar can only guide in principle what should be done during abnormal times, but cannot determine on behalf of that person when to use relaxation and how much.

For example:

- When a person is sick or water is unavailable, perform Tayammum (dry ablution).
- When a person cannot pray standing, they may pray sitting, walking, or lying down.
- When traveling, wiping on socks is enough, and there is no need to wash your feet.
- When one cannot go to the mosque to join the congregation for a valid reason, one may assemble at home; otherwise, pray alone.
- If you are in a traveling-like situation, reduce and combine Zuhr and Asr, and Maghrib and Isha.
- If you cannot fast for any genuine reason during Ramadan, skip it and make it up later, after Ramadan.

Other Terms: Fiqh and Ijtihad

Fiqh

- It is a term used to describe the application of Shariah to real-life situations where details of Shariah are missing.
- It is generally a human understanding of the Shariah guided by the principles already given.
- There is some Fiqh in the Quran, and Prophet Muhammad also provided guidance on this during his lifetime.
- It is narrow in scope and applies to specific issues that depend on time, place, and circumstances.
- It can be changed when new information is available.
- Muslim jurists issue rulings on specific situations or matters called fatwas.

Ijtihad

- It is an extension of Fiqh and applies to human efforts to understand and decide on matters not addressed in the Quran and Sunnah, or, in other words, issues on which the Quran and Sunnah are silent.
- It does not apply to matters which are explicitly stated in the Quran and Sunnah.
- If a matter is mentioned in the Quran and Sunnah, then deliberation on them is the right approach, not ijtihad.
- It is deduced from the relevant guiding principles already given in Shariah.
- Ijtihad is usually performed in new matters where there is no precedent—for example, organ donation.

Examples

Shariah	Fiqh	Ijtihad
God asks us to pray, and the basic method of praying is given through Sunnah.	Some details of praying that were left out (not mandatory). For example, should we raise our hands before going to the bowing position?	How to pray while flying in a plane, and the time zone keeps changing?
Asking for interest is prohibited on loans.	Can someone factor in the currency devaluation when asking for the loaned money back?	Is there an interest involved when someone buys a house on a mortgage, or how to purchase a house?
Generally, a dead Muslim should be bathed, clothed, and buried.	Are there differences between bathing men and women?	Organ donation

Shariah	Fiqh	Ijtihad
Start and end your Ramadan when the new moon is sighted (whether on the 29th or 30th day).	How many people should witness the new moon before the start and the end of Ramadan can be announced?	Can a lunar calendar created with the help of accurate scientific data be used to start and end Ramadan?
Fasting is prescribed in Ramadan from dawn to dusk every day.	What is the exact time when one should start and stop fasting?	How should people fast in Norway where sun does not set or rise for months?

Laws given to previous nations

- While preserving the spirit behind the laws, the Shariah was always slightly different among the Prophets and nations due to the evolution and changes occurring in human civilizations and societies.
- However, the laws related to morality usually remained the same, with few minor differences.
- Before Prophet Muhammad, Shariah was given to the Children of Israel through Torah, which was given to Musa.
- All Prophets who came to the Children of Israel followed the Torah as their book of Shariah.
- On the other hand, the Gospel is full of wisdom and discusses the essence of the law given in the Torah.
- The Quran has replaced all previous Shariah of God for anyone who has accepted Islam as their religion till the day of judgment.

إِنَّا أَنْزَلْنَا التَّوْرٰىةَ فِيْهَا هُدًى وَّ نُوْرٌ ۚ يَحْكُمُ بِهَا النَّبِيُّوْنَ الَّذِيْنَ أَسْلَمُوْا لِلَّذِيْنَ هَادُوْا وَ الرَّبَّانِيُّوْنَ وَ الْأَحْبَارُ بِمَا اسْتُحْفِظُوْا مِنْ كِتٰبِ اللّٰهِ وَ كَانُوْا عَلَيْهِ شُهَدَآءَ

We have revealed this Torah, which contains both guidance and light. Through it, the obedient prophets of God, the rabbis and the jurists would deliver verdicts for these Jews because they had been made custodians of this Book of God and witnesses to it. (5:44)

- Identify 2 or 3 examples of this modern world where Ijtihad is used

- Can anyone do Ijtihad, or is it limited to those with special skills and knowledge? Why? And in what matter do I have to do my own ijtihad?

Chapter 5

Shariah of Worship Rituals

Prayers – Salah

This chapter discusses the first and foremost ritual of worship prescribed in Shariah: Prayers/Salah.

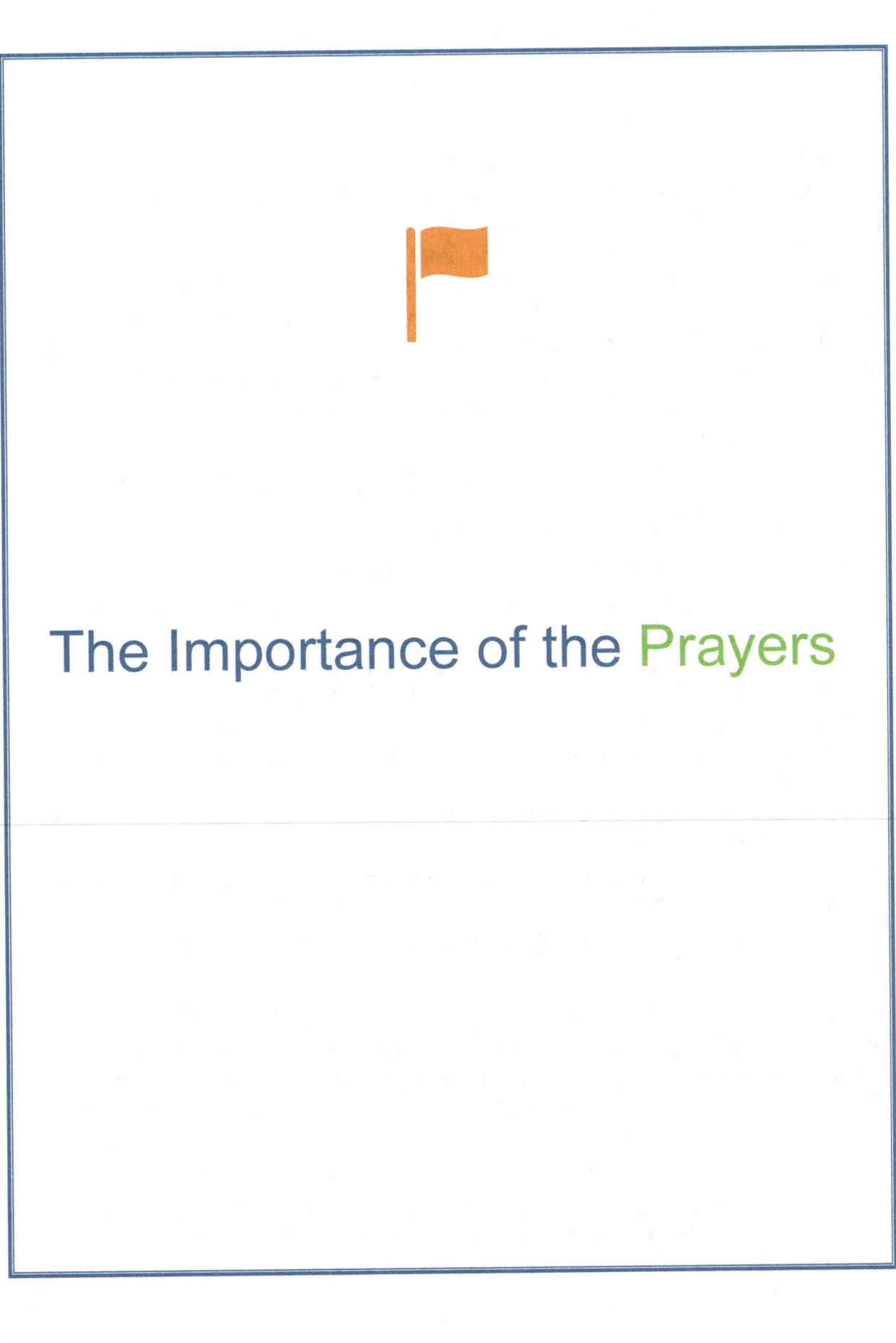

The Importance of the Prayers

History of the Prayers & its Importance

History of the prayers

- The history of the prayers is as old as the religion itself.
- Its remnants can be witnessed in hymns of Hindus, chants of the Zoroastrians, the invocations of the Christians, and Jews.
- The Quran has informed us that all the prophets of God have directed their followers to pray. It occupies a central position in the Abrahamic tradition.
- There are numerous narratives from the time of Prophet Muhammad that suggest that Jews and Christians of that time used to pray.
- Many verses in the Bible suggest that Jesus, Moses, and other prophets of the Children of Israel prayed at specific times, as Muslims do today.
- The form remained the same, but recitations changed.
- When the Quran directed people to pray, it was not unknown worship for them.

Prayers in the Bible (A few examples)

- Abram bowed down in prostration, and God spoke to him. (Genesis, 17:3)
- In the morning, O Lord, you will hear my voice. I will wait for you in your presence after the prayer. (Psalm 5:3)
- Then Jesus went with his disciples to a place called Gethsemane, and he said to them, "Sit here while I go over there and pray." (Matthew, 26:36)
- "And he went a little further and fell on his face, and prayed, saying, O my Father, if it is possible, let this cup pass from me; nevertheless not as I will, but as You will." (Matthew 26:39)
- Very early in the morning, while it was still dark, Jesus got up, left the house, and went to a solitary place where he used to pray. (Mark, 1:35)
- "But Peter put them all forth, knelt down, and prayed; turning him to the body said, Tabitha, arise". (Acts 9:40)
- He knelt with all of them and prayed when he said this. (Acts 20:36)

وَ كَانَ يَأْمُرُ آهْلَهُ بِالصَّلوةِ وَ الزَّكوةِ	رَبِّ اجْعَلْنِى مُقِيمَ الصَّلوةِ وَ مِنْ ذُرِّيَّتِى	رَبَّنَا لِيُقِيمُوا الصَّلوةَ
And he (Ismail) used to instruct his people to pray. (19:55)	(Ibrahim said) O Lord! Make me and my progeny diligent in the prayer. (14:40)	(Ibrahim said) Lord! So that they show diligence in the prayer. (14:37)

قَالُوا يٰشُعَيْبُ اَصَلوتُكَ تَأْمُرُكَ اَنْ نَّتْرُكَ مَا يَعْبُدُ اٰبَآؤُنَآ

They said, O Shoaib, does your prayer teach you that we leave the deities of our forefathers? (11:87)

Why should we pray?

Objective of the prayers

اِنِّیْ اَنَا رَبُّکَ فَاخْلَعْ نَعْلَیْکَ ۖ اِنَّکَ بِالْوَادِ الْمُقَدَّسِ طُوًی ۖ وَ اَنَا اخْتَرْتُکَ فَاسْتَمِعْ لِمَا یُوْحیٰ اِنَّنِیْ اَنَا اللّٰهُ لَاۤ اِلٰهَ اِلَّاۤ اَنَا فَاعْبُدْنِیْ ۙ وَ اَقِمِ الصَّلٰوةَ لِذِکْرِیْ

I am your Lord. Take off your shoes, for you are now in the sacred valley of Tuwa. And [be informed] that I have chosen you for prophethood. Therefore, listen to what shall be revealed.   I am God. Indeed, there is no god but Me. So, worship Me, and for My remembrance, pray with vigilance. (20:12-14)

یٰۤاَیُّهَاالَّذِیْنَ اٰمَنُوا اذْکُرُوا اللّٰهَ ذِکْرًا کَثِیْرًا ۙ وَّ سَبِّحُوْهُ بُکْرَةً وَّ اَصِیْلًا

Believers! Celebrate the praises of Allah in abundance and glorify Him morning and evening. (33:41-42)

- Believers are asked in the Quran to remember their Lord at all times.
- The best way to remember the Lord is through prayer.
- Five daily prayers are given to keep the remembrance of God alive throughout the day.
- When Prophet Musa was given prophethood, he was told to establish prayer as a means of remembering God.

1 The Foremost Directive

- It is the foremost directive of Islam.
- If monotheism is the core of beliefs, prayer is the core of deeds.
- It is the necessary outcome of understanding God, arising from the emotions of love and gratitude.
- It is the first deed mentioned in the Quran, right after belief in the unseen.
- It is considered the deed necessary for attaining purification and, hence, essential for success in the Hereafter.

اِنَّ الَّذِیْنَ اٰمَنُوْا وَ عَمِلُوا الصّٰلِحٰتِ وَ اَقَامُوا الصَّلٰوةَ وَ اٰتَوُا الزَّکٰوةَ لَهُمْ اَجْرُهُمْ عِنْدَ رَبِّهِمْ ۚ وَ لَا خَوْفٌ عَلَیْهِمْ وَ لَا هُمْ یَحْزَنُوْنَ

Indeed, those who believe and do righteous deeds and are diligent in their prayers and pay their charity, for them is a great reward from their Lord; they will have no fear of the future and no regret of the past. (2:277)

قَدْ اَفْلَحَ مَنْ تَزَکّٰی ۙ وَ ذَکَرَ اسْمَ رَبِّهٖ فَصَلّٰی

In fact, he succeeded who purified himself, remembered God, and offered prayers. (87:14-15)

2 A requisite for Muslim citizenship (a distinguishing factor)

- In a Muslim society, prayer is one of the minimum requirements for a person to be considered a Muslim (belief, prayer, and pay Zakah).
- The prayers in an Islamic society are so fundamental that, at the time when Prophet Muhammad was asked by Allah to punish the disbelievers, he was told that if they accept Prophet Muhammad as the messenger, establish Salah, and pay their Zakah, then they can avoid this punishment.
- We also see in our daily life (office or school) that for us to distinguish between a Muslim and a non-Muslim is usually the Salah, when we see that Muslims go for their prayers or Salah on a regular basis.
- The Quran subtly alluded to that which would be the case in the Hereafter, too. (68:42-43)

فَاِنْ تَابُوْا وَ اَقَامُوا الصَّلٰوةَ وَ اٰتَوُا الزَّكٰوةَ فَاِخْوَانُكُمْ فِى الدِّيْنِ

So, if they repent, diligently pray, and pay the Zakah, they shall become your brothers in religion. (9:11)

Note: This was the minimum condition set for the disbelievers to be spared from the punishment of death given to them for rejecting God's messenger. That shows that, in the sight of God, prayer is a symbol of Islam.

بَيْنَ الرَّجُلِ وَ بَيْنَ الشِّرْكِ وَالكُفْرِ تَرْكُ الصَّلَاةِ

Between a man and idolatry and disbelief is abandoning the prayer. (Sahih Muslim #247)

خَمْسُ صَلَوَاتٍ افْتَرَضَهُنَّ اللَّهُ تَعَالَى مَنْ أَحْسَنَ وُضُوءَهُنَّ وَصَلَّاهُنَّ لِوَقْتِهِنَّ وَأَتَمَّ رُكُوعَهُنَّ وَخُشُوعَهُنَّ كَانَ لَهُ عَلَى اللَّهِ عَهْدٌ أَنْ يَغْفِرَ لَهُ وَمَنْ لَمْ يَفْعَلْ فَلَيْسَ لَهُ عَلَى اللَّهِ عَهْدٌ إِنْ شَاءَ غَفَرَ لَهُ وَإِنْ شَاءَ عَذَّبَه

These are five prayers that the Almighty has made obligatory on people: a person who did ablutions in a befitting manner, offered the prayer on time, and prostrated both his inner and outer self before he has promised the Almighty forgiveness. And a person who does not do these things is not promised anything. If He wants, He will forgive him; if He wants, He will punish him. (Abu Dawood #425)

3   Means of strong adherence to Islam

- The prayer is a means to remain steadfast in Islam.
- The Quran says a devil is deputed on a person who becomes indifferent to God's remembrance.
- Prayers continue to ward off Satan and protect a person's mind and heart from his offensive.
- For this reason, we are asked to pray in any condition (standing, sitting, walking, driving, etc.).
- Prayers act like a preacher, protecting us when desires and emotions are strong enough to distract us from the right path.

وَ مَنْ يَّعْشُ عَنْ ذِكْرِ الرَّحْمٰنِ نُقَيِّضْ لَهٗ شَيْطٰنًا فَهُوَ لَهٗ قَرِيْنٌ

Whoever withdraws himself from the remembrance of the Most Gracious, We appoint for him a Satan, who becomes an intimate companion to him. (43:36)

وَ اَقِمِ الصَّلٰوةَ ۖ اِنَّ الصَّلٰوةَ تَنْهٰى عَنِ الْفَحْشَآءِ وَ الْمُنْكَرِ

And be steadfast in the prayer because it deters (a person) from lewdness and evil acts. (29:45)

4   An eraser of sins

- When a person stands in prayer, he renews his commitment to God to refrain from disobeying Him.
- Feeling ashamed of his wrongdoings in front of God makes him repent and cleans him from sins (that are committed against God).

وَ اَقِمِ الصَّلٰوةَ طَرَفَيِ النَّهَارِ وَ زُلَفًا مِّنَ الَّيْلِ ۖ اِنَّ الْحَسَنٰتِ يُذْهِبْنَ السَّيِّاٰتِ ۖ ذٰلِكَ ذِكْرٰى لِلذّٰكِرِيْنَ

And be diligent in your prayers at both ends of the day and in a portion of the night. No doubt, good deeds make amends for sins. This is a reminder for those who benefit from reminders. (11:114)

Tell me if there is a stream flowing near your door in which a person bathes five times a day, then will he still have a stain of dirt on him?" The people replied: "In this case, no speck of dirt would remain on him." The Prophet remarked: "This is an example of the five prayers; through them, the Almighty, in a similar manner, wipes out sins."
(Sahih Al-Bukhari 528)

5 Means of Countering Hardship

- The Quran's recipe for countering life's hardships is to seek God's help through prayer and patience.
- God advised the prophet to stick to prayers to persevere through the persecution of the disbelievers.
- From the Seerah of the Prophet Muhammad, it is known that whenever he would encounter a difficult situation, he would stand to pray.
- In the major battles of Badr and Ahzab, Prophet Muhammad resorted to prayers to seek God's help.

يَٰٓأَيُّهَا الَّذِينَ ءَامَنُوا اسْتَعِينُوا بِالصَّبْرِ وَ الصَّلَوٰةِ ۚ إِنَّ اللَّهَ مَعَ الصَّٰبِرِينَ

O Believers, seek God's assistance through perseverance and prayers; Allah is with those who patiently persevere. (2:153)

6 Symbol of True Dawah

- According to the Quran, the true reformers (who bring goodness into other people's lives) are the ones who hold fast to the divine book, and they are diligent in their prayers.
- All the movements and undertakings that aim at the revival of Muslims and their reformation must have prayers at the core of their struggle (for themselves) and invitation (for others).

وَ الَّذِينَ يُمَسِّكُونَ بِالْكِتَٰبِ وَ أَقَامُوا الصَّلَوٰةَ ۚ إِنَّا لَا نُضِيعُ أَجْرَ الْمُصْلِحِينَ

And those who hold the Book of God tightly and who are diligent in prayer (are the ones who reform), We shall not deny these reformers their reward. (7:170)

7 Means of Perseverance on the Truth

- It is only in the companionship of the Almighty that one can persevere on the path of truth, and prayer nurtures that companionship.
- God has commanded Prophet Muhammad to seek assistance, especially through midnight prayers (*Tahajjud*).
- Tahajjud is the time when one's heart and mind are fresh and receptive to the deeper understanding of matters at hand.

يَا أَيُّهَا الْمُزَّمِّلُ قُمِ اللَّيْلَ إِلَّا قَلِيلًا ۝ نِصْفَهُ أَوِ انْقُصْ مِنْهُ قَلِيلًا ۝ أَوْ زِدْ عَلَيْهِ وَ رَتِّلِ الْقُرْآنَ تَرْتِيلًا ۝ إِنَّا سَنُلْقِي عَلَيْكَ قَوْلًا ثَقِيلًا ۝ إِنَّ نَاشِئَةَ اللَّيْلِ هِيَ أَشَدُّ وَطْأً وَّ أَقْوَمُ قِيلًا ۝ إِنَّ لَكَ فِي النَّهَارِ سَبْحًا طَوِيلًا ۝ وَ اذْكُرِ اسْمَ رَبِّكَ وَ تَبَتَّلْ إِلَيْهِ تَبْتِيلًا ۝

O, you wrapped in a shawl! Stand [in prayer] by night, but not all night. Half the night, or even less or a little more, and [in this prayer of yours] recite the Quran in a slow, measured tone. Because soon We shall lay on you the burden of a heavy word. Indeed, standing up at night is very suitable for the mind's peace and heart's resolve and for the correctness of the speech. Because during the daytime, you will be hard-pressed [with this task; so, pray at this time] and remember the name of your Lord and [in this loneliness of the night] devote yourself entirely to Him. (73:1-8)

Every night, the Almighty descends to our nearest sky. When one-third of the night remains, He says: 'Who is offering supplications that I may accept them? Who is asking that I may give him? Who is calling for forgiveness that I may forgive him?' (Sahih Al-Bukhari # 1145)

8 Nature of every object of the Universe

- If we look closely, we can notice that everything in this universe is submitting to God's will and bowing down to His commands.
- The sun, the moon, the stars, the mountains, the clouds, the trees, and the animals are all following the divine law (their nature) upon which they have been created.
- The Quran tells us that these animate and inanimate creations of God praise Him and glorify Him in their way, which we cannot comprehend.
- When a human being stands in prayer, he brings himself in harmony with the rest of the creation in answering the call for prayers, prostration, and glorification.

تُسَبِّحُ لَهُ السَّمَاوَاتُ السَّبْعُ وَ الْأَرْضُ وَ مَنْ فِيهِنَّ ۚ وَ إِنْ مِنْ شَيْءٍ إِلَّا يُسَبِّحُ بِحَمْدِهِ وَ لَكِنْ لَّا تَفْقَهُونَ تَسْبِيحَهُمْ

The seven heavens, the earth, and all whoever dwells in them exalt Him. And there is not one thing that does not exalt Him as we praise and thank Him. Yet you cannot understand their exaltation. Benevolent is He and Forgiving. (17:44)

أَلَمْ تَرَ أَنَّ اللهَ يُسَبِّحُ لَهُ مَنْ فِي السَّمَاوَاتِ وَ الْأَرْضِ وَ الطَّيْرُ صَافَّاتٍ ۖ كُلٌّ قَدْ عَلِمَ صَلَاتَهُ وَ تَسْبِيحَهُ

Do you not see how God is exalted by those in the heavens, those on earth, and the birds as they wing their way [across the sky]? Each knows his prayer and exaltation of the Almighty, and God knows all they do. (24:41)

- The message of the messengers has been called 'the life' in the Quran.
- The inner calm, peace, and faith in harmony with the rest of the creation of the world can only be secured through the remembrance of God.
- The only way one can keep his soul 'alive' is through the remembrance of God.
- Prayers bring proper comprehension of God and a sense of nearness to Him, which keeps the soul of a believer alive.
- The Quran made a subtle reference to this by placing "the prayer" parallel to "life" and "sacrifice" parallel to "death."

يَآأَيُّهَا الَّذِينَ أَمَنُوا اسْتَجِيبُوا لِلَّهِ وَ لِلرَّسُولِ إِذَا دَعَاكُمْ لِمَا يُحْيِيكُمْ

Believers! Respond to Allah and His Messenger when He calls you to that which will give you life. (8:24)

قُلْ اِنَّ صَلَاتِي وَ نُسُكِي وَ مَحْيَايَ وَ مَمَاتِي لِلّهِ رَبِّ الْعَلَمِينَ

Say My prayer and my sacrifice and my life and my death are all for God, Lord of this Universe. (6:162)

Rise, O Bilal! And soothe us through prayer! (Abu Dawood #4986)
The coolness of my eyes has been placed in the prayer. (An-Nisai #3391)

Summary

- After Eeman, Allah expects that this will be our first deed to prove.
- In Islamic societies, it is/was used as a distinction for being a Muslim.
- It helps a person remain steadfast in Islam and the straight path.
- It erases sins done against Allah.
- It helps to go through hardships and difficulties.
- It is a symbol that the caller to Islam is true in his commitment.
- It helps a person to persevere in the struggle on the path of Truth.
- Every creation on Earth prays one way or the other.
- It keeps our faith a true living faith.

Quran's Warning on not praying

يَوْمَ يُكْشَفُ عَنْ سَاقٍ وَّ يُدْعَوْنَ اِلَى السُّجُوْدِ فَلَا يَسْتَطِيْعُوْنَ

خَاشِعَةً اَبْصَارُهُمْ تَرْهَقُهُمْ ذِلَّةٌ ۖ وَ قَدْ كَانُوْا يُدْعَوْنَ اِلَى السُّجُوْدِ وَ هُمْ سٰلِمُوْنَ

On that day, there shall be a severe affliction, and they shall be called upon to prostrate before God, but they shall not be able to (their backs will become hard). Their looks were cast down, abasement shall overtake them, and they were called upon to prostrate (call to prayer) while they were safe and healthy (in their worldly life). (68:42-43)

Now that you know the importance of prayers and also that prayers were present in every nation. Investigate how Jews, Christians, Baha'is, Hindus, and Buddhists pray today.

Do you feel a need to pray? And how does it help you in your daily life?

Shariah of the Prayers

Shariah of the Prayers/Salah

Prayer Timings and Units (Rakah)

- Muslims are asked to pray five times a day: Fajr (Dawn), Zuhr (Right after midday), Asr (late afternoon), Maghrib (right after sunset), Isha (night).

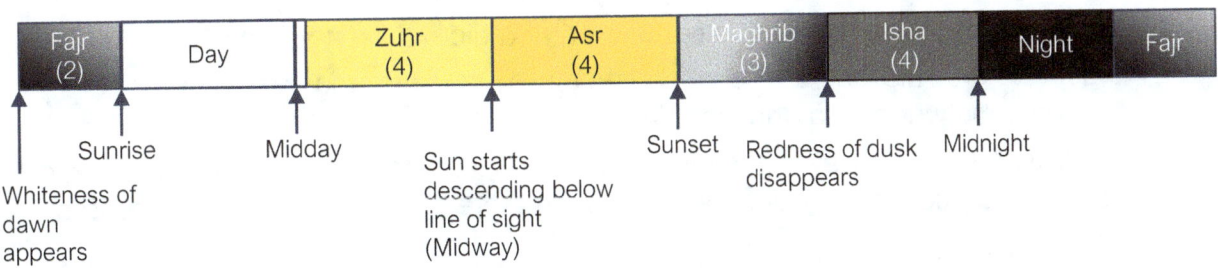

- The times of sunrise and sunset are prohibited for prayer, since the sun was once worshiped in the old days.
- These timings are transmitted to us through the consensus of the Sunnah; the Quran mentions them briefly, but not the exact times.
- It is believed that these timings also remained the same for other prophets.
- Besides these obligatory units (Rakah), all other units are optional and earn a person a great reward. Some of these optional prayers were regularly recited by the Prophet, and people refer to them as Sunnah (the Prophet's practice).

أَقِمِ الصَّلٰوةَ لِدُلُوْكِ الشَّمْسِ اِلٰى غَسَقِ الَّيْلِ وَ قُرْاٰنَ الْفَجْرِ ۭ اِنَّ قُرْاٰنَ الْفَجْرِ كَانَ مَشْهُوْدًا

Diligently attend to your prayers from the time of the sun's descent to nightfall, and especially the recital in the Fajr prayer, because the Fajr prayer is in the presence [witnessed by the angels]. (17:78)

وَ اَقِمِ الصَّلٰوةَ طَرَفِ النَّهَارِ وَ زُلَفًا مِّنَ الَّيْلِ

And diligently attend to your prayer in both parts of the day and in some part of the night too. (11:114)

وَ سَبِّحْ بِحَمْدِ رَبِّكَ قَبْلَ طُلُوْعِ الشَّمْسِ وَ قَبْلَ غُرُوْبِهَا ۚ وَ مِنْ اٰنَآئِ الَّيْلِ فَسَبِّحْ وَ اَطْرَافَ النَّهَارِ لَعَلَّكَ تَرْضٰى

And give glory to your Lord and praise Him before sunrise and before sunset and [in a similar manner], glorify Him at night and the two sides of the day so that you may become content. (20:130)

Prophet Muhammad's best example:

In all aspects of Shariah, we will learn two things: first, the Shariah, or ruling itself, and then how Prophet Muhammad acted on that Shariah, which is called *"Uswa e Hasanah"*.

Guidance from Prophet Muhammad

- He used to pray Fajr earlier, when it was still dark.
- He asked people not to pray Zuhr at midday and, in summer, preferred to delay it a little when the heat lessened.
- He used to pray Asr earlier, when the sun was still high and bright.
- He used to pray Maghrib right after sunset, and did not like to delay it.
- He used to pray his Isha a little late, just before sleeping, and avoided doing anything in between Isha and sleeping.
- If one rakah (unit) of prayer has already been offered and the time has passed (for example, sunrise), he instructs people to complete it, and it will be considered on time.
- If prayer is missed due to a situation beyond our control (e.g., sleeping over), he asked people to pray it immediately once that situation is over, and it will be considered on time.
- He has repeatedly reminded people to observe prayer times vigilantly.

Prerequisites of the prayer

- The prerequisites of prayers mean that all these conditions must be there before Salah can be performed. Salah would be invalid if any of these conditions did not exist.

1. The person must be sober and must not be intoxicated.

2. Women should be completely clean and not be in their state of menstruation or puerperal discharge (after childbirth).

3. The person must be in the state of ceremonial ablution (Wudu).

4. If the person was in the state of *Janabah* (after ejaculation of semen for any reason) or coming from the state of menstruation or puerperal discharge (women), then the person must have taken the ceremonial bath.

5. If water is unavailable or the person is sick, the person can perform Tayammum (dry ablution) in place of both ceremonial ablution and bath.

6. The person must face the *Qiblah* (direction towards Makkah; whatever is known at that time).

يَٰٓأَيُّهَا ٱلَّذِينَ ءَامَنُوا۟ لَا تَقْرَبُوا۟ ٱلصَّلَوٰةَ وَأَنتُمْ سُكَٰرَىٰ حَتَّىٰ تَعْلَمُوا۟ مَا تَقُولُونَ وَلَا جُنُبًا إِلَّا عَابِرِى سَبِيلٍ حَتَّىٰ تَغْتَسِلُوا۟ ۚ وَ

إِن كُنتُم مَّرْضَىٰٓ أَوْ عَلَىٰ سَفَرٍ أَوْ جَآءَ أَحَدٌ مِّنكُم مِّنَ ٱلْغَآئِطِ أَوْ لَٰمَسْتُمُ ٱلنِّسَآءَ فَلَمْ تَجِدُوا۟ مَآءً فَتَيَمَّمُوا۟ صَعِيدًا طَيِّبًا

فَٱمْسَحُوا۟ بِوُجُوهِكُمْ وَأَيْدِيكُمْ ۗ إِنَّ ٱللَّهَ كَانَ عَفُوًّا غَفُورًا

Believers! Do not approach the place of the prayer when you are drunk till you know what you are saying, nor when you are [ceremonially] unclean until you have bathed yourselves, except if the intention is to pass through [the prayer place]. And if you are sick or on a journey, or when you have relieved yourselves or had intercourse with women, and you find no water, take some clean mud and wipe your faces and hands with it. Gracious is God and forgiving. (4:43)

يَٰٓأَيُّهَا ٱلَّذِينَ ءَامَنُوٓا۟ إِذَا قُمْتُمْ إِلَى ٱلصَّلَوٰةِ فَٱغْسِلُوا۟ وُجُوهَكُمْ وَأَيْدِيَكُمْ إِلَى ٱلْمَرَافِقِ وَٱمْسَحُوا۟ بِرُءُوسِكُمْ وَأَرْجُلَكُمْ إِلَى

ٱلْكَعْبَيْنِ ۚ وَإِن كُنتُمْ جُنُبًا فَٱطَّهَّرُوا۟ ۚ وَإِن كُنتُم مَّرْضَىٰٓ أَوْ عَلَىٰ سَفَرٍ أَوْ جَآءَ أَحَدٌ مِّنكُم مِّنَ ٱلْغَآئِطِ أَوْ لَٰمَسْتُمُ

ٱلنِّسَآءَ فَلَمْ تَجِدُوا۟ مَآءً فَتَيَمَّمُوا۟ صَعِيدًا طَيِّبًا فَٱمْسَحُوا۟ بِوُجُوهِكُمْ وَأَيْدِيكُم مِّنْهُ ۚ مَا يُرِيدُ ٱللَّهُ لِيَجْعَلَ عَلَيْكُم مِّنْ حَرَجٍ

وَّلَٰكِن يُرِيدُ لِيُطَهِّرَكُمْ وَلِيُتِمَّ نِعْمَتَهُۥ عَلَيْكُمْ لَعَلَّكُمْ تَشْكُرُونَ

Believers! When you rise to pray, wash your face and your hands as far as the elbow, wipe your head, and wash your feet to the ankle. And if you are [ceremonially] unclean, bathe yourselves. But if you are sick or on a journey, or when you have just relieved yourselves or had intercourse with women, you find no water, take some clean mud and wipe your faces and your hands with it. God does not wish to burden you; He seeks only to purify you and perfect His favor so that you may express gratitude. (5:6)

How did Prophet Muhammad perform Wudu?

The method described in the Quran is sufficient for performing Wudu, but we learned from the narrations how Prophet Muhammad performed it, and he is the best example for us.

- Clean your teeth first (Miswak or toothbrush in our times).
- Start wudu from the right side (for example, right hand first).
- Wash both hands properly and rinse the mouth three times (one/two times are also reported).
- Pour water into the nose three times and clean it properly.
- Wash your face three times and run your fingers through your beard to make sure water reaches inside.
- Wash your hands to the elbows.

- Take some water in your hands and wipe the head (from the forehead to the back of the head and back).
- Clean your ears from the inside and the outside.
- Wash the right foot first and then the left.
- At the end, say the following and perform two Rakah (optional):

اَشْهَدُ اَنْ لَا اِلهَ الا اللهُ وَحْدَهُ لاَ شَرِيْكَ لَهُ وَ اَشْهَدُ اَنَّ مُحَمَّدًا عَبْدُهُ وَ رَسُوْلُهُ

How did Prophet Muhammad perform Bath?

This is the method that we have learned from the narrations of how Prophet Muhammad used to perform ceremonial baths, and he is the best example for us

- Wash both your hands first, starting with the right hand.
- Wash the genital area thoroughly using the left hand.
- Perform complete Wudu as it should be done, except for washing your feet.
- Either wash your hair completely, or pour three handfuls of water over your head and insert your wet fingers so the water reaches the roots and the hair is soaked.
- Pour water all over the body like in a regular bath.
- Wash both feet thoroughly.

What expires Wudu

- Urination
- Defecation
- Passing the wind, whether with sound or without it.
- Discharge of pre-seminal fluid in men or sexual discharge in women (without sexual activity).
- Sleep or unconsciousness (because our wudu state becomes unknown).

Wiping on Socks/Shoes

- Prophet Muhammad allowed people to wipe their socks and shoes during Wudu instead of washing their feet.
- When local, this can be done for 1 day; when traveling, for 3 days/nights.
- The person should perform wudu, washing their feet for the very first time, before putting on socks/shoes.

Rituals & Utterances of Prayers

Note: There are minor differences among various schools of thought regarding certain rituals and utterances. These differences are OK because they do not cause any major impact on the overall shape and form of the prayer, which is intended to be universal.

- In this section, we will cover the exact method to pray. For every step, first the ritual or action is described, and then what to say in that position or with that action in front of that step. The mandatory step is marked with M, and the optional step is marked with an O.

1   **Rafa al-Yadayn**: Raise both hands up to the ears or shoulders while keeping the fingers a little apart and palms facing the Qibla. **(M)**

Say: *Allah o Akbar* (God is the greatest), also called Takbir, while raising hands or right after it. **(M)**

2   **Qiyam**: Stand straight with hands tied in front in such a way that the right hand will be on top of the left. **(M)**

Read: Opening Dua **(O)**
Recite: *Surah Fatiha* (Must) **(M)**
Recite: *Some parts of the Quran* **(M)**

3   **Ruku**: Bow down while placing hands on the knees as one grabs them. Keep your back straight as much as possible. **(M)**

Say: *Allah o Akbar* (when going in *Ruku*) **(M)**
Read: *Subhana Rabbi Al-Azeem* (3 to 5 times) **(O)**

4   **Qawamah**: Stand up straight from *Ruku* such that your back would go back to its original place, like in *Qiyam*. **(M)**

Say: *Sami Allah o Leman Hamidah* **(M)** *Rabbana Wa Lak Al Hamd* **(O)**

5   **Sajdah**: Go in prostration. Place hands on both sides of the head with fingers joined but palms spread. The fingers would face the Qibla. Keep arms apart. Place feet upright while toe fingers are turned and pointing toward the Qibla. The forehead, nose, hands, knees, and forefeet must touch the ground. **(M)**

Say: *Allah o Akbar* (when going in *Sajdah* and in between *Sajdah* and *Jalsah*) **(M)**
Say: *Subhana Rabi al Aala* (3 to 5 times) **(O)**

6   **Jalsah**: This is done in between two prostrations. The person would fold his left foot and composedly sit on it. The right foot should be kept straight, as it was in Sajdah. **(M)**

Say (Optional) : *Rabbi Ighfirli* **(O)**

7 *Qadah*: This is like sitting in Jalsah. This is done at the end of the 2nd and 4th Rakah. **M**

Dua: Make dua as recommended by Prophet Muhammad. **O**

8 *Salam*: Turn face right first and then left. **M**

Say: *Assalam O Alaikum Wa Rehmatullah* on both sides **M**

Guidance from Prophet Muhammad

- He advised people, "Pray as you see me praying" – we should learn how Prophet Muhammad used to pray.

- He encouraged people to perform wudu before going to bed.

- When we make wudu, our minor sins get wiped out – a good incentive for us to make wudu.

- He said, "When my nation is called out on the day of judgment, their foreheads, hands, and feet will appear bright because of the effects of wudu."

- For women, if their hair is plaited, they don't need to disentangle it when soaking it in water during a ceremonial bath.

- Some narratives mention that he used to raise his hands (just like when saying *takbeer*), going into Ruku and coming back from it (it is called *Rafa al-Yadayn*).

- He advised us not to pray in haste and that all rituals must be performed calmly (the person should remain in a position until all his joints are at rest). He warned that people who do not straighten their back (for some time) while doing Ruku and prostration have, in fact) not prayed and should repeat their prayers.

- There are many duas reported from him before reciting the Fatiha to celebrate the praises of the Lord.

- The prayer without reading the Fatiha is considered incomplete.

- He instructed us to recite the Quran slowly in prayers. In one hadith, he mentioned that when a believer recites Surah Fatiha, God responds with every verse he recites.

- It is recommended to beautify our voice when reciting the Quran in prayers.

- He used to recite longer surahs in Isha and Fajr.

- He stopped people from making duas in the ruku position.

- He used to make many duas while in prostration, as this is the position closest to God.

- The last ritual (*Qaadah*) is the time to make duas before finishing the prayer.

- He has taught us to say: **Allah O Akbar (33), Subhan Allah (33), Alhamdulillah (33), and La Ilaha Illalah (1)** after finishing the prayers.

What to recite before Fatihah

- Three opening duas are reported in various Ahadith, and people have been reading them. You can pick any one, but it's optional.

سُبْحَانَكَ اللَّهُمَّ وَبِحَمْدِكَ وَتَبَارَكَ اسْمُكَ وَتَعَالَى جَدُّكَ وَلاَ إِلَهَ غَيْرُكَ

"Glorious You are O Allah, and with Your praise, and blessed is Your Name, and exalted is Your majesty, and none has the right to be worshipped but You."

إِنَّ صَلَاتِي وَنُسُكِي وَمَحْيَايَ وَمَمَاتِي لِلَّهِ رَبِّ الْعَالَمِينَ لاَ شَرِيكَ لَهُ وَبِذَلِكَ أُمِرْتُ وَأَنَا مِنَ الْمُسْلِمِينَ اللَّهُمَّ اهْدِنِي لِأَحْسَنِ الأَعْمَالِ وَأَحْسَنِ الأَخْلَاقِ لاَ يَهْدِي لِأَحْسَنِهَا إِلاَّ أَنْتَ وَقِنِي سَيِّئَ الأَعْمَالِ وَسَيِّئَ الأَخْلَاقِ لاَ يَقِي سَيِّئَهَا إِلاَّ أَنْتَ

Indeed, my salah (prayer), my sacrifice, my living, and my dying are for Allah, the Lord of all that exists. He has no partner. And of this, I have been commanded and am one of the Muslims. O Allah, guide me to the best of deeds and the best of manners, for none can guide to the best of them but You. And protect me from bad deeds and manners, for none can protect against them but You.

اللَّهُمَّ بَاعِدْ بَيْنِي وَبَيْنَ خَطَايَايَ كَمَا بَاعَدْتَ بَيْنَ المَشْرِقِ وَالمَغْرِبِ ، اللَّهُمَّ نَقِّنِي مِنْ خَطَايَايَ كَمَا يُنَقَّى الثَّوْبُ الأَبْيَضُ مِنَ الدَّنَسِ ، اللَّهُمَّ اغْسِلْنِي مِنْ خَطَايَايَ بِالثَّلْجِ وَالمَاءِ وَالْبَرَدِ

O Allah, distance me from my sins just as You have distanced The East from The West, O Allah, purify me of my sins as a white robe is purified of filth, O Allah, cleanse me of my sins with snow, water, and ice.

In Qaadah before Salam

Note: Most people say *At-Tahiyyat* and *Durood-e-Ibrahimi* in Qadah. Both are also duas. The other duas shown below are also recorded from the Prophet before saying, Salam.

اللَّهُمَّ إِنِّي أَعُوذُ بِكَ مِنْ عَذَابِ القَبْرِ، وَمِنْ عَذَابِ جَهَنَّمَ، وَمِنْ فِتْنَةِ المَحْيَا وَالمَمَاتِ، وَمِنْ شَرِّ فِتْنَةِ المَسِيحِ الدَّجَّالِ

O Allah, I take refuge in You from the punishment of the grave (*Barzakh*), from the torment of the Fire, from the trials and tribulations of life and death, and from the evil affliction of *Al-Maseeh Ad-Dajjal* (the Deceptive Leader who will appear at the end of time).

اللَّهُمَّ إِنِّي ظَلَمْتُ نَفْسِي ظُلْماً كَثِيراً وَلَا يَغْفِرُ الذُّنوبَ إلاّ أَنْت ، فَاغْفِرْ لِي مَغْفِرَةً

مِنْ عِنْدِكَ وَارْحَمْني، إِنَّكَ أَنْتَ الغَفورُ الرَّحيم

O Allah, I have indeed oppressed my soul excessively, and none can forgive sins except You, so forgive me a forgiveness from Yourself and have mercy upon me. Surely, You are The Most-Forgiving, The Most-Merciful.

اللَّهُمَّ إِنِّي أَعوذُ بِكَ مِنَ البُخْل، وَأَعوذُ بِكَ مِنَ الجُبْن، وَأَعوذُ بِكَ مِنْ أَنْ أُرَدَّ إلى أَرْذَلِ العُمُر،

وَأَعوذُ بِكَ مِنْ فِتْنَةِ الدُّنْيا وَعَذابِ القَبْر

O Allah, I take refuge in You from miserliness and cowardice, I take refuge in You lest I be returned to the worst of lives, "i.e., old age, being weak, incapable, and in a state of fear," and I take refuge in You from the trials and tribulations of this life and the punishment of the grave.

اللَّهُمَّ إِنِّي أَسْأَلُكَ الجَنَّةَ وَأَعوذُ بِكَ مِنَ النَّار

O Allah, I ask You to grant me Paradise, and I take refuge in You from the Hellfire.

After Salam

لا إلَهَ إلاّ اللهُ وحَدَهُ لا شريكَ لهُ، لهُ المُلْكُ ولهُ الحَمْد، وهوَ على كلّ شَيءٍ قَدير،

اللّهُمَّ لا مانِعَ لِما أَعْطَيْت، وَلا مُعْطِيَ لِما مَنَعْت، وَلا يَنْفَعُ ذا الجَدِّ مِنْكَ الجَد

None has the right to be worshipped except Allah, alone, without a partner, to Him belongs all sovereignty and praise, and He is over all things Omnipotent. O Allah, none can prevent what You have willed to bestow, and none can bestow what You have willed to prevent, and no wealth or majesty can benefit anyone, as from You is all wealth and majesty.

أَسْتَغْفِرُ الله . اللّهُمَّ أَنْتَ السَّلامُ ، وَمِنْكَ السَّلام ، تَبارَكْتَ يا ذا الجَلالِ وَالإِكْرام

I ask Allah for forgiveness. (three times)
O Allah, You are As-Salam (Peace), and from You is all peace; blessed are You, O Possessor of Majesty and Honor.

Other rulings about Salah

The Temperament of Shariah – Review

- We learned about this earlier, but let's review it because we will be using it in some of the rulings related to Salah.

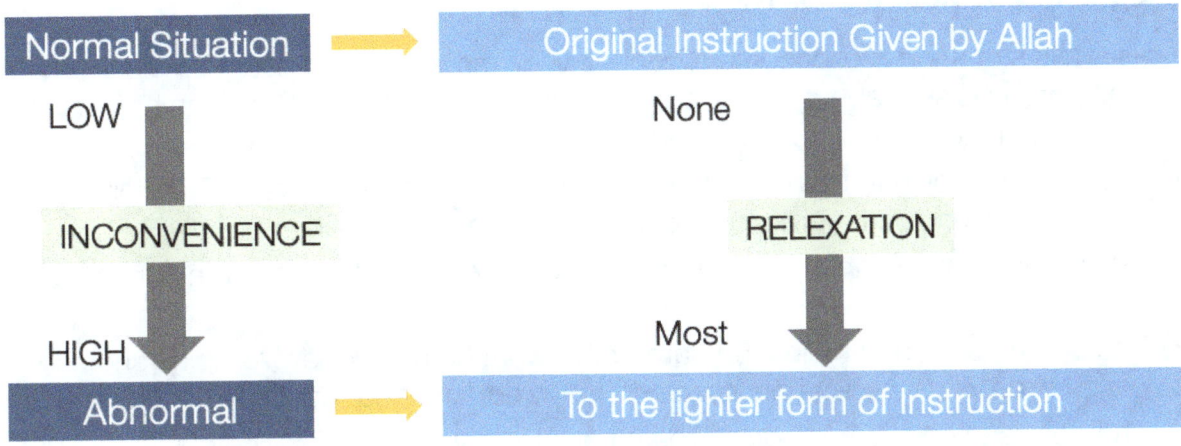

Concession in the prayers

- If the time of the prayer arrives in a situation when it is not safe to pray normally, then it is allowed to pray:
    - While walking or riding, whenever possible.
    - Reduce the number of Rakah.
    - Combine the prayers.
- Prophet Muhammad inferred from this directive (of fear and safety) and applied it to the uneasiness and discomfort of travel as well.
- During these times, people may shorten their prayers, a practice called Qasr.
- The general rule is to reduce 4 rakah to 2 and keep 3 rakah as it is. Also, Zuhr and Asr can be combined (at Zuhr time or Asr time), and Maghrib and Isha can be combined (at Maghrib time or Isha time).
- The Prophet sometimes prayed his optional prayers while walking or riding under normal circumstances.

وَ إِذَا ضَرَبْتُمْ فِى الْأَرْضِ فَلَيْسَ عَلَيْكُمْ جُنَاحٌ أَنْ تَقْصُرُوْا مِنَ الصَّلٰوةِ * اِنْ خِفْتُمْ أَنْ يَّفْتِنَكُمُ الَّذِيْنَ كَفَرُوْا ۚ اِنَّ الْكٰفِرِيْنَ كَانُوْا لَكُمْ عَدُوًّا مُّبِيْنًا

And when you travel, there is no blame on you to shorten your prayers if you fear that the disbelievers may put you through some trial, because these disbelievers are your open enemies. (4:101)

It is left up to each person to decide when to take this concession, as only they are aware of the situation. It is not just related to travel. The scholars can only describe the law given by Allah.

Rectifying mistakes in prayers

- There is a method prescribed by Prophet Muhammad to correct a known mistake (the person is sure about it) or a possible mistake (the person thinks he has made a mistake) in the prayer (ritual or utterance).

- The person should first correct the mistake, then make two extra prostrations (Sajda Sahu) at the end of the prayer, before Salam (or after the Salam).

- If a mistake is not fixable, then just making two extra prostrations at the end would be OK.

- The person should not think too hard about what he has done wrong; he should base his decision on what he is sure of, leave doubts, and rectify the mistake.

- The goal is to do two additional prostrations to fix your prayers. The placement of those prostrations can vary in different schools of thought, or Fiqh. The best way is to fix your placement, for example, before Salam.

- If the Imam makes a mistake and does not realize it, the followers should correct him. They should say, Subhan Allah. The Imam should rectify the mistake the same way as prescribed above.

- If the Imam forgets the Quran or makes a mistake in recitation, then one of the followers should remind him or correct him immediately (if the followers notice that).

Ibn Buhaynah says that once, the Prophet led our Zuhr prayer but did not sit down after the first two Rakah and stood up for the third Rakah. People also stood up with him until the prayer was about to end, and as they waited for the Salam to be said, the Prophet uttered the takbir. Before saying the Salam, he offered two prostrations. (Sahih Al-Bukhari #1224, #1225)

Once, when the Prophet led the Zuhr congregational prayer, he prayed five Rakah. He was asked: "Has the prayer been lengthened?" He replied: "What happened?" The people declared that he had prayed five Rakah. At this, the Prophet turned his feet while sitting, faced the Qiblah, offered two prostrations, and then said the Salam. Then he turned towards the people and said: "If some new directive had been revealed about the prayer, I would have told you; the fact is that I am a human being like you; I also forget the way you do, so when I forget, remind me and remember that if any of you has any doubt in the prayer, he should ascertain what is the right course and then complete his prayer according to it, say Salam and then offer two prostrations. (Sahih Al-Bukhari #401, #404)

The Prophet is reported to have said: "When anyone among you is doubtful whether he has prayed three Rakah or four, he should try to base his decision on which he is surer and leave aside what is doubtful; he should then offer two prostrations before the Salam. If [ultimately] he has prayed five Rakah, these prostrations will make them into an even number, and if he has prayed four, then these prostrations will become a source of humiliation for Satan." (Sahih Muslim #1272)

Etiquette of Prayers

- Conversation during prayers is not allowed. The prayers are only for glorifying the Almighty and earnestly presenting one's supplication before Him.
- One should look down at the place of prostration and avoid looking around them.
- The prayer should be offered with complete calmness and serenity, with every ritual (action) completed properly.
- During the prayer, hair and clothes should not be played with (dress properly to avoid that).
- There should not be anything in front of the prayer place that could distract the praying person.
- If the food is ready and the person is hungry, then one should eat it and then calmly offer the prayer, so that he is not thinking of food during the prayer.
- If a person is compelled to do something during prayer, they should not prolong the prayer. This is usually valid for things that cannot be avoided (for example, a child is about to touch something harmful).
- The person should not take support when standing or sitting in prayer.
- Yawning should be refrained from during the prayer (curb it as much as possible).
- A person should be decently and appropriately dressed while praying. One should not be lazy and sluggish during prayer.

Improving your Salah & Optional Prayers

How to improve the quality of your prayer

- One should not be lazy and sluggish during prayer. This is a very common form of negligence in prayer, and a person guilty of it cannot focus on the Almighty during the prayer.
- Some measures that can be adopted to improve one's prayers are:
  - Realize the importance of prayers in Islam – it is the first manifestation of your faith in God.
  - Realize that prayer is the foundation of the building of the religion. Virtues like charity and compassion cannot bear any fruit in the hereafter without that foundation in place.
  - Be vigilant in your prayers. As soon as you hear Adhan, make it a habit to leave everything aside and start preparing for the prayers.
  - If possible, pray in the congregation, whether with other people in the house or, preferably, in the mosque.
  - Work towards praying Isha and Fajr – if you can pray them every day, the other prayers will be easy.
  - Protect your prayers from latent thoughts and suggestions that keep bombarding a person.
  - Seek refuge in Allah when such thoughts come.
  - Learn the meaning of the portion of the Quran (that you recite every day) and other utterances. You should know what you are reading or saying.
  - Understanding the meaning of the Quran recitation and utterances helps you reflect on the words while praying. This will make your prayer a living moment rather than just a display of mechanically performed rituals. For example, if you are reciting a verse of punishment, seek refuge in God; if the verse asks for forgiveness, ask for forgiveness immediately.
  - Audibly recite the Quran and other utterances so you can keep your focus and attention on the meanings (loud enough to hear yourself).
  - In your general life, keep your thoughts pure and engage yourself in activities that benefit you and others in both worldly and religious affairs.
  - One should carefully notice that the prayer does not become a pretentious display, which is usually the most common and most dangerous affliction of the prayer.
  - The best way to deal with the disease of the show-off is to pray Tahajjud occasionally (or more if possible).

> ## REMEMBER
>
> - Always pray to be firm in your religion and relationship with Allah, not to gain worldly benefits.
> - Prayer is your opportunity to talk to the King of this Universe who controls the destiny of everything.

The Optional Prayer

- What has been mentioned up to now constitutes the minimum requirements in the worship of prayers, which are incumbent on Muslims.
- In addition to obligatory prayers, Muslims are encouraged to offer optional prayers. This is also one way to improve your Salah.
- The following optional prayers are learned from the life of Prophet Muhammad:
    - 2 Rakah before Fajr
    - 2 or 4 Rakah before Zuhr
    - 2 Rakah after Zuhr
    - 2 Rakah after Maghrib
    - 2 Rakah after Isha
    - 4 Rakah after Friday prayer

Note: Voluntary acts of Shariah are kept to grade people on the Day of Judgment because there are many levels of Jannah.

Special Prayers

- 2 Rakah at mid-morning when the sun is out and bright.
- At the time of the eclipse, he offered 2 Rakah with very long Ruku and Prostrations. He even repeated Qiyam multiple times until the eclipse was over.
- 2 Rakah in order to ask for rain in drought conditions.

وَ مَنْ تَطَوَّعَ خَيْرًا ۝ فَإِنَّ اللهَ شَاكِرٌ عَلِيمٌ

He who does a virtue of his own will, God will accept it and is fully aware of it. (2:158)

Zayd ibn Thabit reported: The Messenger of Allah said, "O people, perform prayer in your houses, for the best prayer of a man is in his house, except for the obligatory prayers." (Sahih Bukhari #731)

Prophet Muhammad said that God said, "My slave keeps on coming closer to Me through performing Nawafil (voluntary prayers or doing extra deeds besides what is obligatory) until I love him, (so much so that) I become his hearing with which he hears, and his sight with which he sees, and his hand with which he strikes, and his leg with which he walks; and if he asks Me something, I will surely give him, and if he seeks My Protection (refuge), I will surely protect him". (Riyad al Saliheen #386)

> Umm Habiba reported from Prophet Muhammad, "Whoever performs twelve units of (additional) prayers in each day and night, a house will be built for him/her in Paradise." (Sahih Muslim #728)

Tahajjud prayer

- Besides the five daily prayers, Prophet Muhammad was instructed to pray another prayer called the night prayer, also known as Tahajjud. Tahajjud was obligatory for the Prophet.
- For common Muslims, it is an optional prayer, but a great reward is promised for those who offer it.
- Prophet Muhammad used to offer up to 11 Rakah for this prayer (also called Witr because it has an odd number of Rakah).
- Multiple ways are reported for this prayer:
  - Pray 2 Rakah with Salam and then one Rakah to make it odd in number.
  - Pray in groups of 2 Rakah, and at the end, pray 3 or 5 Rakah to make it odd.
  - Pray in groups of 4 Rakah, and at the end, pray 3.
- The Quran is recited loudly with a medium pitch.

اَقِمِ الصَّلٰوةَ لِدُلُوكِ الشَّمْسِ اِلٰى غَسَقِ الَّيْلِ وَ قُرْاٰنَ الْفَجْرِ ۖ اِنَّ قُرْاٰنَ الْفَجْرِ كَانَ مَشْهُوْدًا

وَ مِنَ الَّيْلِ فَتَهَجَّدْ بِهٖ نَافِلَةً لَّكَ

Establish prayer when the sun declines until the darkness of the night, and also the recitation at the time of Fajr. Certainly, the recitation of the Fajr is witnessed. And during a part of the night, pray Tahajjud, which is extra for you. (17:78-79)

وَ لَا تَجْهَرْ بِصَلَاتِكَ وَ لَا تُخَافِتْ بِهَا وَ ابْتَغِ بَيْنَ ذٰلِكَ سَبِيْلًا

And in your night prayer, recite neither too loudly nor too lowly but seek a middle way. (17:110)

Taraweeh prayer

- Prophet Muhammad allowed his companions to offer Tahajjud with Isha instead of its original time in the middle of the night (or the third part of the night before Fajr).
- Usually, he prayed it alone at night, but on one occasion, he prayed with companions for a few days in the middle of the night before abandoning the congregation (stating he feared it might become obligatory for common Muslims).

- At the time of Umar, he revived this practice after seeing people offering Tahajjud with Isha in the mosque, their voices mixing as they prayed individually. Umar appointed an Imam and asked everyone to join behind that Imam to resolve that problem; however, Umar did not join the prayer with everyone.
- Since then, people have been praying like this, especially during Ramadan, in the form of Taraweeh prayers.
- Since this is an optional prayer, people have added to or subtracted Rakah. Some prayed 11 as the Prophet did, and some prayed 20 or more, but there is no fixed number of Rakah for these prayers.

أَيُّكُمْ خَافَ أَنْ لَا يَقُومَ مِنْ آخِرِ اللَّيْلِ فَلْيُوتِرْ ثُمَّ لِيَرْقُدْ وَمَنْ وَثِقَ بِقِيَامٍ مِنَ اللَّيْلِ فَلْيُوتِرْ مِنْ آخِرِهِ فَإِنَّ قِرَاءَةَ آخِرِ اللَّيْلِ مَحْضُورَةٌ وَذَلِكَ أَفْضَلُ

Whoever among you fears that he would not be able to get up in the last part of the night should offer the *Witr* before going to sleep; but he who is certain that he will be able to get up, should offer this prayer in the last part of the night because the recital [of the Qur'an] at that time is in the presence of the Almighty and it is this which is more blessed. (Sahih Muslim #1767)

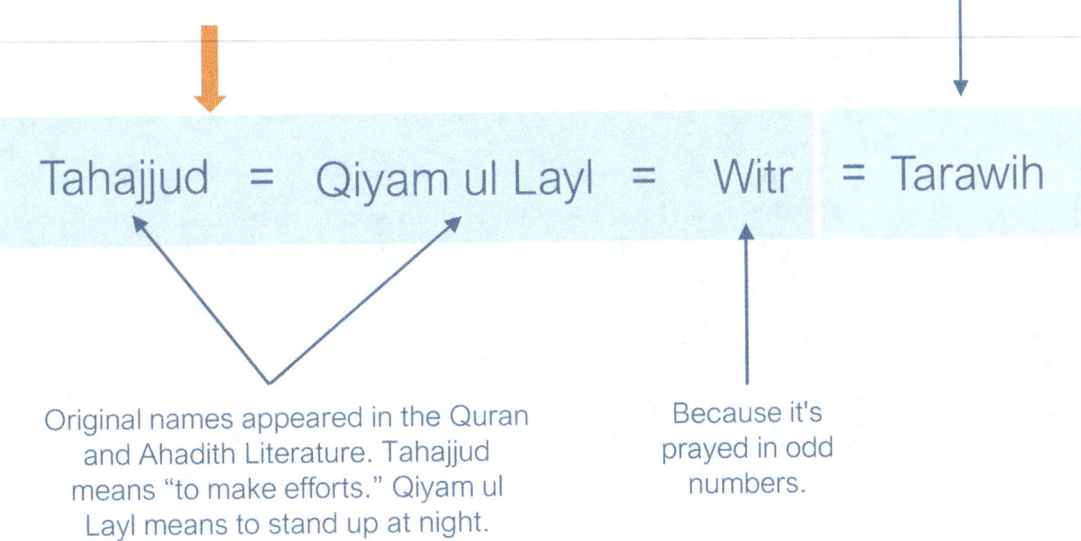

It got its name from Tarweeha, which means to rest (like after four units). **This is now specific to Tahajjud in Ramadan but is prayed with Isha.** Umar regularized it, but the Prophet and his companions only prayed Tahajjud at its original time.

Recommended if you can wake up at night and pray.

Tahajjud = Qiyam ul Layl = Witr = Tarawih

Original names appeared in the Quran and Ahadith Literature. Tahajjud means "to make efforts." Qiyam ul Layl means to stand up at night.

Because it's prayed in odd numbers.

Prayer for Istikhara

- Prophet Muhammad also taught Muslims that when they are unsure about a matter (one that is allowed) and need guidance from God, they should offer two Rakah prayers and recite the following dua before finishing the prayer.
- Do it multiple times until the heart is content with either option.
- We are asked to decide and then put our trust in God.

اللّهُمَّ إِنِّي أَسْتَخِيرُكَ بِعِلْمِكَ وَأَسْتَقْدِرُكَ بِقُدْرَتِكَ وَأَسْأَلُكَ مِنْ فَضْلِكَ الْعَظِيم فَإِنَّكَ تَقْدِرُ وَلَا أَقْدِرُ وَتَعْلَمُ وَلَا أَعْلَمُ وَأَنْتَ عَلَّامُ الْغُيُوب اللّهُمَّ إِنْ كُنْتَ تَعْلَمُ أَنَّ هَذَا الْأَمْرَ خَيْرٌ لِي فِي دِينِي وَمَعَاشِي وَعَاقِبَةِ أَمْرِي فَاقْدِرْهُ لِي وَ يَسِّرْهُ لِيْ ثُمَّ بَارِكْ لِي فِيه وَإِنْ كُنْتَ تَعْلَمُ أَنَّ هَذَا الْأَمْرَ شَرٌّ لِي فِي دِينِي وَمَعَاشِي وَعَاقِبَةِ أَمْرِي فَاصْرِفْهُ عَنِّي وَاصْرِفْنِي عَنْهُ وَاقْدِرْ لِي الْخَيْرَ حَيْثُ كَانَ ثُمَّ أَرْضِنِي

O Allah! I seek what is better through Your Knowledge, and through Your Might, I seek strength, and I beg from You Your great blessings because You have the might and I do not. And You know everything, and I do not know, and You have knowledge of the unseen. O Allah! If in Your Knowledge this action [which I intend to do] is better for my religion, life, and fate, then destinate it for me, make it easy, and then bless it for me. And O Allah! In Your knowledge, if this action is bad for me, for my religion, and for my fate, then turn it away from me and turn me away from it, and [O Allah!] whatever is better for me, ordain that for me wherever it is, and then make me satisfied with it.

> It is an important practice to build a consistent relationship with God in the matters that concern you the most. It can be as simple as choosing between college classes.

Abu Salamah, the son of 'Abd al-Rahman, said he asked Aishah: "Describe the Prophet's prayer in Ramadan?" She replied: "Never did the Prophet pray more than eleven Rakah either in Ramadan or in any other month." (Sahih Al-Bukhari #1147)

Every night, the Almighty directs His attention upon our world. When one-third night remains, He says: 'Who is there at this moment to call me so that I can respond to his call; who is it that can ask from Me so that I give him; who is it that seeks mercy that I forgive him. (Sahih Al-Bukhari #1145)

Aishah informed Urwah ibn Al-Zubair that the Prophet came out at midnight and offered the prayer in the mosque. Some people also prayed behind him there. When these people mentioned [this incident] in the morning, more people gathered the next day. On this night, when he prayed in the mosque, people also prayed behind him. When they gathered again in the morning, people mentioned that on the third night, a large number had gathered at the mosque. The Prophet came out on this night, and people prayed behind him. On the fourth night, the mosque was packed to capacity, but he did not come out until it was time for Fajr. He offered the Fajr prayer, and then he turned to the people and bore witness to the oneness of the Almighty and said: "I was not unaware of your presence; I only feared that it might be made obligatory upon you and then you would not be able to offer it." (Sahih al Bukhari #2012)

- If Prayers are transmitted through Sunnah (perpetual practice), why are there differences in how people pray?
- Some people complain: "I have been praying and making dua regularly, but it looks like my prayers are not answered by God." Why?
- Many Muslims pray regularly, and Muslims are the only nation on earth who have kept this alive in its true form, but why does prayer not show its impact on their lives?

Prayers in the Community

Shariah of praying in a community

Mosques

وَأَنَّ الْمَسَاجِدَ لِلَّهِ فَلَا تَدْعُوا مَعَ اللَّهِ أَحَدًا

And (say) that mosques belong to Allah, so do not call upon anyone along with Allah. (72:18)

- Mosques are built and reserved for worshiping the Almighty alone – they are not built for entertainment, trade, and festive activities.
- It is recommended to build a separate area alongside the "Musallah" (where people pray) for other social activities (as most mosques in the US do).
- The oldest mosque on earth is the *Bayt al-Haram*, built by Prophet Ibrahim.
- The three mosques (*Bayt al-Haram, Masjid Nabawi, and Masjid Aqsa*) hold unique significance in Islam, and Prophet Muhammad reported that praying in these mosques earns great rewards (he encouraged them to travel to these mosques ONLY).
- Traveling to your local mosque for prayers is considered a rewarding activity, and the reward increases with the distance traveled.
- In terms of etiquette for entering the mosque, it is highly recommended to offer two Rakah before sitting down.

Dua for Entering the Mosque	Dua for Leaving the Mosque
اللّهُمَّ ، افْتَحْ لِى أَبْوَابَ رَحْمَتِكَ	اللّهُمَّ ، إِنِّي أَسْأَلُكَ مِنْ فَضْلِكَ

The Congregational Prayer

- The sunnah of Prophet Muhammad was to offer all 5 prayers in congregation, preferably in a place of worship for collective purification – he used to pray sunnah at home (before or after).
- Prophet Muhammad built a mosque as soon as he reached Madinah, and that's why Muslims build a mosque in every locality and settlement all over the world.
- Since the time of the Prophet Muhammad, it has been an established sunnah among Muslims to call the Adhan to announce congregational prayer.
- In Medinah, during the Prophet's time, a time came when it was mandatory for Muslims to join the prayers in the mosque. It was used as a criterion for Muslims to show loyalty to Islam.
- Women were exempted from this special directive and encouraged to pray at home; however, they were allowed to come to the mosque to pray if they wished.

- Prophet Muhammad reported that "the prayer in congregation is 27 times more rewarding than individual prayer" (an encouragement to pray in congregation).
- Both men and women are encouraged to pray in the mosque – praying together builds bonds of brotherhood/sisterhood and allows people to know each other in the community.

What societal benefits do you see in people praying in a congregation five times a day?

Special Instructions during the Time of the Prophet

A blind person once asked the Prophet for permission not to come to the mosque; he was initially granted permission, and then the Prophet asked him, "Do you hear the voice of the adhan?" When he answered affirmatively, the Prophet said he would have to come to the mosque. (Sahih Muslim #1486)

The Prophet warned people: "I would like to burn the houses of those who do not come for the prayer and would like to have them thrown over these people. (Sahih Al Bukhari #1481)

[Note: The above two reports are specific to when Muslims needed to join the prayer in congregation, and there was no excuse accepted to pray at home. This was the time when the Prophet's mission was going towards the final punishment, and Allah wanted to separate hypocrites from true Muslims.

Merits and Rewards of praying in congregation

A person who prayed the Isha prayer in congregation is like a person who stood [for worship] till midnight, and a person who prayed the Fajr prayer in congregation is like a person who spent the whole night standing [in worship]. (Sahih Muslim #1491)

If people had known how highly rewarding it was to reach the mosque at the time of the adhan and stand in the first row, they would have done so even if they had to cast lots. And if they knew the reward of outdoing others for the Zuhr prayer, they would have done so. And if they knew the reward for the Fajr and Isha prayer, they would have reached [the mosque] even if they had to drag themselves for this. (Sahih Al-Bukhari #653, 654)

The Adhan & Iqamah

- It is reported that one of the companions had a dream regarding the wording of the Adhan, as Muslims discussed how to call people to prayer.
- It is also reported that in times of rain and severe cold, the Prophet would ask the Muaddhin to add: (People! Pray in your homes.)
- To raise the voice and increase its reach, the Muaddhin would insert his fingers into his ears and turn his face right and left when making adhan.
- In response to the Adhan, the Prophet urged Muslims to repeat the Muaddhin's words and to send blessings on the Prophet at its end.
- Respond with (*La Hola Wa La Quwwata Illah Billah*) when Muaddhin says: Hayya Ala Salah and Hayya Ala Falah.
- The following supplication is reported at the end of the Adhan:

اللّهُمَّ ، رَبَّ هَذِهِ الدَّعْوَةِ التَّامَّةِ ، وَالصَّلَاةِ الْقَائِمَةِ ، آتِ مُحَمَّدًا الْوَسِيلَةَ وَالْفَضِيلَةَ ، وَ ابْعَثْهُ مَقَامًا مَحْمُودًا الَّذِي وَعَدْتَهُ

O Lord of this complete call and of the prayer which stands as its result! Bless Muḥammad and grant him a rank of nearness and raise him up on the Day of Judgement in a manner that he earns the praise of the people – something which you had promised him.[185]

The Method

- The words of the Iqamah are like the Adhan, except that they are generally recited once.
- One additional statement is also reported in Iqamah to announce the standing (*Qad Qaamatis Salah, Qad Qaamatis Salah*).

اللهُ اَكْبَرُ ، اللهُ اَكْبَرُ ، اللهُ اَكْبَرُ ، اللهُ اَكْبَرُ ؛ اَشْهَدُ اَنْ لَا اِلَهَ اِلَّا اللهُ ، اَشْهَدُ اَنْ لَا اِلَهَ اِلَّا اللهُ ؛
اَشْهَدُ اَنَّ مُحَمَّدًا رَسُولُ اللهِ ، اَشْهَدُ اَنَّ مُحَمَّدًا رَسُولُ اللهِ

Adhan

حَيَّ عَلَى الصَّلوةِ ، حَيَّ عَلَى الصَّلوةِ ؛ حَيَّ عَلَى الْفَلَاحِ ، حَيَّ عَلَى الْفَلَاحِ ؛ اللهُ اَكْبَرُ ، اللهُ اَكْبَرُ
؛ لَا اِلَهَ اِلَّا اللهُ

اللهُ اَكْبَرُ ، اللهُ اَكْبَرُ ؛ اَشْهَدُ اَنْ لَا اِلَهَ اِلَّا اللهُ ، اَشْهَدُ اَنَّ مُحَمَّدًا رَسُولُ اللهِ ، حَيَّ عَلَى الصَّلوةِ ؛
حَيَّ عَلَى الْفَلَاحِ ؛ قَدْ قَامَتِ الصَّلوةُ ، قَدْ قَامَتِ الصَّلوةُ؛ اللهُ اَكْبَرُ ، اللهُ اَكْبَرُ ؛ لَا اِلَهَ اِلَّا اللهُ

Iqamah

The Imam

- The prayer can be performed behind any Muslim with no distinction – their beliefs or actions do not affect your prayers.
- However, when hiring/selecting an Imam, Prophet Muhammad advised entrusting this responsibility to someone who knows or has memorized more of the Quran and has greater knowledge of the religion.
- The Imam should not prolong the prayer because there may be sick, weak, or elderly people behind him.
- The Imam should ensure that the rows behind him are straight, with no gaps, and that there is visible discipline.
- The Imam should read the Quran loudly in Fajr, Maghrib, and Isha – these are the times when people usually do not work and have more time to listen to the Quran.

Anas reported: I have never seen anyone offer the prayer lightly and in a more thorough manner than the Prophet (sws); such was his concern that he would shorten the prayer if he heard a child crying, thinking that his mother would be apprehensive for him. (Sahih Al-Bukhari #709)

"O People! Be gentle with your brothers and do not leave spaces for Satan in between the rows, and remember, he who endeavors to unite a row, the Almighty will unite him [with others], and he who breaks a row, the Almighty will break his relationship with people. (Sunan Al Daud #666)

The Followers

- A person praying behind an Imam MUST not supersede him. They should repeat and/or act on *Takbeer* only after the Imam has said it and moved to the new position.
- If the Imam is reciting the Fatiha, they should say (medium voice) Ameen at the end of it.
- When the Imam is reading the Fatihah loud, the follower must listen quietly. If the Imam is reciting the Fatihah quietly, they may recite it on their own, including the Surah after it. Staying quiet behind the Imam or reciting it to yourself are both acceptable.
- They should say "*Rabbana Wa Lakal Hamd*" when the Imam says "*Samiallahu Liman Hamidah*".

- Mature adults should take the first rows, and children should stand behind them.
- The Prophet recommended that his followers make an effort to pray in the first row, as there are more blessings in praying there. This advice was given to encourage people to arrive at the mosque a little earlier (rather than coming very late and trying to reach the first row).
- If a person is missing a Rakah, they should walk calmly, join the prayer, and complete the remaining Rakahs after the congregation has finished.
- The followers should stand up and make rows only when the Imam says so or when he is reaching his place to lead – the Imam is the leader of the prayer, and he must be followed.
- Women make rows behind men in the mosque (this was the practice at the time of the Prophet, and it was never changed. (Technically, they can also be on either side, like in Masjid al-Haram and Masjid al-Nabawi. At home, women can also pray on the side.)

The Friday Prayer

- Organizing Friday Prayers is the responsibility of a Muslim State. The Sunnah is that a government official or one of their representatives must lead the Friday prayers.
- It is incumbent upon Muslims to pray in the congregation on Friday instead of Zuhr.
- The Adhan should be recited when the Imam reaches the place where he will deliver the sermon.
- The Imam should deliver two small sermons (Khutbahs) in any language in which he should praise God, recite some verses of the Quran, and remind and counsel people.
- It is highly recommended (some consider it mandatory) for followers to reach the Masjid before Khutbah and not skip it – the Friday sermon is part of the Friday prayers.
- Followers are required to listen to the Khutbah attentively, without distractions (for example, checking email on their phones).
- There are two rakah for this prayer, and the Imam recites the Quran loudly.

يَٰٓأَيُّهَا ٱلَّذِينَ ءَامَنُوٓا إِذَا نُودِيَ لِلصَّلَوٰةِ مِن يَوْمِ ٱلْجُمُعَةِ فَٱسْعَوْا إِلَىٰ ذِكْرِ ٱللَّهِ وَ ذَرُوا ٱلْبَيْعَ ۚ ذَٰلِكُمْ خَيْرٌ لَّكُمْ إِن كُنتُمْ تَعْلَمُونَ

فَإِذَا قُضِيَتِ ٱلصَّلَوٰةُ فَٱنتَشِرُوا فِى ٱلْأَرْضِ وَ ٱبْتَغُوا مِن فَضْلِ ٱللَّهِ وَ ٱذْكُرُوا ٱللَّهَ كَثِيرًا لَّعَلَّكُمْ تُفْلِحُونَ

Believers! When you are summoned to Friday prayer, hasten to the remembrance of God and cease your trading. This is best for you if you knew it. Then, when the prayer ends, disperse and go your ways in quest of God's bounty. And keep remembering God a lot so that you may prosper. (62:9-10)

The Prophet has given glad tidings to people – who take a bath, fully cleanse themselves, are befittingly adorned and attired, try not to cut and sit between two people, pray whatever they can at the summoning of the Almighty, and sit silently to listen to the sermon of the Imam – glad tidings that the Almighty will forgive the sins they have committed between the two Fridays. (Sahih Al-Bukhari #883)

On Friday, angels stand at the mosques' doors and write the people's names in order of their entry to the mosques. Consequently, those who come very early are similar to a person who has sent a camel for sacrifice, then he who sends a cow for this purpose, and then he who sends a sheep for this purpose, and then a hen, and then an egg. Then, once the Imam delivers his sermon, they fold their scrolls and listen to his advice and counsel. (Sahih Al-Bukhari #881)

If you say to your companion when the imam gives Khutbah on Friday, 'Be quiet and listen,' you have engaged in idle talk." (Sahih Al-Bukhari # 892; Muslim #851). (It is disliked to get distracted during Khutbah)

The Eid Prayers

- On the days of Eid al-Fitr and Eid al-Adha, it is essential for Muslims (as a community) to arrange a collective prayer (2 rakah) like the Friday prayer.
- It is preferred to pray this prayer in a large open area.
- It is recommended that everyone, including women and children, attend the Eid prayers.
- There is no Adhan or Iqamah for this prayer.
- Additional Takbiraat (Saying Allah u Akbar) are said in the prayer, and no exact count is fixed for them. Any additional numbers can be said during Qiyam and before Ruku. Some reports suggest that Prophet Muhammad said 7 Takbiraat in the first rakah and 5 in the second.
- The two sermons will be delivered after the prayers.
- As on Friday, the sermon should be delivered by the rulers or their representatives.

The Funeral Prayer

- It is the Sunnah of the prophets to pray for the deceased, and it is obligatory in the community. The prayer is performed after the body of the deceased is bathed and enshrouded.
- Followers stand straight in multiple rows behind the Imam, while the dead body is placed in front of the Imam. It is recommended to use an odd number of rows (3, 5, etc.).
- There is no Adhan or Iqamah for the prayer, and it is performed only while standing.

- The following is the procedure for the prayer:
- The Imam says Takbir by raising hands, and everyone reads Surah Fatiha (there is no loud recitation in this prayer).
- On the second takbir, everyone reads Durood (*Allahumma Salli Alaa .....*).
- On the third takbir, everyone makes dua for the deceased.
- On the fourth takbir, everyone makes dua for other Muslims.
- The imam ends the prayer by saying Salam on both sides (or one side).

Duas for the deceased

اللَّهُمَّ اغْفِرْ لَهُ وَارْحَمْهُ وَاعْفُ عَنْهُ وَعَافِهِ وَأَكْرِمْ نُزُلَهُ وَوَسِّعْ مُدْخَلَهُ وَاغْسِلْهُ بِمَاءٍ وَثَلْجٍ وَبَرَدٍ وَنَقِّهِ مِنَ الْخَطَايَا كَمَا يُنَقَّى الثَّوْبُ الْأَبْيَضُ مِنَ الدَّنَسِ وَأَبْدِلْهُ دَارًا خَيْرًا مِنْ دَارِهِ وَأَهْلًا خَيْرًا مِنْ أَهْلِهِ وَزَوْجًا خَيْرًا مِنْ زَوْجِهِ وَقِهِ فِتْنَةَ الْقَبْرِ وَ عَذَابَ النَّارِ

DUA 1

O Lord! Forgive him, pardon him, have mercy on him, and [O Lord!] Grant him prosperity and be a good host to him. Broaden his grave and wash him with water and with snow and with hail. Cleanse him of his sins just as a white piece of cloth is cleansed from dirt. [O Lord!] Grant him a better house in place of his own house and a better family than his own family and a wife better than his own and protect him from the punishment of the grave and from the torment of the Fire.[264]

اللَّهُمَّ اغْفِرْ لِحَيِّنَا وَمَيِّتِنَا وَشَاهِدِنَا وَغَائِبِنَا وَصَغِيرِنَا وَكَبِيرِنَا وَذَكَرِنَا وَأُنْثَانَا اللَّهُمَّ مَنْ أَحْيَيْتَهُ مِنَّا فَأَحْيِهِ عَلَى الْإِسْلَامِ وَمَنْ تَوَفَّيْتَهُ مِنَّا فَتَوَفَّهُ عَلَى الْإِيمَانِ اللَّهُمَّ لَا تَحْرِمْنَا أَجْرَهُ وَلَا تُضِلَّنَا بَعْدَهُ

DUA 2

O Lord! Forgive our living and our dead, those [who are] present [here] and those who are not and forgive our young ones and old ones, our men and our women. Lord! Whoever you give life, give him life such that he [follows] Islam and whoever you give death, let him die on faith. Lord! Do not deprive us of the reward of this deceased person and do not lead us astray after him.[265]

A person who walks in the funeral procession of a Muslim while professing full faith in the Almighty and with a feeling of accountability [to Him] then remains there till the funeral prayer is offered. The deceased is buried and returns with two *carats* worth of reward, each *carat* being as big as the mountain of Uhud. And he who offers the funeral prayer, but comes back before the burial, also returns with one *carat* from them. (Sahih Al-Bukhari #47)

"Do not speak ill of the dead because they have reached the place where their deeds led them to." (Sahih Al-Bukhari #1393)

In Middle Eastern countries, the state appoints Friday Imams and provides them with the text of the Khutbah, whereas in some South Asian Muslim countries, Muslim groups organize them independently. Which approach is preferable and why?

Quick recap

- We can shorten and combine our prayers when traveling – it's a gift from God.
- We can fix our mistakes by completing what is missing (if possible) and then offering two prostrations at the end, before or after Salam.
- There are some etiquette and steps described that we should follow when praying to reap the benefits of prayer.
- If possible, pray in the congregation, whether with other people in the house or, preferably, in the mosque.
- One should take care that the prayer does not become a pretentious display, which is usually the most common and most dangerous affliction of the prayer.
- In addition to the obligatory prayers, Muslims are encouraged to offer the optional prayers.
- For common Muslims, Tahajjud is an optional prayer, but a great reward is promised for those who offer it.
- Taraweeh prayer in Ramadan is nothing but Tahajjud prayer offered after Isha.
- It is highly recommended to offer prayer for Istikhara when we are not sure about a matter (a matter that is allowed) and need guidance from God.

Chapter 6

Shariah of Worship Rituals

Zakah – Obligatory Charity

This chapter discusses the second most important ritual of worship prescribed in Shariah: Zakah (Obligatory Charity).

Shariah of Zakah

History of the prayers

- The history of Zakah is the same as that of the prayer, and it always existed in the Shariah of the prophets.
- In other belief systems, people have generally adopted the practice of offering their wealth, livestock, etc., to their deities.
- The Quran referred to it as the "specified or known right" of the people when addressing the people of Quraish, as it was a pre-existing Sunnah.
- The Quran mentioned that other prophets used to give Zakah along with offering prayer.
- It is mentioned in the Bible also:

A tithe of everything from the land, whether grain from the soil or fruit from the trees, belongs to the LORD; it is holy to the LORD. If a man redeems any of his tithes, he must add a fifth of their value. The entire tithe of the herd and flock – every tenth animal that passes under the shepherd's rod – will be holy to the LORD. (Leviticus 27:30-31)

The LORD said to Moses, Speak to the Levites and say: When you receive the tithe I give you as your inheritance from the Israelites, you must present a tenth of that tithe as the LORD's offering. (Numbers 18:25-26)

وَ كَانَ يَأْمُرُ أَهْلَهُ بِالصَّلٰوةِ وَ الزَّكٰوةِ

And he (Ismail) would instruct his family to pray and to give Zakah. (19:55)

وَ قَالَ اللهُ اِنِّیْ مَعَكُمْ ۚ لَئِنْ اَقَمْتُمُ الصَّلٰوةَ وَ اٰتَیْتُمُ الزَّكٰوةَ

(Saying to the children of Israel) I am with you if you are diligent in prayer and pay Zakah. (5:12)

وَ وَیْلٌ لِّلْمُشْرِكِیْنَ ۙ الَّذِیْنَ لَا یُؤْتُوْنَ الزَّكٰوةَ وَ هُمْ بِالْاٰخِرَةِ هُمْ كٰفِرُوْنَ

And woe to the idolaters, who do not pay the Zakah, and it is these who reject the Hereafter. (41:6-7)

Objective of Zakah

- The root of the Arabic word Zakah has two meanings: "purity" and "growth".
- Thus, wealth given in the path of Allah is to obtain the purity of the heart and grow in Eeman.
- It cleanses the soul of the stains that can corrode it because of love of wealth and infuses blessings into wealth.
- It is the minimum financial obligation on a person to spend his wealth in the way of God.

خُذْ مِنْ اَمْوَالِهِمْ صَدَقَةً تُطَهِّرُهُمْ وَ تُزَكِّيْهِمْ بِهَا

[O Prophet!] Take Zakah from their wealth in order to purify them with it. (9:103)

مَآ اٰتَيْتُمْ مِّنْ زَكٰوةٍ تُرِيْدُوْنَ وَجْهَ اللّٰهِ فَاُولٰٓئِكَ هُمُ الْمُضْعِفُوْنَ

And that which you give as Zakah, seeking Allah's countenance, it is these people who will increase their wealth [in the Hereafter]. (30:39)

"For wherever your treasure is, your heart will also be." (Mathew 5:21)

Importance of Zakah

- Muslims are directed to pay Zakah in numerous places in the Quran, and it is the second most important act of worship after prayer.
- It is considered the second manifestation of one's faith in God.
- When disbelievers were given the punishment of death, Muslims were asked to leave them if the disbelievers agreed to offer prayer and pay their Zakah.
- It is considered a sign of righteousness in the Quran.
- This is not a financial matter in religion, but rather a ritual, like prayer.
- Zakah is a share imposed by Allah on one's wealth and has been reserved for Allah.
- In our Shariah, we are directed to pay Zakah to our rulers so that the state's needs can be met.
- It is like a tax that rulers are asked to collect to run their affairs, but God fixes its proportion, and He did not leave it to the rulers.
- The Quran has talked about severe consequences for people who do not pay their Zakah.

وَ اَقِيمُوا الصَّلٰوةَ وَ اٰتُوا الزَّكٰوةَ وَ اَقْرِضُوا اللهَ قَرْضًا حَسَنًا ۚ وَ مَا تُقَدِّمُوا لِاَنْفُسِكُمْ مِّنْ خَيْرٍ تَجِدُوهُ عِنْدَ اللهِ هُوَ خَيْرًا وَّ اَعْظَمَ اَجْرًا

And [in the daytime and at night] be diligent in the prayer and pay Zakah and [for the cause of your religion and state] lend to Allah a befitting loan, and [remember] whatever good you send forth for yourselves you shall find it with Allah better than before and greater in reward. (73:20)

وَ مَا تَفَرَّقَ الَّذِينَ اُوتُوا الْكِتٰبَ اِلَّا مِنْ بَعْدِ مَا جَاءَتْهُمُ الْبَيِّنَةُ

وَ مَا اُمِرُوا اِلَّا لِيَعْبُدُوا اللهَ مُخْلِصِينَ لَهُ الدِّينَ حُنَفَاءَ وَ يُقِيمُوا الصَّلٰوةَ وَ يُؤْتُوا الزَّكٰوةَ وَ ذٰلِكَ دِينُ الْقَيِّمَةِ

And [those among them] who were given the Book [before] became divided only after such a clear sign had come to them. And [in this Book also] they had been directed to worship Allah, obeying Him exclusively with sincere devotion. and to be diligent in the prayer and to pay Zakah [and the truth is that] this is the religion of the Upright Nation. (98:4-5)

وَ الَّذِينَ يُؤْتُونَ مَا اٰتَوا وَّ قُلُوبُهُمْ وَجِلَةٌ اَنَّهُمْ اِلٰى رَبِّهِمْ رٰجِعُونَ

And those who, whenever they give, give such that their hearts are filled with awe, knowing that they will have to return to their Lord. (23:60)

اَلَمْ يَعْلَمُوا اَنَّ اللهَ هُوَ يَقْبَلُ التَّوْبَةَ عَنْ عِبَادِهِ وَ يَأْخُذُ الصَّدَقٰتِ وَ اَنَّ اللهَ هُوَ التَّوَّابُ الرَّحِيمُ

Do they not know that God Himself accepts the repentance of His servants and takes their charities? (9:104)

فَاِنْ تَابُوا وَ اَقَامُوا الصَّلٰوةَ وَ اٰتُوا الزَّكٰوةَ فَاِخْوَانُكُمْ فِي الدِّينِ

So if they repent, become diligent in the prayers, and pay Zakah, they are your brethren in religion (9:11)

Consequences of not paying Zakah

- Failing to pay Zakah has serious consequences, as mentioned in the Quran.
- This is especially true when people have money, and the society needs it, but they keep hoarding without sharing any of it.

وَ الَّذِينَ يَكْنِزُونَ الذَّهَبَ وَ الْفِضَّةَ وَ لَا يُنْفِقُونَهَا فِىْ سَبِيلِ اللهِ ۙ فَبَشِّرْهُمْ بِعَذَابٍ اَلِيْمٍ

يَّوْمَ يُحْمٰى عَلَيْهَا فِىْ نَارِ جَهَنَّمَ فَتُكْوٰى بِهَا جِبَاهُهُمْ وَ جُنُوْبُهُمْ وَ ظُهُوْرُهُمْ ۙ هٰذَا مَا كَنَزْتُمْ

لِاَنْفُسِكُمْ فَذُوْقُوْا مَا كُنْتُمْ تَكْنِزُوْنَ

And to those who hoard gold and silver and spend it not in the way of Allah, give them glad tidings of dreadful punishment. The day when in Hell their treasures shall be heated, then their foreheads, sides, and backs branded with them: "These are the riches which you hoarded. So taste then what you were hoarding." (9:34-35)

Concept of Nisaab

- Nothing except the following is exempt from Zakah:
  - Tools and means used for production, trade, and business (for example, machines, factories, offices, etc.).
  - Personal items of daily use, regardless of how expensive they are (as per a person's status in society).
  - Considering the circumstances, a fixed quantity called **Nisaab** can be adjusted (added to or subtracted from). Prophet Muhammad fixed the following as Nisab (You don't have to pay Zakah on this):
    - Wealth – 642 grams of Silver or equivalent.
    - Produce – 653 kilograms of dates or equivalent.
    - Livestock – 5 camels, 30 cows, and 40 goats.
- Nisaab is the minimum amount of wealth, produce, and livestock that makes Zakah an obligation upon you. Before reaching Nisab, you are not supposed to pay Zakah.
- For brevity, we can use the minimum Nisaab amount in dollars. Prophet set it at 642 grams of silver, or its equivalent (it turns out to be around $500 in the US today).
- The concept is explained in the following picture.

- For you to pay Zakah, the Nisaab amount must stay with you for the entire year. If at any time your savings go below the Nisaab amount, you have to wait for that amount to reach Nisaab and start counting the year again.
- The wisdom behind waiting one year is to ensure your savings are consistent, not temporary before you pay Zakah.

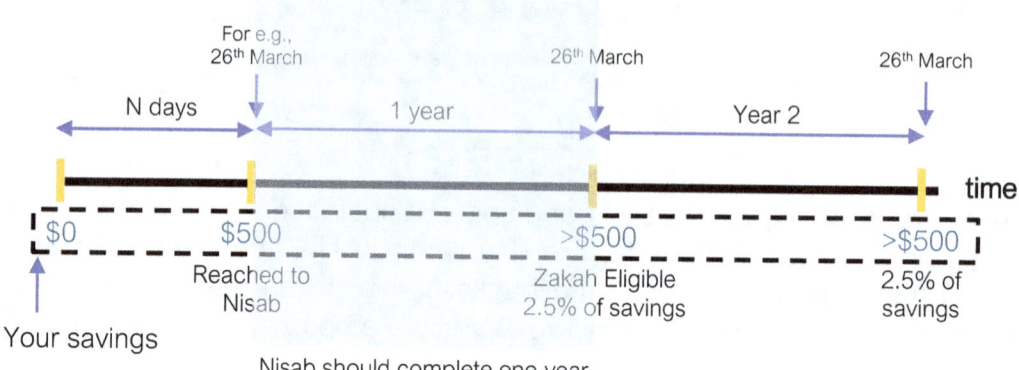

Nisab should complete one year

$$\text{لَيْسَ فِيمَا دُونَ خَمْسَةِ أَوْسُقٍ مِنَ التَّمْرِ صَدَقَةٌ وَلَيْسَ فِيمَا دُونَ خَمْسِ أَوَاقٍّ مِنَ الْوَرِقِ صَدَقَةٌ وَلَيْسَ}$$
$$\text{فِيمَا دُونَ خَمْسِ ذَوْدٍ مِنَ الْإِبِلِ صَدَقَةٌ}$$

There is no Zakah below five *wasaqs* of dates (a unit of measurement); there is no Zakah below five *uqiyahs* of silver, and there is no Zakah below five camels. (Al-Muwatta #683)

Rates of Zakah

- There is no single Zakah rate, as some people think. It depends on the item for which Zakah is collected.
- The following are the rates given to us by Prophet Muhammad through his Sunnah:

Wealth

- 2.5% annually.
- Wealth includes all cash on hand, money in the bank, savings, gold, silver, and anything equivalent to the currency in use.

Production

- 5% of the produce when it is ready if both capital and labor are involved.
- 10% if either capital or labor is involved.
- 20% if no capital or labor is involved, and it is a gift from God.

Livestock

Camels
- From 5 to 24: 1 she-goat for every 5 camels
- From 25 to 35: 1, one-year-old she-camel or, in its absence, 1, two-year-old camel
- From 36 to 45: 1, a two-year-old she-camel
- From 46 to 60: 1, a three-year-old she-camel
- From 61 to 75: 1, a four-year-old she-camel
- From 76 to 90: 1, two-year-old she-camels
- From 91 to 120: 2, three-year-old she-camels
- Over 120: 1, two-year-old she-camel on every 40 camels, and 1, three-year-old
- old on every fifty camel

Cows
- One one-year-old calf on every thirty cows and one, two-year-old calf on every forty cows

Goats/Sheep
- From 40 to 120: 1 she-goat
- From 121 to 200: 2 she-goats
- From 201 to 300: 3 she-goats
- Over 300: 1 she-goat for every 100 goats

When Zakah is due
- Since Zakah is due on many things, the due time also varies.
- The Zakah on non-production items is due annually – a day (date) should be fixed, and Zakah should be paid on that day every year. The example of $ was shown before.
- The Zakah on production is due as soon as the product is ready.
- All new forms of wealth and production will be associated with existing forms, and their rates will be applied to the new forms.
- For example:
  - Rental property is like a production unit, and it produces the rent on which the Zakah of 5% of the production (rental income) is applied (you are using your capital and labor), and it is due when rent is received.
  - The same applies to the monthly salary, which acts like a production.
- Land (non-agriculture) is another form of wealth, and 2.5% of the land price should be paid annually.

The heads of Zakah expenditure

إِنَّمَا الصَّدَقَٰتُ لِلْفُقَرَآءِ وَ الْمَسَٰكِينِ وَ الْعَٰمِلِينَ عَلَيْهَا وَ الْمُؤَلَّفَةِ قُلُوبُهُمْ وَ فِي الرِّقَابِ وَ الْغَٰرِمِينَ وَ فِي سَبِيلِ اللهِ وَ ابْنِ السَّبِيلِ ۖ فَرِيضَةً مِّنَ اللهِ ۗ وَ اللهُ عَلِيمٌ حَكِيمٌ

Zakah is only for the poor and the needy, and for those who are in charge of it, and for those whose hearts are to be reconciled [to the truth], and for the emancipation of the slaves and for those who have been inflicted with losses, and for the way of Allah and the welfare of the wayfarers. This is an obligation decreed by God, and God is All-Knowing and Wise. (9:60)

1. The poor.
2. The needy.
3. The salaries of all state employees.
4. All political expenditures in the Interest of Islam and Muslims.
5. For the liberation of people from the slavery of all kinds.
6. For helping people suffering economic losses and/or who are burdened with a fine or a loan.
7. For the welfare of the citizens, which includes multiple things, such as some types of social security.
8. For helping travelers and for the construction of roads, bridges, and rest houses.

Other details

- If the state is not collecting Zakah for any reason, the person must pay it himself and distribute it according to the heads identified on the previous slide.
- Zakah and its laws are only applicable to Muslim citizens of a state.
- It is expected from a believer that the best of wealth, produce, and livestock should be given in Zakah.
- Zakah can be given in an individual's personal possession or spent on social welfare projects.
- A state can exempt certain items from Zakah each year, taking into account the circumstances and situation of the masses and the state.
- The Nisaab can be set by the government, but rates cannot be changed.
- If the state is already imposing income tax and collecting it every month from your salary, then the person can subtract that from the Zakah due – if the rate of income tax is more than the Zakah, then there is no need to pay Zakah in that month (however, Zakah should be calculated on the savings at the end of the year).

- There is an opinion that Zakah cannot be given to the people who claim to be from the family of Prophet Muhammad (called Syeds). Discuss the opinion.

- Can I give Zakah for the construction of the Mosque in my community?

Chapter 7

Shariah of Worship Rituals

Fasting – Saum

This chapter discusses the ritual of fasting that the Quran describes as a means of attaining God-consciousness.

Shariah of Fasting

The history of fasting

- The history of fasting is the same as that of prayer and zakah.
- The Quran states that it was prescribed for other nations.
- The concept, similar to fasting as a ritual to train and discipline the soul, also exists in other belief systems.
- It is also mentioned in the Bible.
- In pre-Islamic Arab times, the existence of the word for fasting (Saum or Siyam) shows that people were aware of this ritual.
- Some narratives state that the Quraish used to fast on the day of Ashura (10th Muharram). They fast on this day to atone for a sin they had committed in the days of Jahiliyyah – a sin whose burden lay heavily upon them.
- They were fully aware of its religious status and details; its bounds and limits.
- The source of the fast is also the consensus and the practical perpetuation among Muslims; only certain rules related to travelers and the sick were mentioned in the Quran.

Then the Israelites, all the people, went up to Bethel, where they sat weeping before the LORD. They fasted that day until evening and presented burnt and fellowship offerings to the LORD. (Judges 20:26)

David pleaded with God for the child. He fasted and went into his house and spent the nights lying on the ground. (2 Samuel 12:16)

Yet when they were ill, I put on sackcloth and humbled myself with fasting. When my prayers returned to me unanswered. (Psalms 35:13)

Objective of Fasting

- In the Arabic language, the word used for fasting is "Sawm," which means "to abstain from something."
- The Quran stated the objective of fasting as "so that you become God-conscious" (called Taqwa).
- Having Taqwa means that a person should lead his life within the limits set by God and remain conscious of His accountability for everything he does.

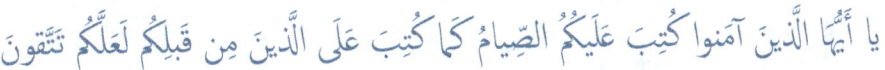

يا أَيُّهَا الَّذِينَ آمَنوا كُتِبَ عَلَيْكُمُ الصِّيامُ كَما كُتِبَ عَلَى الَّذِينَ مِن قَبْلِكُم لَعَلَّكُم تَتَّقونَ

Believers! Fasting has been obligatory upon you as it was made obligatory upon those before you, so that you become God-conscious. (2:183)

How fasting engenders *Taqwa*?

1 Feeling of Servitude & Obedience

- It revives, with full force, the concept in a person's mind that he is God's servant.
- The feeling of servitude arises and intensifies when the body's natural desires are given up (for example, the desire for food).
- A person does not consume a single bite of food or a single drop of water merely because his Lord has directed him to refrain from them.
- It is befitting for a fasting person to obey God in other affairs of life as he submits during fasting.

2 Awareness of Accountability

- When the onslaught of thirst, hunger, and carnal desire makes life difficult, it is only the awareness of being answerable before the Almighty that stops a person from fulfilling these needs.
- This abstention requires a lot of effort, which is only possible when the person knows that breaking the law of fasting will have consequences he will have to face on the day of judgment.

3 Lots of Patience

- Patience is one of the key traits in developing Taqwa, and fasting is the best way to engender that.
- Fasting is the best training one can have to practice and develop patience.
- Outside the fast, the trial of this life requires us to exercise patience at every step.
- If the traits of honesty, veracity, justice, forbearance, forgiveness, keeping promises, perseverance on the truth, avoiding evil, and shunning lust are not present in a person, Taqwa has no basis, and without patience, these traits cannot be espoused in a person.

Taqwa is the objective of the fast, and the month of Ramadan has been fixed for it. It is a 30-day training period that God requires Muslims to undergo to train their minds and bodies to obey God's commands.

Importance of fasting and Ramadan

- One of the most practical ways a person can express his worship is by obeying his Lord's commands.
- Fasts are a symbolic expression of this obedience.
- The Quran was revealed (began to be revealed) in the month of Ramadan (*Lailatul Qadr*), and fasting is also made obligatory during Ramadan.
- Fasting in the month of the Quran allows Muslims to glorify their Lord and express gratitude for the Quran's blessings by embodying obedience.
- The treasured state that arises from combining the prayer (extra prayers) and the fast with recitals of the Quran and the feeling of being solely devoted to the Almighty, with no one around (*Eitikaf*), helps achieve the objective of the fast in the very best way.
- The night of the decree (Lailatul Qadr) also falls in the last part of Ramadan.
- The Quran informed us that Angel Jibrael and other angels descend on this night, and important decisions are made.
- The nearness of God that can be achieved on this night is equivalent to worshiping the Almighty for one thousand months.

A person who fasts in Ramadan with faith and while holding himself accountable to God, his previous sins are forgiven. (Sahih Al-Bukhari #3009)

A person who prays during the night in Ramadan with faith and while holding himself accountable to God, his previous sins are forgiven. (Sahih Al-Bukhari #37)

"When Ramadan comes, the doors of Paradise are opened, and the doors of Hell are closed, and the devils are enchained." (Sahih Al-Bukhari #1899)

Whatever pious deed a person does, he is rewarded from ten to seven hundred times, but the fast is an exception to this. The Almighty says: It is for Me, and only I will reward [a person] for it) because he gave up eating and drinking and abstained from sexual desires for My sake. (Sahih Al-Bukhari #1894)

There is a door in Paradise called Rayyan. People who fast will enter Paradise from this door on the Day of Judgement. No other person will be able to pass through this door. It shall be asked: "Where are the people who fast?" At this, they will get up, and no one else will enter with them. Once they enter [Paradise], it shall be closed. No one else after them would be able to pass through it. (Sahih Al-Bukhari # 1896)

The Shariah of Fasting

يَا أَيُّهَا الَّذِينَ آمَنُوا كُتِبَ عَلَيْكُمُ الصِّيَامُ كَمَا كُتِبَ عَلَى الَّذِينَ مِن قَبْلِكُمْ لَعَلَّكُمْ تَتَّقُونَ

أَيَّامًا مَّعْدُودَاتٍ ۚ فَمَن كَانَ مِنكُم مَّرِيضًا أَوْ عَلَىٰ سَفَرٍ فَعِدَّةٌ مِّنْ أَيَّامٍ أُخَرَ ۚ وَعَلَى الَّذِينَ يُطِيقُونَهُ فِدْيَةٌ

طَعَامُ مِسْكِينٍ ۖ فَمَن تَطَوَّعَ خَيْرًا فَهُوَ خَيْرٌ لَّهُ ۚ وَأَن تَصُومُوا خَيْرٌ لَّكُمْ ۖ إِن كُنتُمْ تَعْلَمُونَ

شَهْرُ رَمَضَانَ الَّذِي أُنزِلَ فِيهِ الْقُرْآنُ هُدًى لِّلنَّاسِ وَبَيِّنَاتٍ مِّنَ الْهُدَىٰ وَالْفُرْقَانِ ۚ فَمَن شَهِدَ مِنكُمُ

الشَّهْرَ فَلْيَصُمْهُ ۖ وَمَن كَانَ مَرِيضًا أَوْ عَلَىٰ سَفَرٍ فَعِدَّةٌ مِّنْ أَيَّامٍ أُخَرَ ۗ يُرِيدُ اللَّهُ بِكُمُ الْيُسْرَ وَلَا يُرِيدُ

بِكُمُ الْعُسْرَ وَلِتُكْمِلُوا الْعِدَّةَ وَلِتُكَبِّرُوا اللَّهَ عَلَىٰ مَا هَدَاكُمْ وَلَعَلَّكُمْ تَشْكُرُونَ

Believers! Fasting has been obligatory upon you as it was made obligatory upon those before you, so that you become God-conscious. These are but a few days, but if anyone among you is ill or on a journey, let him fast the same number of days later (after Ramadan); those who have the capacity [to feed a needy] should feed a needy in place of it. Then he who does a virtuous deed of his own accord, it is better for him, and if you fast, then this is even better for you if you but knew. It is the month of Ramadan in which the Qur'an was revealed as a book of guidance for mankind, and in the form of manifest arguments, which are a means of total guidance and a means of distinguishing right from wrong. Therefore, whoever among you is present this month should fast. And he who is ill or on a journey should fast the same number of days later. [This concession is because] God desires ease for you, not discomfort. And [the permission given to travelers and the sick to feed the needy has been withdrawn because] you can complete the fasts [and thus not be deprived of the blessings of fasting] and [for this purpose, the month of Ramadan has been fixed so that in the form of the Qur'an] the guidance God has bestowed upon you; you glorify God and express your gratitude to Him. (2:183-185)

- Fasting is made obligatory for Muslims in the month of Ramadan.
- The fasting period is from Fajr to Nightfall (after sunset).
- Abstention from the following is required during the fast:
  - No eating or drinking.
  - No marital relations between spouses.
- Initially, people who were unable to fast due to illness or travel were allowed to either make up the fast later or feed a poor person – however, later, God directed people that they should make up their fast later.
- Fasting during the menstrual or childbirth cycles is forbidden, and women should make up the fast later.
- If a person decides to sit in Eitikaf, he is permitted to eat and drink during the night; however, he cannot engage in physical marital relations with his spouse. The Almighty has prohibited this.

Some other details

- When the moon is sighted, Ramadan should begin, and when the moon is sighted, fasting should end.
- It is recommended not to fast for a few days before Ramadan unless the person is used to fasting on those days.
- One should eat Sahur (the pre-fast meal) before beginning the fast. The Prophet asked people to eat it because eating it brings blessings.
- During the fast, husband and wife can be intimate in whatever way they choose, except for having a physical marital relationship.
- If a person eats forgetfully, then this does not break the fast. The Prophet remarked that it was Allah who had fed him.
- The prophet is reported to have said that one should try to seek *Laylatul Qadr* in the last ten days of Ramadan, particularly on the odd nights.
- It is better to observe *Eitikaf* during the second or third portion (the last 10 days) of Ramadan, preferably for the full 10 days.
- Intentionally breaking the fast is a grave sin. If a person commits this sin, he should atone for it by fasting for two consecutive months (although the Prophet did not insist on it).

Optional fasts

- The prophet observed the following optional fasts or urged people to fast:
  - The day of Ashura (10th of Muharram)
  - The day of Arafah (9th of Dhul Hijjah)
  - Six days in Shawwal after Ramadan.
  - The three days of each month (like the 13th, 14th, and 15th).
  - Mondays and Thursdays.

Missing the objective

- People who do not fully understand the true purpose of fasting often indulge in activities during the fast, thereby stripping it of its blessings. Some of those activities are highlighted here:
  1. Ramadan becomes the month of a food fest when people savor the flavors.
  2. The Fast becomes an excuse for people who lose their temper quickly and easily, especially when hunger and thirst are at their peak.

3. People try to find replacements for the things they have given up – for example, food, drinks, and other activities like playing cards, reading novels, listening to songs, watching movies, and gossiping. The idea is to 'kill time'.

4. Some people do not fast for God but merely to avoid criticism and condemnation from their family members and acquaintances.

When the last ten days of Ramadan would arrive, the Prophet would fully prepare himself to worship the Almighty. He would worship the Almighty late at night and wake up his family members for this as well. (Sahih Al-Bukhari #2024)

Ibn Abbas says that even in normal times, the Prophet was the most generous; however, in Ramadan, he would become an embodiment of generosity. (Sahih Al-Bukhari #6009)

The fast is a shield; whoever among you fasts should not indulge in lewd talk nor be overcome by his emotions; if anyone abuses him or initiates a fight, he should respond by saying: 'I am fasting, my brother, I am fasting.' (Sahih Al-Bukhari #1894)

A person who does not desist from lying and practicing it, then the Almighty does not need him to abandon eating and drinking." (Sahih Al-Bukhari #1903)

Whoever kept the fasts of Ramadan and followed them up with six fasts in Shawwal is like a person who kept fasts all his life. (Sahih Muslim #2758)

Moonsighting to start and end fasting

- The prophet instructed Muslims to begin fasting when the moon of Ramadan is sighted, as the Quran commands fasting for the entire month. This instruction was given to ensure that people carefully observe the start of the month, as in those days, sighting the moon was the only method available to mark it.
- Similarly, Prophet asked them to stop fasting when the moon is sighted for the next month to complete the month of fasting.
- In a lunar calendar, a month can have 29 or 30 days. Realizing that people may misunderstand that they have to fast for a complete 30 days, the Prophet is reported to have said:

"A month can also be of twenty-nine days; so, if you sight the moon, begin the fast, and if you sight it, break the fast; if the weather is not clear, end the month of Shaban by completing thirty days." (Sahih Muslim #2503 & 2514)

- It is clear from the instructions above that the only purpose of sighting the moon is to determine if the month is 29 days, so people do not insist on completing 30 days.
- If, today, we can determine the number of days in the month by any other means (e.g., creating a lunar calendar through science), then there is no need to see the moon.
- We can also conclude that seeing the moon was not a condition for starting or ending the month of Ramadan, because he did not insist on seeing the moon when the count reached 30 due to the overcast.
- Today, this is a big issue among Muslims. Due to not fully understanding the instructions and advancements in communications, Muslims are divided into three groups when it comes to starting and ending the month of Ramadan.
    1. Those who perform local sighting for the moon within the boundary of a country.
    2. Those who rely purely on scientific methods to estimate the start and end of the month have made a lunar calendar.
    3. Those who believe in international moon sighting, meaning they would look for a report of sighting anywhere in the world. Usually, they coincide with moon sighting done in Saudi Arabia.

If you don't want to fast because of your family's pressure, what is the best way to convince yourself to fast?

Chapter 8

Shariah of Worship Rituals

Fasting – Saum

This chapter discusses the ritual of fasting that the Quran describes as a means of attaining God-consciousness.

History and Innovations

The history of Hajj

- It begins with the declaration of Ibrahim referred to in verses 22:27-29.
- Before Prophet Muhammad became the Messenger, the people of Arabia would come in multitudes to perform this ritual.
- When the Quran discussed Hajj, it was not a new concept to its addressees, who were already aware of its rites and rituals.
- However, a few innovations and deviations were introduced, which the Quran corrected to restore the ritual to its original form.

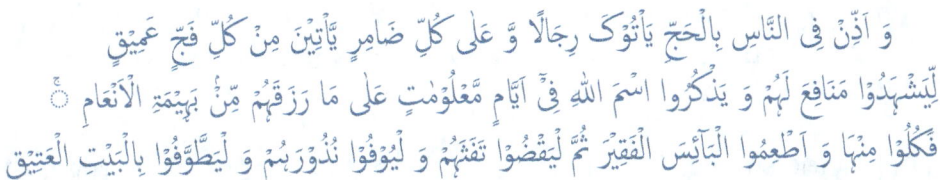

And proclaim the pilgrimage among the people. They will come to you on foot and the backs of lean camels from distant mountainous ways so that they can reach places of benefit and, on a few appointed days, invoke the name of God over their cattle which He has bestowed upon them. [So when you slaughter them] eat of their flesh and feed the deprived beggar. Then let the pilgrims cleanse themselves of their dirt and fulfill their vows and circle the Ancient House. (22:27-29)

وَ لِلّٰهِ عَلَى النَّاسِ حِجُّ الْبَيْتِ مَنِ اسْتَطَاعَ اِلَيْهِ سَبِيْلًا

And pilgrimage to the House has always remained a duty to God for all who can make the journey. (3:97)

Jubayr bin Mut'im reported an incident (who accepted Islam later) before Prophet Muhammad was given the Messengerhood: "I lost my camel. On the day of 'Arafah, while trying to find it, I went up to the field of 'Arafat and found Muhammad standing there. I said to myself: "By God! He belongs to the Quraysh; then what is he doing here?" (because Quraish introduced an innovation of not going to Arafat for anyone who is from the tribe of Quraish). The incident described suggests that before Islam, Prophet Muhammad and others in Makkah were fully aware of those innovations and performed Hajj in accordance with Ibrahim's legacy. (Sahih Al-Bukhari #1664)

Innovations and corrections

1   Being the custodian, the Quraish wanted to maintain authority on who could come for Hajj and Umrah – the Quran did not accept it and said no one has the right to stop any person from coming to the house of Allah.

اِنَّ الَّذِیْنَ کَفَرُوْا وَ یَصُدُّوْنَ عَنْ سَبِیْلِ اللہِ وَ الْمَسْجِدِ الْحَرَامِ الَّذِیْ جَعَلْنٰهُ لِلنَّاسِ سَوَآءَ الْعَاكِفُ فِیْهِ وَ الْبَادِ ؕ وَ مَنْ یُّرِدْ فِیْهِ بِاِلْحَادٍۭ بِظُلْمٍ نُّذِقْهُ مِنْ عَذَابٍ اَلِیْمٍ

Those who disbelieved and are now preventing others from the path of God and from the Sacred Mosque, which We regarded for mankind, natives and strangers alike [are indeed committing grave oppression], and [the matter of this Mosque is such that] those who seek to practice something non-religious, some polytheism within it, We shall make them taste a grievous penalty. (22:25)

2   The filth of polytheism was introduced into the foremost center of monotheism, i.e., the Kabaah – the Quran declared that this house would be handed over to those who would keep it cleansed of this filth.

وَ اِذْ بَوَّاْنَا لِاِبْرٰهِیْمَ مَکَانَ الْبَیْتِ اَنْ لَّا تُشْرِکْ بِیْ شَیْئًا وَّ طَهِّرْ بَیْتِیَ لِلطَّآئِفِیْنَ وَ الْقَآئِمِیْنَ وَ الرُّکَّعِ السُّجُوْدِ

And recall when We made for Abraham the site of the sacred mosque as an abode [with the guidance]: "Worship none besides Me. Keep clean My House for those who walk around it, and those who stand upright or kneel in worship." (22:26)

3   Due to safety concerns, the month of Rajab was reserved for Umrah, and the months of Dhul Qadah, Dhul Hijjah, and Muharram were reserved for Hajj, but Quraish violated this rule. To suit their fighting needs, they used to switch months. Also, sometimes, to have Hajj fall in the same season as the next year, they used to add one month (called Kabisa) to the lunar calendar to bring it into line with the solar calendar. The Quran declared such practices as evidence of increased disbelief and rejected them.

اِنَّمَا النَّسِیْٓءُ زِیَادَةٌ فِی الْکُفْرِ یُضَلُّ بِهِ الَّذِیْنَ کَفَرُوْا یُحِلُّوْنَهٗ عَامًا وَّ یُحَرِّمُوْنَهٗ عَامًا لِّیُوَاطِـُٔوْا عِدَّةَ مَا حَرَّمَ اللہُ فَیُحِلُّوْا مَا حَرَّمَ اللہُ ؕ زُیِّنَ لَهُمْ سُوْٓءُ اَعْمَالِهِمْ ؕ وَ اللہُ لَا یَهْدِی الْقَوْمَ الْکٰفِرِیْنَ

The annulment of sacred months is only an addition in disbelief that has been made a means to misguide the disbelievers. In one year, they regard one month as allowed [for bloodshed], and in another year, they regard the same month as forbidden so that they may make up for the months that God has regarded as forbidden, thus making lawful what God has forbidden. Their evil deeds seem fair to them. [They are disbelievers], and God does not guide such disbelievers. (9:37)

4 Quraish stopped sacrificing certain animals as they had forbidden those animals for themselves – the Quran termed it as "attributing lying to Allah" and outrightly rejected it.

ذٰلِكَ وَ مَنْ يُّعَظِّمْ حُرُمٰتِ اللهِ فَهُوَ خَيْرٌ لَّهٗ عِنْدَ رَبِّهٖ ۗ وَ أُحِلَّتْ لَكُمُ الْأَنْعَامُ إِلَّا مَا يُتْلٰى

عَلَيْكُمْ فَاجْتَنِبُوا الرِّجْسَ مِنَ الْأَوْثَانِ وَ اجْتَنِبُوا قَوْلَ الزُّورِ

حُنَفَآءَ لِلّٰهِ غَيْرَ مُشْرِكِينَ بِهٖ ۗ وَ مَنْ يُّشْرِكْ بِاللهِ فَكَأَنَّمَا خَرَّ مِنَ السَّمَآءِ

فَتَخْطَفُهُ الطَّيْرُ أَوْ تَهْوِىْ بِهِ الرِّيحُ فِىْ مَكَانٍ سَحِيْقٍ

ذٰلِكَ وَ مَنْ يُّعَظِّمْ شَعَآئِرَ اللهِ فَإِنَّهَا مِنْ تَقْوَى الْقُلُوْبِ

لَكُمْ فِيْهَا مَنَافِعُ إِلٰى أَجَلٍ مُّسَمًّى ثُمَّ مَحِلُّهَآ إِلَى الْبَيْتِ الْعَتِيْقِ

Be diligent in these things and [remember] he who reveres the sacred things of God, it is better for him in [the eyes of] God. And the cattle are made lawful to you, except for those which have been spelled out to you before. So, abstain from the filth of idols and this falsehood [you attribute to God], dedicating yourselves to God and not associating others with Him. And [remember] he who associates other deities with God is like a person who falls from heaven, and then birds will snatch him away, or the wind will carry him away and throw him in some far-off region. Adhere to these things and [remember that] he who reveres the symbols of God [should know that] this is from the piety of the hearts. (22:30-32)

5 Benefiting from the services (milk, transportation) of the animals reserved for sacrifice was generally considered prohibited. The Quran stated that until the time of sacrifice, these animals can be used however people wish.

لَكُمْ فِيْهَا مَنَافِعُ إِلٰى أَجَلٍ مُّسَمًّى ثُمَّ مَحِلُّهَآ إِلَى الْبَيْتِ الْعَتِيْقِ

You can use these [animals] of [sacrifice] until an appointed time. Then they are to reach this Ancient House. (22:33)

6 Jews living in that area had prohibited the camel themselves because of a weak tradition. The Quran called it an innovation and encouraged Quraish to sacrifice camels, as they are dear to them.

وَ الْبُدْنَ جَعَلْنٰهَا لَكُمْ مِّنْ شَعَآئِرِ اللهِ لَكُمْ فِيْهَا خَيْرٌ ۖ فَاذْكُرُوا اسْمَ اللهِ عَلَيْهَا صَوَآفَّ ۗ فَإِذَا وَجَبَتْ جُنُوْبُهَا فَكُلُوْا مِنْهَا وَ

أَطْعِمُوا الْقَانِعَ وَ الْمُعْتَرَّ ۚ كَذٰلِكَ سَخَّرْنٰهَا لَكُمْ لَعَلَّكُمْ تَشْكُرُوْنَ

And We have made the camels a part of God's symbols. They are of much use to you. So, pronounce over them the name of God while you draw them up in line. Then, when they fall on their sides, eat of their flesh and feed the uncomplaining beggar and the demanding suppliant. Thus, have We subjected these [animals] to your service so that you may be grateful? (22:36)

7 It was believed that the Almighty was pleased with the flesh and blood of a sacrificed animal. The Quran states that God is pleased only with the piety engendered in those who offer such sacrifices.

لَنْ يَّنَالَ اللهَ لُحُوْمُهَا وَ لَا دِمَآؤُهَا وَ لٰكِنْ يَّنَالُهُ التَّقْوٰى مِنْكُمْ ۚ كَذٰلِكَ سَخَّرَهَا لَكُمْ لِتُكَبِّرُوا اللهَ عَلٰى مَا هَدٰىكُمْ ۚ وَ بَشِّرِ الْمُحْسِنِيْنَ

Flesh and blood of these [sacrifices of yours] do not reach God; your piety reaches Him. Thus, He has subjected them to your service so that you may give glory to God for guiding you. [This is the way of those who are righteous] and [O Prophet!] Give glad tidings to these righteous (22:37)

8 Jews created doubts about the *tawaf* of the *Safa* and *Marwah* due to their hostility towards Prophet Ismail. The Quran admonished them for concealing that Ismail was prostrated for sacrifice on the hill of Marwah. God called Safa and Marwah among His symbols.

إِنَّ الصَّفَا وَ الْمَرْوَةَ مِنْ شَعَآئِرِ اللهِ ۚ فَمَنْ حَجَّ الْبَيْتَ أَوِ اعْتَمَرَ فَلَا جُنَاحَ عَلَيْهِ أَنْ يَّطَّوَّفَ بِهِمَا ۚ وَ مَنْ تَطَوَّعَ خَيْرًا ۙ فَإِنَّ اللهَ شَاكِرٌ عَلِيْمٌ   إِنَّ الَّذِيْنَ يَكْتُمُوْنَ مَآ أَنْزَلْنَا مِنَ الْبَيِّنٰتِ وَ الْهُدٰى مِنْ بَعْدِ مَا بَيَّنّٰهُ لِلنَّاسِ فِي الْكِتٰبِ ۙ أُولٰئِكَ يَلْعَنُهُمُ اللهُ وَ يَلْعَنُهُمُ اللّٰعِنُوْنَ

Safa and Marwah are indeed God's symbols. So, it shall be no offense for those who come for hajj or Umrah of this Sacred House to walk around them. [In fact, this is a virtuous deed], and He who does a virtue of his own will, God will accept it and is fully aware of it. Those who conceal the clear proofs and guidance We have revealed [in this matter], even though We had openly proclaimed them for these people in our Book, they shall be cursed by God and cursed by those who curse (2:158-159)

9 In the state of Ihram, coming back from the Hajj, Quraish would not enter their houses from the front but from the back due to a superstition that one should not enter from the same door (with the burden of sins at the time of leaving) after being cleansed from these sins (after Hajj). The Quran called it a foolish act and asserted there is no virtue in it.

وَ لَيْسَ الْبِرُّ بِأَنْ تَأْتُوا الْبُيُوْتَ مِنْ ظُهُوْرِهَا وَ لٰكِنَّ الْبِرَّ مَنِ اتَّقٰى وَ أْتُوا الْبُيُوْتَ مِنْ أَبْوَابِهَا ۚ وَ اتَّقُوا اللهَ لَعَلَّكُمْ تُفْلِحُوْنَ

It is certainly no virtue that you enter your dwellings from the rear [while returning from hajj and being in a state of ihram]. Virtue is that of a man who adopts piety. And enter your dwellings by their doors and keep fearing God so you may attain salvation. (2:189)

10 In those days, the ritual of Hajj had become a form of religious entertainment, and less attention was paid to its real objectives. The Almighty has directed their attention to useless activities and emphasized that in this journey, one's greatest provision is actually piety.

اَلْحَجُّ اَشْهُرٌ مَّعْلُوْمٰتٌ ۚ فَمَنْ فَرَضَ فِيْهِنَّ الْحَجَّ فَلَا رَفَثَ ۟ وَ لَا فُسُوْقَ ۟ وَ لَا جِدَالَ فِى الْحَجِّ ۚ وَ مَا تَفْعَلُوْا مِنْ خَيْرٍ يَّعْلَمْهُ اللّٰهُ ۗ وَ تَزَوَّدُوْا فَاِنَّ خَيْرَ الزَّادِ التَّقْوٰى ۟ وَ اتَّقُوْنِ يٰۤاُولِى الْاَلْبَابِ

The months of the hajj are known. So, anyone who intends to offer it [by wearing the ihram] should not indulge in lustful activities, refrain from being disobedient to the Almighty, and abstain from the altercation. And [remember that] the Almighty is aware of whatever good you do. And [in the journey of hajj] take the provision [of piety] with you because the best provision is piety. And O men of intellect! Keep fearing Me. (2:197)

11 Most people began using the Hajj journey to engage in business, trade, and similar activities. The Quran clarified that there is no harm in engaging in business during Hajj, but in reality, the sites of Hajj are not meant for such activities.

لَيْسَ عَلَيْكُمْ جُنَاحٌ اَنْ تَبْتَغُوْا فَضْلًا مِّنْ رَّبِّكُمْ ۚ فَاِذَاۤ اَفَضْتُمْ مِّنْ عَرَفٰتٍ فَاذْكُرُوا اللّٰهَ عِنْدَ الْمَشْعَرِ الْحَرَامِ ۖ وَ اذْكُرُوْهُ كَمَا هَدٰىكُمْ ۚ وَ اِنْ كُنْتُمْ مِّنْ قَبْلِهٖ لَمِنَ الضَّآلِّيْنَ

[In this journey of hajj], it shall be no offense for you to seek the bounty of your Lord [but remember that Muzdalifah is no place of amusement and trading;] so when you come from Arafat, remember God near the sacred monument [*Mashar al-haram*] and remember Him in the way He has guided you. And before this, you were undoubtedly in error. (2:198)

12 It had become the prerogative of the Quraish not to go beyond Muzdalifah (crossing the limits of Haram). The Quran did not accept the privilege they granted themselves and directed them to go to Arafat as others do.

ثُمَّ اَفِيْضُوْا مِنْ حَيْثُ اَفَاضَ النَّاسُ وَ اسْتَغْفِرُوا اللّٰهَ ۗ اِنَّ اللّٰهَ غَفُوْرٌ رَّحِيْمٌ

Then [O People of the Quraysh! It is also essential that] you return from where other people return and seek the forgiveness of God. God is indeed Forgiving and Ever-Merciful. (2:199)

13 The days at Mina, too, were spent in eulogistic recitals, storytelling, and indulging in proving the superiority of one another. Even if they invoked God, they would ask for worldly benefits. The Quran admonished them for such behavior and asserted that such people would have no share in the hereafter.

فَإِذَا قَضَيْتُمْ مَّنَاسِكَكُمْ فَاذْكُرُوا اللهَ كَذِكْرِكُمْ اٰبَآءَكُمْ اَوْ اَشَدَّ ذِكْرًا ۗ فَمِنَ النَّاسِ مَنْ يَّقُوْلُ رَبَّنَآ اٰتِنَا فِى الدُّنْيَا وَ مَا لَهُ فِى الْاٰخِرَةِ مِنْ خَلَاقٍ وَ مِنْهُمْ مَّنْ يَّقُوْلُ رَبَّنَآ اٰتِنَا فِى الدُّنْيَا حَسَنَةً وَّ فِى الْاٰخِرَةِ حَسَنَةً وَّ قِنَا عَذَابَ النَّارِ اُولٰئِكَ لَهُمْ نَصِيْبٌ مِّمَّا كَسَبُوْا ۗ وَ اللهُ سَرِيْعُ الْحِسَابِ

After this, when you have fulfilled the rites of hajj, remember God as you remember your forefathers; in fact, even more. [This is the time of asking from God], but there are some who [at this instance also] say: "Lord, give us in this world," and [then the result of this is that] these shall have no share in the world to come. But there are others who say: "Lord, give us what is good both in this world and in the world to come, and save us from the torment of the Fire." It is these who will receive a share of what they earned, and swift is God in taking account. (2:200-202)

14 The worst of these innovations was the nude circumambulation of the Kabaah. The Quran prohibited this practice and stressed that at all places of worship, a person must conceal their private parts and be properly dressed.

يٰبَنِيْ اٰدَمَ خُذُوْا زِيْنَتَكُمْ عِنْدَ كُلِّ مَسْجِدٍ وَّ كُلُوْا وَ اشْرَبُوْا وَ لَا تُسْرِفُوْا ۚ اِنَّهُ لَا يُحِبُّ الْمُسْرِفِيْنَ

O Children of Adam! Adorn yourself with your beautiful clothes on all occasions of attending your mosques. Eat and drink well, but do not waste. Indeed, He does not like the wasters. (7:31)

Objective of Hajj and Umrah

- The objectives of Hajj and Umrah are the same:
  - Affirmation of the oneness of God and
  - A reminder of the fact that after embracing Islam, we have devoted and dedicated ourselves to Him.
- It is the comprehension of this objective that allows a person "to reach to the benefits of the places of the Hajj" لِيَشْهَدُوْا مَنَافِعَ لَهُمْ (so that they can reach the places of benefit)
- The objective of Hajj is highlighted by the words we utter as we prepare for It by wearing Ihram.

لَبَّيْكَ اللّٰهُمَّ لبيك ۖ لَبَّيْكَ لَا شَرِيْكَ لَكَ لَبَّيْكَ إِنَّ الْحَمْدَ وَ النِّعْمَةَ لَكَ وَ الْمُلْكَ لَا شَرِيْكَ لَكَ

Here I am; O Lord, here I am; here I am; no one is Your partner; here I am. All gratitude is for You, and all blessings are Yours; sovereignty is for You only, and no one is Your partner.

> Hajj is a symbolic representation of a lifelong struggle and war with Satan.

Shariah – Method and Rulings

Days of Hajj and Umrah

- No time has been fixed for Umrah.
- The days of Hajj have been fixed from the 8th to the 13th of Dhul Hijjah.
- In those days, since people had to reach the city of Makkah from all over the world, the months of Rajab, Dhul Qadah, Dhul Hijjah, and Muharram were dedicated to Hajj, and war was prohibited.
- They are considered the sacred months.

God ordained the months to be twelve in number when He created the heavens and the earth. Of these, four are sacred. This is true faith. Therefore, do not sin against yourselves in them [by violating their sanctity]. (9:36)

Sites of Hajj and Umrah

- The sites of Hajj and Umrah are called the "*Sha'air*" (symbols) of Allah, and He commanded us that His symbols must be revered to gain the piety of the hearts.
- Some sites are common, for example, the first three in the list below are for both Umrah and Hajj.
- **Mawaqit:** The limits around the Bayt-al-Haram where the Haram begins, and these limits can only be crossed in the state of Ihram if one intends to perform Hajj or Umrah.
- **Bayt al-Haram:** the sacred mosque (Masjid al-Haram) where the *Kabaah* is located. The black stone (Hajar-e-Aswad) is placed on one of the corners of this building. The precincts of Baitullah extend for several kilometers on all four sides, and this area is called Haram.
- **Safa and Marwah:** These are two hills located very near the *Baitullah*, where Ismail's sacrifice occurred (Marwah). The tawaf between these two hills is called "Sai".

The Almighty has declared this city sacred since He created the heavens and the earth. It is sacred till the Day of Judgement because of this sanctity declared by God. No one before me was ever permitted to wage war in it. For me, this prohibition was lifted for part of the day. Hence, it is sacred till the Day of Judgement because of this sanctity declared by God; neither will its thorny trees be cut, nor its prey be chased for hunting, nor will anything found in it be picked except if it is picked by someone to have it delivered to its owner, nor will its grass be cut. (Sahih Al-Bukhari #1834)

Sites of Hajj

- **Mina:** This vast field between two hills is situated about 5 Km from Makkah. Pilgrims stay here (twice), once they return from Makkah and also from Arafat.
- **Arafat:** This vast field is about 10 Km from Mina. It is here that the imam of the Muslims delivers a sermon, and then till sunset, the pilgrims stand ceremoniously (Waquf). This is a place for dua, and Prophet Muhammad called this day of visiting Arafat the central day of Hajj.
- **Muzdalifah:** This is a second field where pilgrims spend the night on their way back from Arafat. The limits of Haram begin here and are therefore called Mashar al-Haram.
- **Jamarat:** Three columns situated in the middle of Mina, where people throw stones.
  - Jamrah Al-Ukhra/Aqabah – largest
  - Jamrah al-Ula
  - Jamrah al-Wusta

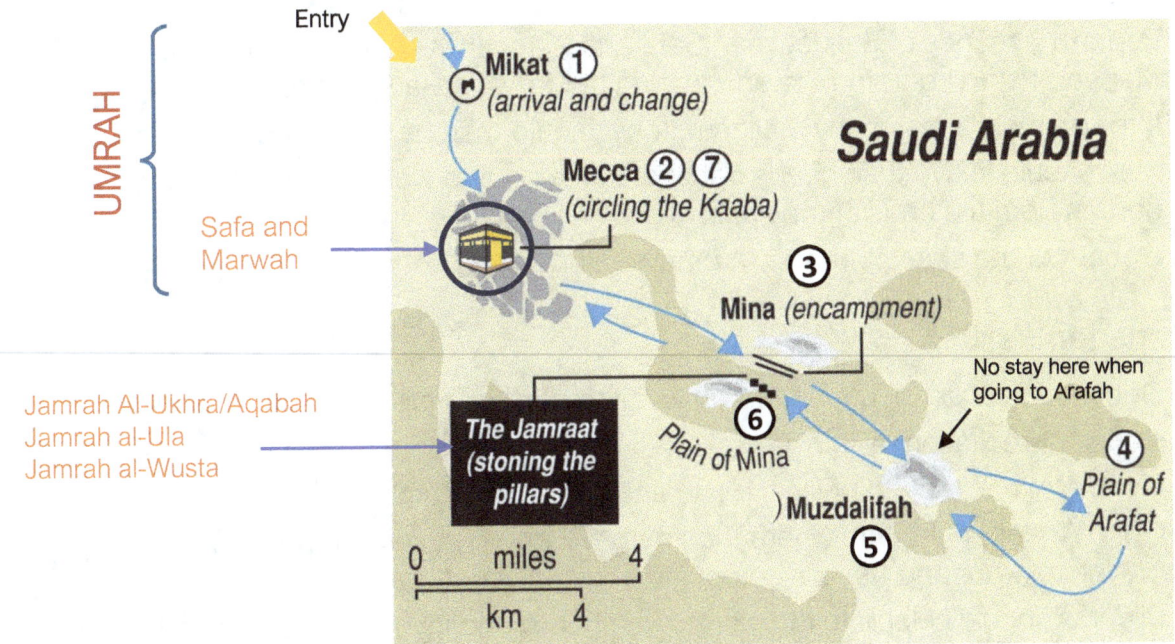

Steps for Umrah

- Ihram (two unstitched sheets) should be put on with the intention of Umrah from one of the Mawaqit or limits of Haram. In Ihram:
  - They cannot wear stitched cloth and should expose their heads, faces, and upper parts of their feet.
  - One cannot indulge in lewd talk.
  - Cannot use any adornments, such as perfume or nail polish, or shave or cut hair.
  - Cannot remove any dirt from outside, even to the extent of killing a louse.
  - Cannot hunt.
  - Women can wear stitched cloth and cover their heads and feet, but must leave their hands and face exposed.
  - The constant recitation of the Talbiyah

لَبَّيْكَ اللّٰهُمَّ لبيك لَبَّيْكَ لَا شَرِيْكَ لَكَ لَبَّيْكَ إِنَّ الْحَمْدَ وَ النِّعْمَةَ لَكَ وَ الْمُلْكَ لَا شَرِيْكَ لَكَ

- Perform 7 tawafs of Baitullah, starting from the black stone while kissing it or using a gesture.
- Perform 7 rounds of Sai between Safa and Marwah (one round is from Safa to Marwah), starting from Safa and ending at Marwah. Sai is optional.
- If the animals accompany a pilgrim, they should then be sacrificed (optional).
- Men should shave their heads or have a haircut, and women should cut a small portion from the ends of their hair.
- Get out of the state of Ihram by removing Ihram.

Steps for Hajj

- Get into the state of Ihram from Mawaqit to perform Hajj (all conditions apply).
- Constant recitation of Talbiyah.
- Go to Mina on the 8th of Dhul Hijjah and stay in the camps there.
- Go to Arafat on the 9th, where the Imam will deliver a sermon before Zuhr, and the prayers of Zuhr and Asr are combined and shortened.
- Pilgrims should celebrate the glory of their Lord and invoke and beseech Him as much as they can.
- Set off for Muzdalifah after sunset and combine shortened Maghrib and Isha there and spend the night.
- After Fajr, pilgrims should celebrate the glory of their Lord and invoke and beseech Him as much as they can.

- Leave for Mina, and once they reach the *Jamrah Al-Aqabah* (the largest pillar), they should stop reciting the *Talbiyah* and pelt this *Jamrah* with seven stones.
- If the pilgrims have brought their animals or it has become incumbent upon them to sacrifice animals for any reason, then they should sacrifice.
- Men should shave their heads or have a haircut, and women should cut a small portion from the ends of their hair.
- Get out of the state of Ihram by removing Ihram.
- Set off for the Baitullah and offer the tawaf of Hajj, also called "*Tawaf e Ifadah*".
- Optionally, offer Sai.
- Go back to Mina and stay there for 2 or 3 days, and every day, pelt the first, middle, and last *Jamrah* with seven stones each.
- Hajj is considered complete now.

Summary of Hajj

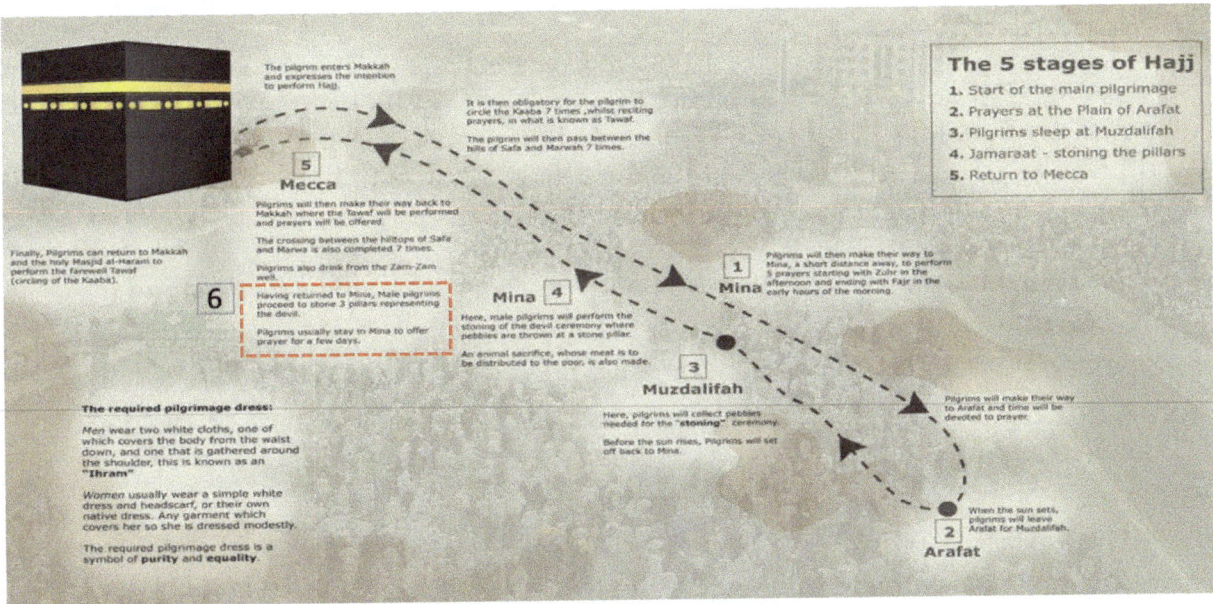

Guidance from Prophet Muhammad

- Ibn Umar reports that when the Prophet would go out for Hajj and Umrah, he would pray two rakah at Dhu al-Hulayfah, then mount a camel near the mosque; when the camel stopped, he would begin reciting the Talbiyah loudly.
- The Prophet has directed the pilgrims to perform another tawaf after Hajj and Umrah before they return home.
- He ran in the first three rounds, shaking his shoulders, and in the four remaining rounds, he walked the way he used to walk.
- He offered two rakah near *Maqam-e-Ibrahim* after performing Tawaf
- During tawaf, he would wear Ihram in such a way that he would expose his right shoulder and cover his left shoulder
- While starting Sai, he would climb Safa, face the Qiblah, declare the oneness of God three times, and make dua. He repeated the same to Marwah also.

لَا اِلَهَ اِلَّا اللهُ وَحْدَهُ , لَا شَرِيْكَ لَهُ , لَه الْمُلْكُ وَ لَهُ الْحَمْدُ , وَ هُوَ عَلَى كُلِّ شَئٍ قَدِيْرٌ , لَا اِلَهَ اِلَّا اللهُ
وَحْدَهُ , أَنْجَزَ وَعْدَهُ , نَصَرَ عَبْدَهُ , وَ هَزَمَ الْأَحْزَابَ وَحْدَهُ (مسلم , رقم: ٢٩٥٠)

There is no God but Allah; He is alone; no one is His partner; sovereignty is His, and all praise and gratitude also are His, and He has power over everything. There is no God but Allah; He is alone; He has fulfilled His promise and helped His servant and defeated all groups who have rejected [the truth]. (Sahih Muslim: 2950)

- During Sai, he would run on the slope and then walk as soon as he reached the incline.
- In Arafat, he would stay there for some time before returning (*Wuquf al Arafat*).
- The Prophet did rami (throwing stones at *Jamaraat*) in mid-morning on the day of sacrifice and on the other days when the sun started to decline.
- On the eighth of Dhu al-Hajj, also when he came to Makkah from Mina, he shortened all his prayers as long as he stayed here.
- He hurled seven pebbles and recited the takbir each time he threw a pebble.
- The Prophet always warned people about the sanctity of Madinah, just as Ibrahim had classified Makkah as sacred, he had also classified Madinah as sacred.

On the occasion of the final hajj, the Prophet himself had his head shaved (Halq), and some of the companions also preferred it. Ibn Omar narrated Prophet prayed three times for those who had shaved their heads and once for those who had haircuts (Sahih Al-Bukhari #1728).

A lady from a tribe asked: "O Messenger of God! The hajj is obligatory upon my father, but he is so old that he cannot even sit on an animal of conveyance; can I offer the Hajj for him?" The Prophet replied: "Yes." (Sahih Al-Bukhari #1855).

- How can a believer benefit from the journey of Hajj?
- It is said that a person whose Hajj is accepted is like a newborn; why is it so?

Shariah of Animal Sacrifice

History of Animal Sacrifice

- The history of sacrifice begins with Adam.
- There is evidence that the concept of animal sacrifice exists in all ancient religions.
- Prophet Ibrahim took this worship ritual to its pinnacle, and its importance, grandeur, and scope are unprecedented.
- Ibrahim had a dream in which he was told to sacrifice his son for the sake of the Almighty.
- Although such a dream is to be interpreted, he took it literally and complied with it without hesitation.
- Ibrahim attested to submitting his will to God through his actions.
- God ransomed Ismail for the sacrifice of a ram, and the ritual of sacrifice was instituted as a great tradition to be carried out on the same day each year.

وَاِذْ قَرَّبَا قُرْبَانًا فَتُقُبِّلَ مِنْ اَحَدِهِمَا وَ لَمْ يُتَقَبَّلْ مِنَ الْاٰخَرِ

When they both presented their sacrifices, one was accepted, and the other was not (5:27)

Adam lay with his wife Eve, and she became pregnant and gave birth to Cain. She said, 'With the help of the LORD, I have brought forth a man.' Later, she gave birth to his brother Abel. Now Abel kept flocks, and Cain worked the soil. With time, Cain brought some of the fruits of the soil as an offering to the LORD. But Abel brought fat portions from some of the firstborn of his flock. The LORD looked with favor on Abel and his offering, but on Cain and his offering, he did not look with favor. (Genesis 4:1-5

فَبَشَّرْنٰهُ بِغُلٰمٍ حَلِيْمٍ

فَلَمَّا بَلَغَ مَعَهُ السَّعْىَ قَالَ يٰبُنَيَّ اِنِّيْٓ اَرٰى فِى الْمَنَامِ اَنِّيْٓ اَذْبَحُكَ فَانْظُرْ مَاذَا تَرٰى ۚ قَالَ يٰٓاَبَتِ افْعَلْ مَا تُؤْمَرُ ۖ سَتَجِدُنِيْٓ اِنْ شَآءَ اللّٰهُ مِنَ الصّٰبِرِيْنَ فَلَمَّآ اَسْلَمَا وَ تَلَّهُ لِلْجَبِيْنِ وَ نَادَيْنٰهُ اَنْ يّٰٓاِبْرٰهِيْمُ قَدْ صَدَّقْتَ الرُّءْيَا اِنَّا كَذٰلِكَ نَجْزِى الْمُحْسِنِيْنَ اِنَّ هٰذَا لَهُوَ الْبَلٰٓؤُا الْمُبِيْنُ وَ فَدَيْنٰهُ بِذِبْحٍ عَظِيْمٍ

So [when he prayed to Us], we gave him news of a forbearing son. And when he reached the age when he could work with him, [one day], his father said to him: "My son! I had a dream that I was slaughtering you. Tell me what you think." He replied: "Father! Do as you are told. God willing, you shall find me steadfast." And when both submitted to God, Abraham laid his son prostrate upon his temples, and We called out to him, saying: "Abraham! You have fulfilled your dream." Thus, do We reward the righteous? This was indeed an open trial. [Abraham succeeded in it] and [as a result], We ransomed his son with a grand sacrifice. (37:97-107)

Objective of Animal Sacrifice

- The objective of sacrifice is to express gratitude to the Almighty.
- When we offer our life symbolically to the Almighty by offering the sacrifice of an animal, we are, in fact, expressing our gratitude for the guidance of submission, which Abraham expressed by sacrificing his only son.

$$لَنْ يَّنَالَ اللهَ لُحُوْمُهَا وَ لَا دِمَآؤُهَا وَ لٰكِنْ يَّنَالُهُ التَّقْوٰى مِنْكُمْ ۚ كَذٰلِكَ سَخَّرَهَا لَكُمْ لِتُكَبِّرُوا اللهَ$$

$$عَلٰى مَا هَدٰىكُمْ ۚ وَ بَشِّرِ الْمُحْسِنِيْنَ$$

The flesh and blood [of] these [sacrificed animals] does not reach God; it is only your piety that reaches Him. Thus, has He subjected them to your service so that you may give glory to God for guiding you? [This is the way of the righteous] and [O Prophet!] Give glad tidings to these righteous. (22:37)

Importance of animal sacrifice

- Throughout the history of religions, the ritual of animal sacrifice has remained a great means of attaining nearness to the Almighty.
- It is essentially a vow to pledge one's life for the sake of God, and an animal is sacrificed symbolically for that.
- It is always seen as "accepting death in the path of God to get real life".
- The Quran, in one verse, placed Salah in comparison to life and sacrifice in comparison to death.
- God called Ibrahim's sacrifice "the great sacrifice".
- Sacrifice is considered the pinnacle of worship.
- It is the essence of Islam – a Muslim is someone who willingly surrenders his will and life to God.

$$قُلْ إِنَّ صَلَاتِيْ وَ نُسُكِيْ وَ مَحْيَايَ وَ مَمَاتِيْ لِلّٰهِ$$

$$رَبِّ الْعٰلَمِيْنَ$$

Say: "My prayer and my sacrifice, my life, and my death, are all for God, Lord of the Universe." (6:162)

$$فَلَمَّآ أَسْلَمَا وَ تَلَّهُ لِلْجَبِيْنِ$$

Then, when both of them submitted and the father made his son lie on his temple, (37:103)

Shariah of Animal Sacrifice

- All four-legged animals (sound and of an appropriate age) that are from cattle can be sacrificed.
- The time of animal sacrifice begins after offering the Eid prayer on the 10th of Dhul Hijjah (Yawm al-Nahr).
- The days fixed for animal sacrifice are the same as those appointed for staying at Mina once the pilgrims return from Muzdalifah. They are also called "the days of Tashriq".
- At the end of each congregational prayer, Muslims are asked to declare "Takbiraat".
- Those who intend to sacrifice an animal should not cut their nails and hair before they have offered a sacrifice (from 01 Dhul Hijjah till the time they offer it).
- Animals should be sacrificed in all circumstances after the Eid prayer. Sacrifice related to the occasion of Eid is invalid before the prayer.

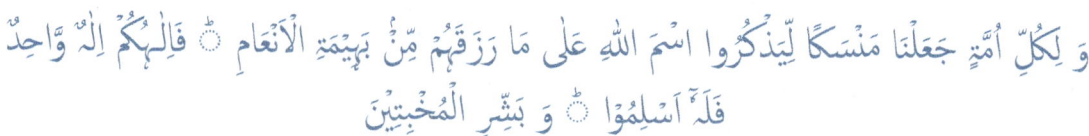

And for every community, We have ordained the ritual of sacrifice so that they may pronounce the name of God over the cattle which He has blessed them with because your God is one God; so, surrender yourselves to Him. [But this will only be done by those whose hearts have bowed down before their God] and [O Prophet!] Give glad tidings [from the Almighty] to those who bow down. (22:34)

- The appropriate age for a sheep/goat is at least 1 year; for a cow/bull, at least 2 years; and for a camel, at least 5 years. It can be male or female.
- Up to 7 people can share in the sacrifice of a cow, bull, or camel.
- The meat can be eaten alone (if the situation demands) or shared with others, and can also be used to feed the poor.
- Animal sacrifice can also be offered as an optional act other than on Eid. For example, on the occasion of the birth of a newborn or any other occasion of joy.

How do you see animal sacrifice in the light of animal rights as advocated by its proponents?

Chapter 9

Social Shariah

Etiquette of Gender Interaction

This chapter introduces Social Shariah and the etiquette of gender interaction in a Muslim society. People often refer to this as a hijab.

The Background

The concept of "Hijab"

View of a Muslim woman   View of the West

- It is a symbol of modesty and dignity worn by faithful Muslim women. It is usually not related to men.
- Generally, the Social Shariah of Islam revolves around the word hijab.
- The word hijab is not used in the Quran or Ahadith in the sense we understand.
- In the West, it is looked at as a sign of the oppression of Muslim women.
- These days, with growing Islamophobia, Muslim women feel fear and anxiety about being identifiable in public.

> The better words for what Islam has prescribed are "etiquette of gender interaction".

The basic unit of family

> "The family is one of nature's masterpieces." — George Santayana, Spanish-American philosopher.

- Man, as a social animal, loves to build relationships.
- We are not born in the prime of our youth, but we go through a life cycle – from a feeble infant to an old age, which is similar to being an infant.
- The family is the nucleus of civilization, the basic unit of society, and an important social concept in Islam.
- To God, the welfare of the child is the most important aspect of this unit of family.
- God wants to protect this unit of the family from all dangers that can jeopardize its survival, and hence He gave us detailed guidelines on gender interaction.
- God's social laws, specifically related to gender interaction, revolve around protecting the sanctity of family and the welfare of the children.

Illicit relationships are prohibited by God

- The family is formed of a sacred and pure relationship that is only possible through marriage (a legal contract).
- This demands zero tolerance for any illicit relationship between a man and a woman before and after marriage.
- To make sure that the sexual relationship is limited to husband and wife, God declared any illicit relationship outside of marriage as prohibited.
- Relationships with concubines were tolerated because of the enormous social consequences of prohibiting them.
- Islam's guidance on gender interaction is given for two main reasons:
  - To save society from becoming one where sexual relations are taken casually and are morally bankrupt.
  - To protect the sanctity of the family.

يَٰٓأَيُّهَا ٱلنَّاسُ ٱتَّقُوا۟ رَبَّكُمُ ٱلَّذِى خَلَقَكُم مِّن نَّفْسٍ وَٰحِدَةٍ وَّ خَلَقَ مِنْهَا زَوْجَهَا وَ بَثَّ مِنْهُمَا رِجَالًا كَثِيرًا وَّ نِسَآءً ۚ وَ ٱتَّقُوا۟ ٱللَّهَ ٱلَّذِى تَسَآءَلُونَ بِهِۦ وَ ٱلْأَرْحَامَ ۚ إِنَّ ٱللَّهَ كَانَ عَلَيْكُمْ رَقِيبًا

O mankind! Fear your Lord who created you from a single person, created of the same species his mate, and from these two, scattered countless men and women [in this world], and fear Allah through whom you seek mutual help, and fear breaking blood relationships. Indeed, God is watching over you. (4:1)

وَ لَا تَقْرَبُوا۟ ٱلزِّنَىٰٓ إِنَّهُۥ كَانَ فَٰحِشَةً ۖ وَ سَآءَ سَبِيلًا

"You shall not approach near to adultery, for it is lewd and its way is evil." (17:32)

Consequence of Illicit relationships

- Illicit relationships (infidelity) often cause family breakdown, leading to divorce, financial strain, and severe emotional distress in children, including anxiety, depression, and trust issues.
- It is a leading cause of divorce, resulting in single-parent households and reduced financial stability.
- Children may experience emotional distress, poor academic performance, behavioral changes (acting out), and difficulty trusting others in future relationships.
- Parents are considered the first teachers. If children grow up seeing a lack of boundaries or "anything goes" behavior, it becomes much harder for them to develop their own sense of self-discipline, modesty, and respect for sacred boundaries later in life.
- Children may have higher risks of future relationship issues and psychological difficulties.

1 - The Shariah of Gender Interaction

- The Shariah of gender interaction is comprehensively described in Surah Nur, verses 27-31.
- We will study the Shariah by studying these verses of the Quran.

يَٰٓأَيُّهَا ٱلَّذِينَ ءَامَنُوا۟ لَا تَدْخُلُوا۟ بُيُوتًا غَيْرَ بُيُوتِكُمْ حَتَّىٰ تَسْتَأْنِسُوا۟ وَ تُسَلِّمُوا۟ عَلَىٰ أَهْلِهَا ۚ ذَٰلِكُمْ خَيْرٌ لَّكُمْ لَعَلَّكُمْ تَذَكَّرُونَ

فَإِن لَّمْ تَجِدُوا۟ فِيهَآ أَحَدًا فَلَا تَدْخُلُوهَا حَتَّىٰ يُؤْذَنَ لَكُمْ ۖ وَ إِن قِيلَ لَكُمُ ٱرْجِعُوا۟ فَٱرْجِعُوا۟ هُوَ أَزْكَىٰ لَكُمْ ۚ وَ ٱللَّهُ بِمَا تَعْمَلُونَ عَلِيمٌ ۚ لَيْسَ عَلَيْكُمْ جُنَاحٌ أَن تَدْخُلُوا۟ بُيُوتًا غَيْرَ مَسْكُونَةٍ فِيهَا مَتَٰعٌ لَّكُمْ ۚ وَ ٱللَّهُ يَعْلَمُ مَا تُبْدُونَ وَ مَا تَكْتُمُونَ

قُل لِّلْمُؤْمِنِينَ يَغُضُّوا۟ مِنْ أَبْصَٰرِهِمْ وَ يَحْفَظُوا۟ فُرُوجَهُمْ ۚ ذَٰلِكَ أَزْكَىٰ لَهُمْ ۗ إِنَّ ٱللَّهَ خَبِيرٌۢ بِمَا يَصْنَعُونَ

وَ قُل لِّلْمُؤْمِنَٰتِ يَغْضُضْنَ مِنْ أَبْصَٰرِهِنَّ وَ يَحْفَظْنَ فُرُوجَهُنَّ وَ لَا يُبْدِينَ زِينَتَهُنَّ إِلَّا مَا ظَهَرَ مِنْهَا وَ لْيَضْرِبْنَ بِخُمُرِهِنَّ عَلَىٰ جُيُوبِهِنَّ ۖ وَ لَا يُبْدِينَ زِينَتَهُنَّ إِلَّا لِبُعُولَتِهِنَّ أَوْ ءَابَآئِهِنَّ أَوْ ءَابَآءِ بُعُولَتِهِنَّ أَوْ أَبْنَآئِهِنَّ أَوْ أَبْنَآءِ بُعُولَتِهِنَّ أَوْ إِخْوَٰنِهِنَّ أَوْ بَنِىٓ إِخْوَٰنِهِنَّ أَوْ بَنِىٓ أَخَوَٰتِهِنَّ أَوْ نِسَآئِهِنَّ أَوْ مَا مَلَكَتْ أَيْمَٰنُهُنَّ أَوِ ٱلتَّٰبِعِينَ غَيْرِ أُو۟لِى ٱلْإِرْبَةِ مِنَ ٱلرِّجَالِ أَوِ ٱلطِّفْلِ ٱلَّذِينَ لَمْ يَظْهَرُوا۟ عَلَىٰ عَوْرَٰتِ ٱلنِّسَآءِ ۖ وَ لَا يَضْرِبْنَ بِأَرْجُلِهِنَّ لِيُعْلَمَ مَا يُخْفِينَ مِن زِينَتِهِنَّ ۚ وَ تُوبُوٓا۟ إِلَى ٱللَّهِ جَمِيعًا أَيُّهَ ٱلْمُؤْمِنُونَ لَعَلَّكُمْ تُفْلِحُونَ

O, Believers! Enter the houses other than your own once you have introduced yourselves and wished peace to those in them (say, Salam). That is best for you so that you may be heedful. Then, if you find no one in the house, do not enter until you are given permission, and if you are asked to go back, go back, for it is Purer for you. And Allah knows all that you do. It is no sin for you to enter non-residential places with benefits for you. And Allah knows what you reveal and what you conceal.

Tell believing men to restrain their eyes and guard their private parts [if women are present in these houses]. That is purer for them. And indeed, Allah is well-aware of what they do. And tell the believing women to restrain their eyes and to guard their private parts and to display their ornaments only those which are normally revealed and to draw their coverings over their bosoms. And they should not reveal their embellishments to anyone save their husbands or their fathers or their husbands' fathers or their sons or their husbands' sons or their brothers or their brothers' sons or their sisters' sons or other women of an acquaintance or their slaves or the subservient male servants who are not attracted to women or children who have no awareness of the hidden aspects of women. And they should [also] not stamp their feet to draw attention to their hidden ornaments. Believers! Turn to Allah in repentance that you may prosper.

These verses from Surah Nur sum up the norms and etiquette of gender interaction. We are asked to adhere to these norms in order to avoid getting into the traps of Satan. The objective of these instructions is to attain the purity of hearts.

Context of the Verses

- These verses of the law were given in a specific context that made it mandatory to tell Muslims about the etiquette.

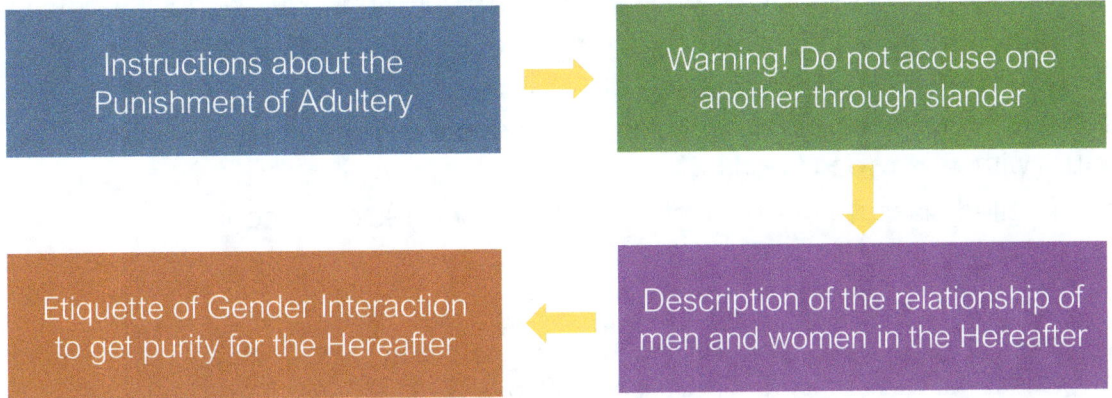

Groups of people & places

- These verses describe the following groups of people and places where the etiquette must be observed.
- The Quran's instructions are given according to the groups of people men and women mix with, and the places they go to.

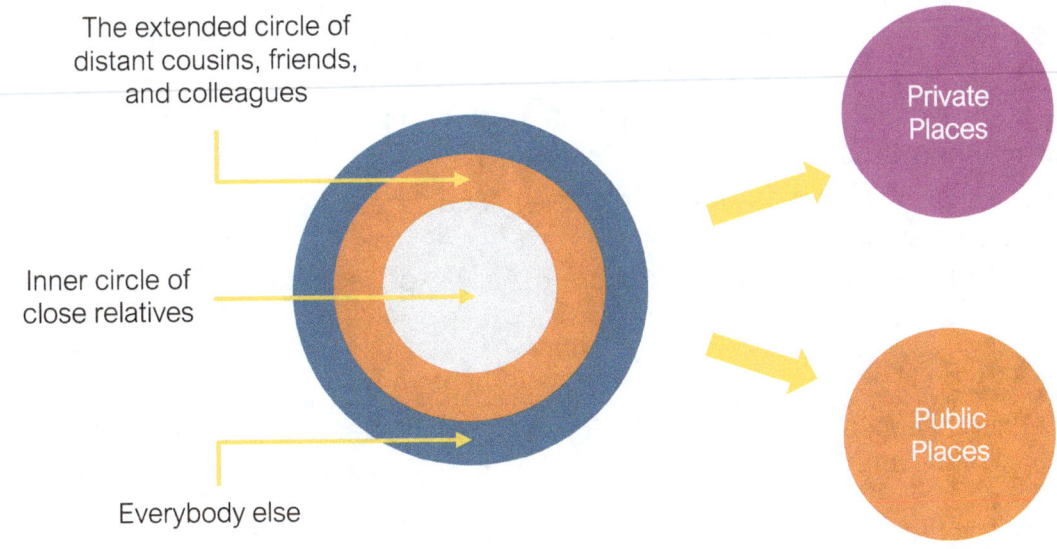

Visiting places

1. When friends, relatives, and acquaintances visit each other, where both men and women are present, we are expected to observe certain decorum.

2. When entering private property, we are asked to announce our name, say Salam to everyone, and ask for permission to enter, so people know who wants to come in.

3. The purpose is to let the residents decide whether they want to meet at this time. These days, it is much better to call in advance.

4. If the residents do not open the door or refuse to meet at that time, we are asked to return without any bad feelings.

5. If the visited place is non-residential, no formal permission is required.

> The prophet instructed the visitor to ask permission three times and leave without bad feelings. He told us to seek permission without any intention to peek through the door or window to see who was inside. (Sahih Bukhari #6245, #6241)

Gender Interaction

6. When men and women are mixing, both should follow some etiquette:
   - Both should restrain their gazes – look at each other the way decent people look at each other when talking. Having modesty in the gaze does not mean that we should not look at each other, but rather, we should not look at each other with sexual desire.
   - Both should 'guard' their private parts by dressing appropriately – this is not just to cover but to cover in such a way that it does not reveal those parts in any shape or form (extended clothing is preferred).
   - A woman's chest is considered a private part, and an appropriate dress should be worn that does not reveal it in any way.
   - If women have worn embellishments, they should not be displayed except before the innermost circle (the list is on the next page). This does not include embellishments on body parts that are usually exposed (hands, face, and feet).

Prophet's Guidance

Jarir ibn Abdullah reports that he asked the Prophet: "What if such a glance (with sexual desire) suddenly occurs?" The Prophet replied: "Immediately turn it away or lower it." Muslim #5644)

Once during the Prophet's farewell pilgrimage, when a lady from the Khatam tribe stopped the Prophet on his way, Fadl ibn Abbas started to stare at her (inappropriately). When the Prophet saw him, he grabbed his face and turned it to the other side. (Sahih Bukhari #1855)

God's guidance on gender interaction

List of close relatives to whom you can expose your embellishment

1. Husband
2. Father & Father-in-law - Implied grandfather, paternal and maternal uncles.
3. Sons, sons of the husband, brothers, brothers' sons, sisters' sons.
4. Women of acquaintance and maids.
5. Slaves.
6. People living in the house as dependents for some reason who are incapable of feeling any attraction.
7. Children who have not reached the age of puberty.

Concept of Guarding

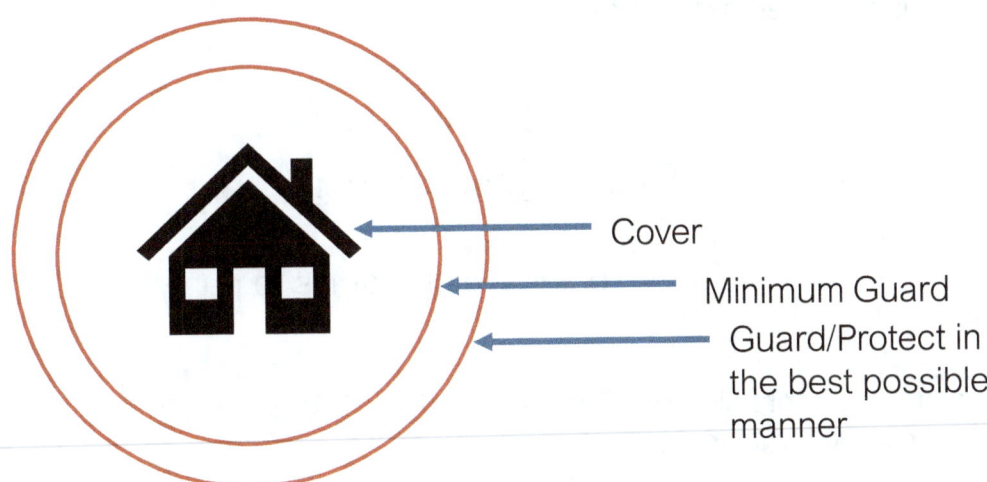

Cover

Minimum Guard

Guard/Protect in the best possible manner

- When God said "guard your chastity or private parts", it means it is more than just covering them.
- We can understand the concept of guarding by looking at how we guard our houses.
- The walls and roof we build provide cover and a shield against external harm. But we don't usually stop at this when it comes to securing or protecting our houses.
- Wealthy people who are more vulnerable to theft and other crimes always build multiple walls or barriers around their houses to feel more secure and protected.
- That's exactly what God wants from us when asking us to guard our private parts. Our attire and behavior must establish the extra boundaries that allow us to feel safe around others and others to feel safe around us.

Some clarifications

- Slave men/women, and younger children don't have to ask for permission whenever entering the bedroom/private area except for three times: before Fajr, siesta time, and after Isha. (24: 58-59)
- Secondly, the directive to cover the chest and neckline does not apply to old women who are no longer of marriageable age, provided they do not intend to display their ornaments (although God likes for them to be careful even at this age). (24:60)
- Thirdly, it is explained in these verses that there is absolutely no harm if men and women from different families eat together or separately in their own houses, of their fathers' or grandfathers', mothers', brothers' and sisters,' of their paternal uncles' and aunts,' maternal uncles' and aunts,' and of their friends' houses. (24:61)
- The guidelines noted in these verses show that God does not intend to deprive people of mutual support or to curtail their social freedom and interaction.

The purpose of the instructions

ذٰلِكَ اَزْكٰى لَهُمْ

That is <u>purer</u> for them.

Remember, the objective of Islam is to purify us.

- This is an important point why God gave us these instructions: to purify us so we become eligible for Jannah.
- People may not follow the instructions given by God and engage in immoral relationships, which will give them some temporary pleasure, but they will never be able to purify themselves and prepare themselves for the eternal pleasures of the hereafter unless they ask for forgiveness from God.
- People who follow these instructions will gain purity in their thoughts and actions and will be able to save themselves from engaging in major sins like adultery.
- God wants us to think big and focus on the permanent life in the Hereafter rather than this temporary life.

In the matter of gender interactions, why has God given precautionary instructions on top of stating the actual prohibition?

2 - Guidance under special circumstance

- What we just learned was the actual Shariah about gender interaction. What we are going to learn now concerns special circumstances in which God wants to protect the honor of Muslim men and women.
- A couple of special circumstances are discussed in Surah Ahzab.

وَ الَّذِيْنَ يُؤْذُوْنَ الْمُؤْمِنِيْنَ وَ الْمُؤْمِنٰتِ بِغَيْرِ مَا اكْتَسَبُوْا فَقَدِ احْتَمَلُوْا بُهْتَانًا وَّ اِثْمًا مُّبِيْنًا

يٰۤاَيُّهَا النَّبِيُّ قُلْ لِّاَزْوَاجِكَ وَ بَنٰتِكَ وَ نِسَآءِ الْمُؤْمِنِيْنَ يُدْنِيْنَ عَلَيْهِنَّ مِنْ جَلَابِيْبِهِنَّ

ۚ ذٰلِكَ اَدْنٰۤى اَنْ يُّعْرَفْنَ فَلَا يُؤْذَيْنَ ۚ وَ كَانَ اللهُ غَفُوْرًا رَّحِيْمًا

لَئِنْ لَّمْ يَنْتَهِ الْمُنٰفِقُوْنَ وَ الَّذِيْنَ فِيْ قُلُوْبِهِمْ مَّرَضٌ وَّ الْمُرْجِفُوْنَ فِى

الْمَدِيْنَةِ لَنُغْرِيَنَّكَ بِهِمْ ثُمَّ لَا يُجَاوِرُوْنَكَ فِيْهَآ اِلَّا قَلِيْلًا

مَّلْعُوْنِيْنَ ۛ اَيْنَمَا ثُقِفُوْٓا اُخِذُوْا وَ قُتِّلُوْا تَقْتِيْلًا

And those who harass believing men and believing women for what they never did [should know that] they shall bear the guilt of slander and a grievous sin. O Prophet! [In this situation] tell your wives, daughters, and true believers' wives to draw over them a shawl [when they go out]. It will become possible for them to be distinguished [from other women] and to avoid harassment. God is Ever-forgiving and Merciful. If, [after these measures, also] these hypocrites and those who have the ailment [of jealousy] in their hearts and the scandal-mongers of Madinah do not desist, We will rouse you against them, and their days in that city will be numbered. Cursed be they, wherever found, they would be seized and put to exemplary death. (Ahzab 58-61)

Context of the Verses

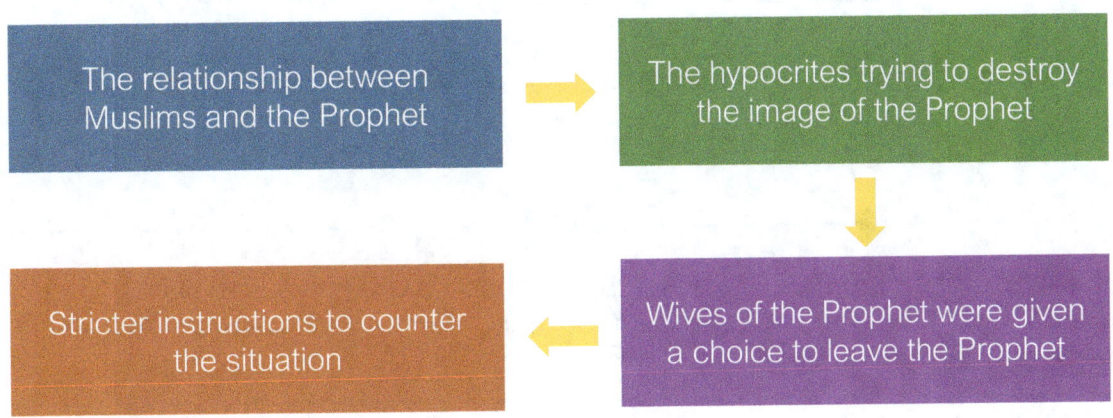

- In the time of Prophet Muhammad, God gave specific instructions regarding a special circumstance. Those instructions are given in Surah Ahzab. (33:58-61)
- Some miscreants started a mischievous smear campaign against the family of Prophet Muhammad and other Muslim women.
- They used to create problems for Muslim women whenever they found them outside.
- Almighty God in Surah Ahzab instructed the wives of the Prophet, his daughters, and other Muslim women to draw over them any of the shawls they have to cover them fully when they go out to insecure places.
- Such attire would distinguish them from women of lewd character, and they would not be teased on the pretext of being outwardly like such women.
- Various narratives showed that when Muslim women used to travel in the dark of night or dawn, the miscreants would go after them and, when they were caught, present an excuse that they thought these were slave-women (whose moral upbringing was lacking).
- It is evident from the statement "so that they be distinguished [from other women] and not be harassed" that the instructions given here are for a specific situation and are not general.

The purpose of the instructions

They are distinguished [from other women] and
<u>should not be harassed</u> (in that situation).

Note: Remember the purpose of the instructions previously given in Surah Nur?

Discuss and compare the purpose of the instructions given in Surah Nur 27-31 vs what's given in Surah Ahzab 58-61, and what makes the latter instructions given in special circumstances?

3 - Special instructions for Prophet's wives (1)

- This is the third type of instructions given specifically to Prophet Muhammad's wives. They were give two instructions: one directly related to them and one related to the household.

يٰنِسَآءَ النَّبِيِّ لَسْتُنَّ كَاَحَدٍ مِّنَ النِّسَآءِ اِنِ اتَّقَيْتُنَّ فَلَا تَخْضَعْنَ بِالْقَوْلِ فَيَطْمَعَ الَّذِىْ فِىْ قَلْبِهٖ مَرَضٌ وَّ قُلْنَ قَوْلًا مَّعْرُوْفًا وَّ قَرْنَ فِىْ بُيُوْتِكُنَّ وَ لَا تَبَرَّجْنَ تَبَرُّجَ الْجَاهِلِيَّةِ الْاُوْلٰى وَ اَقِمْنَ الصَّلٰوةَ وَ اٰتِيْنَ الزَّكٰوةَ وَ اَطِعْنَ اللّٰهَ وَ رَسُوْلَهٗ اِنَّمَا يُرِيْدُ اللّٰهُ لِيُذْهِبَ عَنْكُمُ الرِّجْسَ اَهْلَ الْبَيْتِ وَ يُطَهِّرَكُمْ تَطْهِيْرًا

O wives of the Prophet! You are not like other women. [So], if you fear God, do not be too accommodating in your speech, lest people with a disease in their hearts should lust after you. Talk [with such people] in plain and simple words. And stay in your homes and do not display your finery as women used to do in the days of ignorance. Attend to your prayers, pay Zakah, and obey God and His Messenger. Women of this house! The Almighty wants to cleanse you from the filth [these hypocrites want to besmear you with] and to fully purify you. (Ahzab 32-33)

Background

- When the hypocrites and miscreants embarked upon a campaign to scandalize the private life of Prophet Muhammad, God gave the wives of the Prophet some special instructions that did not apply to common Muslim women. Any damage to the moral repute of the family of Prophet Muhammad would have turned people away from Islam and the Prophet.

Instructions

1. After this time, they should not be kind and friendly to every person who enters their house. They must speak in clear, simple terms so that those among their addressees who intend evil realize they cannot achieve their objective.
2. They should remain in their homes to protect their rank and status.
3. Diligently pray and pay Zakah as much as they can and, with full sincerity, spend their time in obedience to the Almighty and His Prophet.
4. If they must go out to meet some compelling need, they must not go out displaying their ornaments and finery – something which was the way of women of the age of ignorance.
5. They should try to communicate the verses of the Quran, as well as Islam's beliefs and moral teachings, to visitors, and refrain from other general gossip.
6. From reading the Quran, it appears that the miscreants did not mend their ways even after these measures, and consequently, the Almighty gave some stricter instructions to Muslims.

3 - Special instructions for Prophet's wives (2)

م ۛ a يَٰٓأَيُّهَا الَّذِينَ اٰمَنُوا لَا تَدْخُلُوا بُيُوتَ النَّبِيِّ اِلَّآ اَنْ يُؤْذَنَ لَكُمْ اِلٰى طَعَامٍ غَيْرَ نَاظِرِينَ اِنٰىهُ ۛ وَ لٰكِنْ اِذَا دُعِيتُمْ فَادْخُلُوا فَاِذَا طَعِمْتُمْ فَانْتَشِرُوا وَ لَا مُسْتَأْنِسِينَ لِحَدِيثٍ ۛ اِنَّ ذٰلِكُمْ كَانَ يُؤْذِى النَّبِيَّ فَيَسْتَحْيٖ مِنْكُمْ ۛ وَ اللّٰهُ لَا يَسْتَحْيٖ مِنَ الْحَقِّ ۛ وَ اِذَا سَاَلْتُمُوهُنَّ مَتَاعًا فَسْـَٔلُوهُنَّ مِنْ وَرَآءِ حِجَابٍ ۛ ذٰلِكُمْ اَطْهَرُ لِقُلُوبِكُمْ وَ قُلُوبِهِنَّ ۛ وَ مَا كَانَ لَكُمْ اَنْ تُؤْذُوا رَسُولَ اللّٰهِ وَ لَا اَنْ تَنْكِحُوٓا اَزْوَاجَهُ مِنْ بَعْدِهٖ اَبَدًا ۛ اِنَّ ذٰلِكُمْ كَانَ عِنْدَ اللّٰهِ عَظِيمًا

اِنْ تُبْدُوا شَيْـًٔا اَوْ تُخْفُوهُ فَاِنَّ اللّٰهَ كَانَ بِكُلِّ شَيْءٍ عَلِيمًا

لَا جُنَاحَ عَلَيْهِنَّ فٖٓى اٰبَآئِهِنَّ وَ لَآ اَبْنَآئِهِنَّ وَ لَآ اِخْوَانِهِنَّ وَ لَآ اَبْنَآءِ اِخْوَانِهِنَّ وَ لَآ اَبْنَآءِ اَخَوَاتِهِنَّ وَ لَا نِسَآئِهِنَّ وَ لَا مَا مَلَكَتْ اَيْمَانُهُنَّ ۛ وَ اتَّقِينَ اللّٰهَ ۛ اِنَّ اللّٰهَ كَانَ عَلٰى كُلِّ شَيْءٍ شَهِيدًا

O, Believers! Do not enter the houses of the Prophet except if you are permitted some time to enter for a meal. In this case, do not sit waiting for the food to be cooked. But if you are invited, enter, and when you have eaten, disperse. Do not engage in unnecessary conversation, for this would distress the Prophet, and he would feel shy to bid you go; but about the truth, God does not feel shy. And if you ask his wives for anything, speak to them from behind a curtain. This is purer for your hearts and their hearts. And you must not give grief to God's Messenger, nor shall you ever wed his wives after him; this would be a grave offense in the sight of God. Whether you reveal or conceal them, God knows all things. It shall be no offense for these women [– Prophet's wives –] to come in front of their fathers, sons, brothers, brothers' sons, sisters' sons, women of acquaintance, or slaves. [O] Women [of the household of the Prophet!] Be afraid of God; surely God observes all things. (Ahzab 53-55)

1. Muslims were told that no one should enter the house of the Prophet unless he/she was invited or called.

2. If people are invited to eat at the house of the Prophet, they shall come at the time of the meal and leave afterward without engaging in conversation.

3. The wives of the Prophet shall be secluded from the Muslims, and except for close relatives and women of their acquaintance, no one shall come in front of them.

4. Anyone who wants something from their private places must ask for it from behind a veil (called Hijab in verse). The word hijab is taken from here.

5. The wives of the Prophet shall be the mothers of the believers. Every believer should honor and respect them the way he/she honor and respect his/her mother.

6. No one can marry any of the wives of the Prophet in his presence (if he divorces) or after he leaves this world.

The purpose of the instructions (both 1 and 2)

O wives of the Prophet! You are <u>not like other women</u>.

Note: Remember the purposes of the instructions previously given in Surah Nur 27-31 and Surah Ahzab 58-61?

Summary of God's three types of commands

Surah Nur 27-31

General instructions were given to Muslim men and women on how to interact and behave with one another to foster piety in their hearts. These instructions should always be followed regardless of time and place. They are valid until the Day of Judgment.

Surah Ahzab 58-61

Special instructions were given to Muslim women to protect themselves from the mischief of the disbelievers and hypocrites in Medinah. It was an extraordinary situation for Muslims. These and similar measures can be followed in extraordinary circumstances. They are valid until the Day of Judgment if a situation arises. Any other precautionary measures can be taken.

Surah Ahzab 32-33 & 53-55

The special instructions given to the Prophet's wives were neither applied to other common Muslim women at the time nor are they applicable now. This is because of their special status in society and their relationship with the Prophet.

Understanding the differences among these Quranic directives is very important. In many parts of the Muslim world, Muslim men have misplaced these directives and created an environment for Muslim women that is repressive toward them.

The wisdom in Allah's instructions

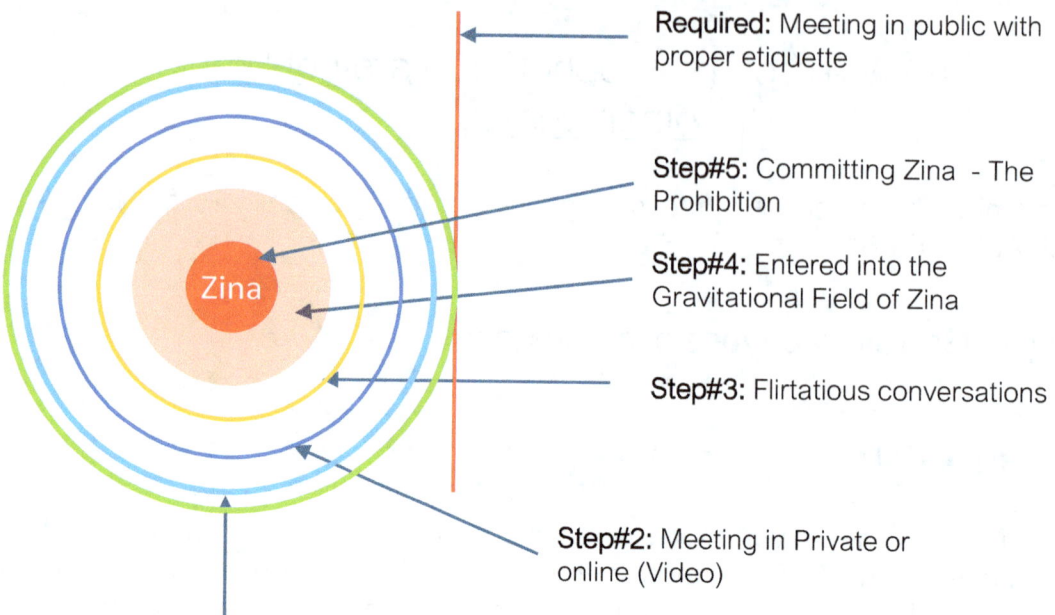

Allah SWT wants us to stop here when He says don't go **near** adultery.

Required: Meeting in public with proper etiquette

Step#5: Committing Zina - The Prohibition

Step#4: Entered into the Gravitational Field of Zina

Step#3: Flirtatious conversations

Step#2: Meeting in Private or online (Video)

Step#1: Meeting in Public in person or social media with bad intention

- Allah wants to protect us and keep us pure, and to protect society and keep it pure as well.
- He wants us to keep our distance from Zina.
- We should never feel bold enough to say, "We know what I am doing, and I am not that stupid." This is the weakest point of a human being, and once you are in the gravitational field of Zina and the circumstances are encouraging, you can't protect yourself from committing it.
- So be aware and follow God's instructions. We all know very well that when we are in steps 2 and 3, we will soon reach step 4.

What etiquette should we follow in an online world that complies with the guidance of the Quran?

Practical tips on following the guidelines

- Realize that it is a hard ask, especially in the time and society that you live in, and if you don't set certain rules for yourself about gender interaction, the chances of failure are high:
- When meeting, follow the fundamental rules: keep your gaze down and dress properly.
- Hang out with people who share your moral values.
- It is OK to develop "feelings" for someone, as long as you understand the limits and follow the guidelines God provides.
- Do not meet a person of the opposite gender in seclusion – even if you like someone, make the meeting a family or friend occasion.
- Make interaction purposeful (avoid just passing the time together).
- Avoid indulging in flirtatious conversations – we all know when that moment.
- Watch your social media interactions and use them – meeting someone on a video call is the same as meeting in person (maybe with fewer consequences, only at that moment).

Remember, the goal of this etiquette is to remain outside the gravitational field of *Zina,* which is at the core of the prohibition and is considered one of the major sins in Islam after Shirk and murder.

Do you think the Hijab attire adopted today meets the core requirements of attaining purity mentioned in the Quran?

Chapter 10

Social Shariah

Nikah (Marriage)

This chapter introduces the concept of Nikah or marriage in Islam. The detailed Shariah related to it is discussed.

Shariah of Nikah

What is Nikah (Marriage)?

> Marriage is an **open declaration** of a contract by a man and a woman to live **permanently** as husband and wife.

- The contract must be declared in the presence of witnesses by a responsible person with great solemnity and gravity.
- Dowry (token money) should be given by the husband to his wife.
- A person may deliver a sermon to counsel and guide the newlywed.

- To firmly establish a society on the core principles, an everlasting bond between the spouses is made essential in the religion of the prophets.
- Remember, family is the nucleus of civilization and the basic unit of society, and is an important aspect of Islam's social concept.
- The verses on the opening slide (24:32-33) assert that, in God's eyes, there is only one legitimate way for a man and a woman to have a conjugal relationship: through marriage (Nikah).
- If it is not possible to marry for any reason, then God wants us to remain chaste until it becomes possible to marry.
- The concept of marriage is nothing new, and Islam did not introduce it. Adam and Eve were made husband and wife. There is nothing Islamic about it.

وَ مِنْ اٰیٰتِهٖ اَنْ خَلَقَ لَكُمْ مِّنْ اَنْفُسِكُمْ اَزْوَاجًا لِّتَسْكُنُوْۤا اِلَیْهَا وَ جَعَلَ بَیْنَكُمْ مَّوَدَّةً وَّ رَحْمَةً ۭ اِنَّ فِیْ ذٰلِكَ لَاٰیٰتٍ لِّقَوْمٍ یَّتَفَكَّرُوْنَ

And among His Signs is that He created for you mates from among your species that you may obtain comfort from them, and [for this purpose], He has put love and sympathy within you; surely, in this are signs for those who reflect. (30:21)

وَ اَنْكِحُوا الْاَیَامٰی مِنْكُمْ وَ الصّٰلِحِیْنَ مِنْ عِبَادِكُمْ وَ اِمَآئِكُمْ ۭ اِنْ یَّكُوْنُوْا فُقَرَآءَ یُغْنِهِمُ اللهُ مِنْ فَضْلِهٖ ۭ وَ اللهُ وَاسِعٌ عَلِیْمٌ   وَ لْیَسْتَعْفِفِ الَّذِیْنَ لَا یَجِدُوْنَ نِكَاحًا حَتّٰی یُغْنِیَهُمُ اللهُ مِنْ فَضْلِهٖ

And marry those among you who are single and those who have the capability for marriage among your slaves, male or female. If they are poor, Allah will give them means out of His grace: Allah is ample-giving and knows everything. And let those who find not an opportunity for marriage keep themselves chaste until Allah gives them means out of His grace. (24:32-33)

A glad tiding

$$....اِنْ يَّكُوْنُوْا فُقَرَآءَ يُغْنِهِمُ اللهُ مِنْ فَضْلِهٖ ...$$

If they are poor, Allah will give them means out of His grace.

- Besides urging people to practice Nikah, they are given glad tidings that, even if they are poor, they should marry to protect themselves from immoral acts; hopefully, the Almighty will bless them with resources if they resolve to enter into a marriage contract.
- The idea is that once a man and a woman marry, their abilities develop, and when both start to strive together in life, the Almighty blesses them in their struggle, and their circumstances also change [for the better].
- In some cultures, Muslim men and women keep delaying their Nikah because they want to get financial stability first. It is primarily due to the poor cultural norms in a society where a marriage ceremony requires a lot of money.
- Allah promised them that they would be helped if they entered into Nikah to protect themselves from entering into haram relationships.

Relations prohibited for marriage

وَ لَا تَنْكِحُوْا مَا نَكَحَ اٰبَآؤُكُمْ مِّنَ النِّسَآءِ اِلَّا مَا قَدْ سَلَفَ ۚ اِنَّهٗ كَانَ فَاحِشَةً وَّ مَقْتًا ۚ وَ سَآءَ سَبِيْلًا

حُرِّمَتْ عَلَيْكُمْ اُمَّهٰتُكُمْ وَ بَنٰتُكُمْ وَ اَخَوٰتُكُمْ وَ عَمّٰتُكُمْ وَ خٰلٰتُكُمْ وَ بَنٰتُ الْاَخِ وَ بَنٰتُ الْاُخْتِ وَ اُمَّهٰتُكُمُ الّٰتِيْ

اَرْضَعْنَكُمْ وَ اَخَوٰتُكُمْ مِّنَ الرَّضَاعَةِ وَ اُمَّهٰتُ نِسَآئِكُمْ وَ رَبَآئِبُكُمُ الّٰتِيْ فِيْ حُجُوْرِكُمْ مِّنْ نِّسَآئِكُمُ الّٰتِيْ دَخَلْتُمْ بِهِنَّ

ۖ فَاِنْ لَّمْ تَكُوْنُوْا دَخَلْتُمْ بِهِنَّ فَلَا جُنَاحَ عَلَيْكُمْ ۖ وَ حَلَآئِلُ اَبْنَآئِكُمُ الَّذِيْنَ مِنْ اَصْلَابِكُمْ ۖ وَ اَنْ تَجْمَعُوْا بَيْنَ

الْاُخْتَيْنِ اِلَّا مَا قَدْ سَلَفَ ۚ اِنَّ اللهَ كَانَ غَفُوْرًا رَّحِيْمًا

وَّ الْمُحْصَنٰتُ مِنَ النِّسَآءِ اِلَّا مَا مَلَكَتْ اَيْمَانُكُمْ ۚ كِتٰبَ اللهِ عَلَيْكُمْ

And marry not women your fathers married – except what has been done in the past: it was shameful and odious – an abominable practice. Prohibited to you [for marriage] are your mothers, your daughters, your sisters, your maternal and paternal aunts, the daughters of your brothers and sisters; your mothers who have suckled you and your sisters through fosterage. [Similarly], the mothers of your wives, your step-daughters raised under you, who were born of your wives with whom you have made physical contact – no offense if you have not made physical contact with their mothers, and the wives of your real sons, and two sisters in wedlock at the same time, except for what has already happened. God indeed is Oft-Forgiving, Most Merciful. Also [prohibited are] women already married, except those your right hands possess; this is a written obligation upon you from God. (4:22-24)

- Women prohibited for marrying are mentioned on three bases of relationship:

Lineage

- Mothers, daughters, sisters, paternal aunts, maternal aunts, and the daughters of brothers and daughters of sisters (nieces).
- Most cultures view these relations as sanctified, and men do not consider them for marriage.
- No distinction is made between real and step relations.
- Mother includes everyone up in the chain, including grandmother.
- Similarly, the daughter includes everyone down in the chain, including the granddaughter.
- The Sister of the maternal grandfather and the sister of the paternal grandmother are, respectively, like paternal and maternal aunts.

Fosterage

- All foster relationships have the same sanctity as real ones. For example, foster mother, sister, aunt, etc.
- Fostering should involve establishing the relationship at the suckling age with full intent, not based on one or two unintended events.
- The Quran only mentions a foster sister, but the intent is to include all foster relations.

Marriage

- Daughter-in-law, mother-in-law, wife's daughter, wife's sister, and both nieces of one's wife, maternal and paternal aunts of wife.
- The daughter of that wife is prohibited from having conjugal contact with anyone with whom one has had conjugal contact.
- Only the daughter-in-law of a real son is prohibited.
- Sister of a wife, her maternal and paternal aunts, and her two nieces are prohibited if the wife is in wedlock with the husband.

Some practices in the Arabs

- The son could inherit his father's wife (stepmother), and he would feel no wrong in doing so. The Quran referred to it as open lewdness and a shameful and abominable practice and strictly prohibited it.

- People would consider marriage to the wives of adopted sons to be prohibited. The Quran has explained the fact that mere adoption does not give the child the status of a begotten child, nor does this adoption entail any prohibition regarding marriage.

وَ مَا جَعَلَ اَدْعِيَاءَكُمْ اَبْنَاءَكُمْ ۚ ذٰلِكُمْ قَوْلُكُمْ بِاَفْوَاهِكُمْ ۚ وَ اللهُ يَقُولُ الْحَقَّ وَ هُوَ يَهْدِى السَّبِيلَ

اُدْعُوهُمْ لِاٰبَآئِهِمْ هُوَ اَقْسَطُ عِنْدَ اللهِ ۚ فَاِنْ لَّمْ تَعْلَمُوٓا اٰبَآءَهُمْ فَاِخْوَانُكُمْ فِى الدِّيْنِ وَ مَوَالِيْكُمْ

And He has not made your adopted sons your [real] sons. Such is only the speech of your mouth, but Allah tells the truth, and only He shows the right way. Call them after [the names of] their fathers: that is more just in the sight of Allah. But if you do not know their fathers, they are your faith brothers and friends. (33:4-5)

Note: God insists that we must not hide a child's lineage. The purpose is to avoid the emotional suffering people often experience when such matters are exposed later in life.

Bounds and conditions for Nikah

- A payment must be made by the man to the woman at the time of the contract, known as a dower. This is the token money to confirm that the man is ready to take financial responsibility for this new family.

- The dower amount has been left to societal norms and traditions.

- The second requisite of marriage is chastity. No adulterer (declared by the court of law) has the right to marry a chaste woman, and no adulteress (declared by the court of law) has the right to marry a chaste man. If the law were not involved, then they must purify themselves of this sin by sincere repentance.

- A Muslim CANNOT marry a polytheist.

- Muslim men can marry women from the people of the book (Christians and Jews). Although this relaxation was given at a time when Muslim society was dominant over others. Today, this decision should be given careful thought.

- Most families with two different religions at home usually struggle when it comes to their children. Their children can't easily make up their minds which direction they should go. Especially in societies where Christianity is dominant, it's hard to convince children of Islam.

وَّ الْمُحْصَنٰتُ مِنَ النِّسَآءِ اِلَّا مَا مَلَكَتْ اَيْمَانُكُمْ ۚ كِتٰبَ اللّٰهِ عَلَيْكُمْ ۚ وَ اُحِلَّ لَكُمْ مَّا وَرَآءَ ذٰلِكُمْ اَنْ تَبْتَغُوْا بِاَمْوَالِكُمْ مُّحْصِنِيْنَ غَيْرَ مُسَافِحِيْنَ ۚ فَمَا اسْتَمْتَعْتُمْ بِهٖ مِنْهُنَّ فَاٰتُوْهُنَّ اُجُوْرَهُنَّ فَرِيْضَةً ۚ وَ لَا جُنَاحَ عَلَيْكُمْ فِيْمَا تَرَاضَيْتُمْ بِهٖ مِنْۢ بَعْدِ الْفَرِيْضَةِ ۚ اِنَّ اللّٰهَ كَانَ عَلِيْمًا حَكِيْمًا

And all other women except for those [specified] are lawful to you, such that you seek them through your wealth, desiring chastity, not lust. [Consequently, if you have not paid their dowers yet], pay them their dowers as an obligation for the benefit you have derived from them. If you agree mutually on something after a dower is prescribed, there is no blame on you, and Allah is All-Knowing, All-Wise. (4:24)

اَلزَّانِيْ لَا يَنْكِحُ اِلَّا زَانِيَةً اَوْ مُشْرِكَةً ۫ وَّ الزَّانِيَةُ لَا يَنْكِحُهَآ اِلَّا زَانٍ اَوْ مُشْرِكٌ ۚ وَ حُرِّمَ ذٰلِكَ عَلَى الْمُؤْمِنِيْنَ

The man guilty of fornication may only marry a woman similarly guilty or an idolatress, and the woman guilty of fornication may only marry such a man or an idolater. The believers are forbidden from such marriages. (24:3)

وَ لَا تَنْكِحُوا الْمُشْرِكٰتِ حَتّٰى يُؤْمِنَّ ۚ وَ لَاَمَةٌ مُّؤْمِنَةٌ خَيْرٌ مِّنْ مُّشْرِكَةٍ وَّ لَوْ اَعْجَبَتْكُمْ ۚ وَ لَا تُنْكِحُوا الْمُشْرِكِيْنَ حَتّٰى يُؤْمِنُوْا ۚ وَ لَعَبْدٌ مُّؤْمِنٌ خَيْرٌ مِّنْ مُّشْرِكٍ وَّ لَوْ اَعْجَبَكُمْ

And wed not idol-worshipper women, unless they embrace faith, and [remember] a believing slave-girl is better than an idolatrous woman, although you may find them attractive. And wed not your women to the Idolaters unless they embrace faith. And [remember] a believing slave is better than an idolater, although you may find them attractive. (2:221)

وَ الْمُحْصَنٰتُ مِنَ الَّذِيْنَ اُوْتُوا الْكِتٰبَ مِنْ قَبْلِكُمْ اِذَآ اٰتَيْتُمُوْهُنَّ اُجُوْرَهُنَّ مُحْصِنِيْنَ غَيْرَ مُسَافِحِيْنَ وَ لَا مُتَّخِذِيْٓ اَخْدَانٍ

And [lawful to you in marriage] are also chaste women from among these People of the Book before you when you give them their dowers with the condition that you desire chastity, not lewdness, nor becoming secret paramours. (5:5)

As discussed earlier, the last allowance was given with the hope that more women from the people of the book would have the opportunity to learn about Islam closely, and their chances of converting were high. If that possibility does not exist today, then it is not advised.

Rights and obligations of the spouses

- God has entrusted responsibilities within the family unit to the spouses' various capacities for the tasks at hand.
- These distinct positions or tasks are assigned based on the physical and emotional states of men and women. Also, this is a suggestion from God based on the prevailing norms of the society. Anytime the norms change, these assignments can change as well.

اَلرِّجَالُ قَوَّامُونَ عَلَى النِّسَاءِ بِمَا فَضَّلَ اللهُ بَعْضَهُمْ عَلَى بَعْضٍ وَّ بِمَآ اَنْفَقُوْا مِنْ اَمْوَالِهِمْ ۗ فَالصّٰلِحٰتُ قٰنِتٰتٌ حٰفِظٰتٌ لِّلْغَيْبِ بِمَا حَفِظَ اللهُ ۗ وَ الّٰتِیْ تَخَافُوْنَ نُشُوْزَهُنَّ فَعِظُوْهُنَّ وَ اهْجُرُوْهُنَّ فِی الْمَضَاجِعِ وَ اضْرِبُوْهُنَّ ۚ فَاِنْ اَطَعْنَكُمْ فَلَا تَبْغُوْا عَلَيْهِنَّ سَبِيْلًا ۗ اِنَّ اللهَ كَانَ عَلِيًّا كَبِيْرًا

Men (husbands) are the guardians of women because God has given one a higher status than the other, and because they financially support them. Consequently, pious women are obedient [to their husbands] and keep their secrets, for Allah also keeps secrets. And as for those from whom you fear rebellion, admonish them [first] and [next] refuse to share their beds and [even then if they do not listen] punish them. Then, if they obey you, take no further action against them. Indeed, Allah is Exalted and Mighty. (4:34)

وَ لَا تَتَمَنَّوْا مَا فَضَّلَ اللهُ بِهٖ بَعْضَكُمْ عَلٰى بَعْضٍ ۗ لِلرِّجَالِ نَصِيْبٌ مِّمَّا اكْتَسَبُوْا ۗ وَ لِلنِّسَاءِ نَصِيْبٌ مِّمَّا اكْتَسَبْنَ ۗ وَ سْئَلُوا اللهَ مِنْ فَضْلِهٖ ۗ اِنَّ اللهَ كَانَ بِكُلِّ شَیْءٍ عَلِيْمًا

And in no way covet those things in which God has bestowed His favors on some of you more than on others: to men is allotted what they earn, and to women what they earn. And ask God of His bounty. For God has full knowledge of all things. (4:32)

يٰاَيُّهَا الَّذِيْنَ اٰمَنُوْا لَا يَحِلُّ لَكُمْ اَنْ تَرِثُوا النِّسَاءَ كَرْهًا ۗ وَ لَا تَعْضُلُوْهُنَّ لِتَذْهَبُوْا بِبَعْضِ مَا اٰتَيْتُمُوْهُنَّ اِلَّاۤ اَنْ يَّأْتِيْنَ بِفَاحِشَةٍ مُّبَيِّنَةٍ ۚ وَ عَاشِرُوْهُنَّ بِالْمَعْرُوْفِ ۚ فَاِنْ كَرِهْتُمُوْهُنَّ فَعَسٰۤى اَنْ تَكْرَهُوْا شَيْئًا وَّ يَجْعَلَ اللهُ فِيْهِ خَيْرًا كَثِيْرًا

Believers! You are forbidden to forcibly inherit women. Nor by treating them with harshness should you take away part of what you have given them, except where they have been guilty of open lewdness; and live with them befittingly. Because if you dislike them, it may be that you dislike something, and Allah brings about a great deal of good through it. (4:19)

Rights and obligations of the spouses

- A family is like a small state or institution, and in every state/institution, we select a president or prime minister to run the affairs smoothly without mayhem.
- In the sphere of the family, God has entrusted men with the responsibility for households because of their innate tendency toward greater activity and physical dominance.
- The 'superiority' that God has talked about in the Quran is only in the realm of family affairs and is relative in nature.
- God has advised that, in contrast to this sphere (taking over responsibilities and thinking of them as 'superiority'), there is another sphere in which people should strive to outdo one another. This is the sphere of earning a reward for oneself through good deeds, high character, and virtue.
- As with any good state or institution, it is expected of the head of state to consult with the other members of the family on every matter before making any decision.
- The expression "*Quwwamuna Ala*" embodies the "responsibility of protection, defending and taking care of the livelihood of the family".
- Women can earn, but they are not given the financial responsibility of the family. They have no responsibility to participate in the financial matters unless they want to do so willingly.
- In the interest of maintaining sanity in the house, God advised pious wives to be accommodating and adaptable to their husbands when decisions are made.
- This demand from wives is based on the fact that women are more patient, forbearing, loving, and accommodating by nature than men.
- The second demand from the wives is that they keep their husbands' and households' secrets and protect their honor and integrity.
- The Quran also refers to a situation when the wife becomes rebellious or takes a position of defying the authority of the husband in the house, and suggests the following course of action:
    - Advise her to mend her ways.
    - Suspend intimate marital relations.
    - Scold her through light physical punishment at the gesture level.
- In Arab society, when these verses were revealed, that was the only way to address this problem; in those days, men used to resort to violence, but God stopped them and suggested the above instead.
- In modern times, political states can enact laws to address it in other ways.
- If the same situation occurs with the husband, it is expected that the wife will address it through family elders, society, and the law.

Application of the verses in our time

Problem 1: The text in the Quran seems to be intrinsically patriarchal and male-dominating.

Problem 2: These days, women contribute equally to family and society. Are these verses invalid now?

- In the Quran, the verses related to 'superiority' are only applicable in the context of marriage (husband and wife) and not in general to men and women.
- Islam sees the family as an organizational unit; it assigns authority to either the husband or the wife over this unit, and gives this authority to the husband for obvious reasons.
- Outside of this relationship, in the eyes of God, men and women are created equally (Surah Nisa verse 1), and they will be rewarded for their deeds equally.
- In the eyes of God, the mother is superior in rank and deserving of respect three times more than the father (Hadith).
- To address changes in societal norms, if applicable, at the time of drafting the marriage contract, if the husband and wife view the situation differently from what the Quran suggests, they can specify the terms agreed upon in the contract.
- E.g., the wife can make it part of the contract that I will be responsible for half of the household's livelihood and, as a result, will have equal decision-making rights. However, it does not solve the problem of whose decision will prevail, since it is between two people, and you need a third person to break the tie.

Does the Quran condone domestic violence?

Problem 1: The text in the Quran suggests that a husband can physically punish his wife under certain conditions.

- The Quran did not 'instruct' believers to physically punish their wives – it's a suggestion to deal with a problem at times when that's the only way the rebellious behavior of the wives can be handled.
- Since Islam sees the family as a small state or institution, it suggests a solution for how to deal with a situation when someone wants to challenge the state/institute.
- The Quran recommended a stepwise procedure, and physical punishment is the last option.
- If the husband does not want to take this step or the norms of society do not allow it, then the rebellious behavior of the wife should be handled by:
    - Temporary separation
    - Divorce
    - If the government has enacted laws to restrict this action, the matter should be resolved through family courts or other appropriate procedures.

Polygamy

- The following verses of Surah Nisaa are usually considered the source of 'polygamy in Islam'. We will see that these verses do not, in any way, serve as the source of this practice, which existed even before the time of Prophet Muhammad.

وَ اِنْ خِفْتُمْ اَلَّا تُقْسِطُوْا فِى الْيَتٰمٰى فَانْكِحُوْا مَا طَابَ لَكُمْ مِّنَ النِّسَآءِ مَثْنٰى وَ ثُلٰثَ وَ رُبٰعَ ۖ فَاِنْ خِفْتُمْ اَلَّا تَعْدِلُوْا فَوَاحِدَةً اَوْ مَا مَلَكَتْ اَيْمَانُكُمْ ۖ ذٰلِكَ اَدْنٰى اَلَّا تَعُوْلُوْا ۖ وَ اٰتُوا النِّسَآءَ صَدُقٰتِهِنَّ نِحْلَةً ۖ فَاِنْ طِبْنَ لَكُمْ عَنْ شَیْءٍ مِّنْهُ نَفْسًا فَكُلُوْهُ بَنِیْٓـًٔا مَّرِیْٓـًٔا

And if you fear that you shall not be able to deal justly with the orphans, marry [their mothers] who are lawful to you, two, three, four; but if you fear that you shall not be able to deal justly [with them], then only one, or those which your right hands possess. That will be more suitable to prevent you from doing injustice. And give these women their dowers also the way dowers are given; but if they, of their good pleasure, remit any part of it to you, take it and consume it gladly. (4:3-4)

- The verses where polygamy is discussed came in the context of guardians of the orphans in a very special situation after a war. God asked the guardians whether, if they could not deal with the orphans justly while discharging their responsibilities in this critical time, they should marry their mothers and bring them into their family.
- The context suggests that the verses were not specifically revealed to permit polygamy, contrary to what most people suggest.
- The verses suggest that, since men were already marrying more than one woman in that society, why not the guardians do the same for the welfare of the children?
- Islam or any other religion did not start the practice of polygamy; social, psychological, political, and cultural needs gave rise to the need for polygamy.
- Considering those needs, one can say that 'Islam allowed this practice in Shariah'.
- However, Islam puts two conditions for this practice:
  - A man cannot marry more than 4 women at a time.
  - All wives/children should be dealt with justice and equality (in financial matters and provisions) as humanely as possible without showing bias towards one or the other (this does not mean that one cannot be more inclined in their heart).

وَ لَنْ تَسْتَطِیْعُوْٓا اَنْ تَعْدِلُوْا بَیْنَ النِّسَآءِ وَ لَوْ حَرَصْتُمْ فَلَا تَمِیْلُوْا كُلَّ الْمَیْلِ فَتَذَرُوْهَا كَالْمُعَلَّقَةِ ۖ وَ اِنْ تُصْلِحُوْا وَ تَتَّقُوْا فَاِنَّ اللّٰهَ كَانَ غَفُوْرًا رَّحِیْمًا

And even if it is your ardent desire, you will never be able to be just between women, so it is enough if you do not completely incline yourself to a woman altogether to leave the other aside. And if you come to a friendly understanding and fear Allah, Allah is Oft-Forgiving, Most Merciful. (4:129)

Marriages of Prophet Muhammad

يٰٓأَيُّهَا النَّبِيُّ إِنَّآ أَحْلَلْنَا لَكَ أَزْوَاجَكَ الّٰتِيٓ اٰتَيْتَ أُجُوْرَهُنَّ وَ مَا مَلَكَتْ يَمِيْنُكَ مِمَّآ أَفَآءَ اللّٰهُ عَلَيْكَ وَ

بَنٰتِ عَمِّكَ وَ بَنٰتِ عَمّٰتِكَ وَ بَنٰتِ خَالِكَ وَ بَنٰتِ خٰلٰتِكَ الّٰتِيْ هَاجَرْنَ مَعَكَ ۗ وَ امْرَأَةً مُّؤْمِنَةً اِنْ

وَّهَبَتْ نَفْسَهَا لِلنَّبِيِّ اِنْ أَرَادَ النَّبِيُّ أَنْ يَّسْتَنْكِحَهَا ۙ خَالِصَةً لَّكَ مِنْ دُوْنِ الْمُؤْمِنِيْنَ ۗ قَدْ عَلِمْنَا مَا

فَرَضْنَا عَلَيْهِمْ فِيٓ أَزْوَاجِهِمْ وَ مَا مَلَكَتْ أَيْمَانُهُمْ لِكَيْلَا يَكُوْنَ عَلَيْكَ حَرَجٌ ۗ وَ كَانَ اللّٰهُ غَفُوْرًا رَّحِيْمًا

تُرْجِيْ مَنْ تَشَآءُ مِنْهُنَّ وَ تُؤْوِيٓ اِلَيْكَ مَنْ تَشَآءُ ۗ وَ مَنِ ابْتَغَيْتَ مِمَّنْ عَزَلْتَ

فَلَا جُنَاحَ عَلَيْكَ ۗ ذٰلِكَ أَدْنٰٓى أَنْ تَقَرَّ أَعْيُنُهُنَّ وَ لَا يَحْزَنَّ وَ يَرْضَيْنَ بِمَآ اٰتَيْتَهُنَّ

كُلُّهُنَّ ۗ وَ اللّٰهُ يَعْلَمُ مَا فِيْ قُلُوْبِكُمْ ۗ وَ كَانَ اللّٰهُ عَلِيْمًا حَلِيْمًا

لَا يَحِلُّ لَكَ النِّسَآءُ مِنْ بَعْدُ وَ لَآ أَنْ تَبَدَّلَ بِهِنَّ مِنْ أَزْوَاجٍ وَّ لَوْ أَعْجَبَكَ

حُسْنُهُنَّ اِلَّا مَا مَلَكَتْ يَمِيْنُكَ ۗ وَ كَانَ اللّٰهُ عَلٰى كُلِّ شَيْءٍ رَّقِيْبًا

O Prophet! We have made lawful to you the wives whom you have paid their dowers and free women whom God gives in your possession [because of a military campaign] and the daughters of your paternal uncles and aunts and the daughters of your maternal uncles and aunts who migrated [from Makkah] with you and any believing woman who gifts her soul to the Prophet on the condition that the Prophet wishes to marry her. **This directive is specifically for you, not for the believers.** We very well know what We have imposed on them as obligations regarding their wives and slave girls – [a special directive for you] so that there be no difficulty for you [in discharging your duties] and [and in case of any blemish], Allah is Forgiving and Merciful. You have the authority to keep any of them away from you, and it is lawful for you to bring any of them near you whom you have kept away. There is no blame on you in this regard. This [explanation] is more proper so that they are contented and not sorrowful, and feel satisfied with whatever you give all of them. And Allah knows what is in your hearts, and Allah is All-Knowing and Most- Forbearing. All other women besides these are not lawful for you, nor can you change them for other wives, even though their beauty attracts you. Slave girls, however, [are still] allowed to you. And [in reality] Allah does watch over all things. (33:50-52)

- After the incident of Prophet Muhammad's marriage to Zaynab, God made a proclamation about his special case of marriage and divorce.
- Bear in mind that Prophet Muhammad was married to Khadijah for 25+ years.
- The Prophet was allowed (in some cases instructed) to marry more than four:
    - To honor free women who were captured in military expeditions.
    - As a gesture of kindness to those who wanted to marry him just for the sake of associating themselves with him, and they wanted to gift themselves to him.
    - To console and sympathize with his maternal and paternal cousin-sisters who had migrated with him from Makkah and left their homes and relatives (in some cases, even their former husbands).
- He was prohibited from marrying any woman other than those specified. Also, he could not divorce any of his wives nor bring a new wife into their place.
- The wives of the Prophet are the mothers of the believers, and for believers, marriage with them is eternally prohibited.

اَلنَّبِيُّ اَوْلٰى بِالْمُؤْمِنِينَ مِنْ اَنْفُسِهِمْ وَ اَزْوَاجُهُ اُمَّهٰتُهُمْ

The Prophet holds priority for the believers over themselves, and his wives are their mothers. (33:6)

لَآ اَنْ تَنْكِحُوٓا اَزْوَاجَهُ مِنْ بَعْدِهٖ اَبَدًا ۜ اِنَّ ذٰلِكُمْ كَانَ عِنْدَ اللّٰهِ عَظِيمًا

Nor is it right for you that you should marry his widows after him at any time. Truly, such a thing is abominable in Allah's sight. (33:53)

Etiquette of Sexual Intimacy

وَ يَسْأَلُونَكَ عَنِ الْمَحِيضِ ۖ قُلْ هُوَ أَذًى ۙ فَاعْتَزِلُوا النِّسَآءَ فِى الْمَحِيضِ ۖ وَ لَا تَقْرَبُوهُنَّ حَتَّى يَطْهُرْنَ ۖ
فَإِذَا تَطَهَّرْنَ فَأْتُوهُنَّ مِنْ حَيْثُ أَمَرَكُمُ اللّٰهُ ۚ إِنَّ اللّٰهَ يُحِبُّ التَّوَّابِينَ وَ يُحِبُّ الْمُتَطَهِّرِينَ
نِسَآؤُكُمْ حَرْثٌ لَّكُمْ ۖ فَأْتُوا حَرْثَكُمْ أَنّٰى شِئْتُمْ ۖ وَ قَدِّمُوا لِأَنْفُسِكُمْ ۚ وَ
اتَّقُوا اللّٰهَ وَ اعْلَمُوٓا أَنَّكُمْ مُّلٰقُوهُ ۗ وَ بَشِّرِ الْمُؤْمِنِينَ

And they ask you about women's cycles. Tell them: "They are an impurity. So keep away from women in their courses and do not approach them until they have cleansed themselves from blood. But when they have purified themselves after taking a bath, approach them in the manner the Almighty has directed you [in your instincts]. Indeed, Allah loves those who constantly repent and keep themselves clean." These women of yours are your cultivated land; go into your lands in any manner you please [and through this] plan for the future [of both this world and the next] and remain fearful of God. And bear in mind that you shall necessarily meet Him [one day]. And [O Prophet!] Give good tidings (of success and salvation) to the believers (on that day). (2:222-223)

- Sexual relations between a man and a woman stem from their instincts, and they do not need any external guidance in this matter, but the Quran discusses this to emphasize the etiquette.
- A husband and wife cannot have sexual intercourse (that's the only restriction) when the wife is going through her menstrual or puerperal cycle (it is prohibited in all major religions).
- The two should approach each other for sexual intercourse only after the woman has taken the ceremonial bath after her cycle.
- Sexual intercourse should be done in the way prescribed by the Almighty, and non-natural methods must be avoided (keeping the goal of purity in mind).

1. Why do people associate polygamy with Islam only?
2. Why can't women marry more than one man at the same time?

Chapter 11

Social Shariah

Divorce (Talaq)

This chapter introduces the Shariah governing the divorce procedure in Islam, which is often misunderstood.

Ending the Marriage Contract

Ending the Marriage Contract

- In Islam, divorce is highly discouraged and should be considered the last resort when settling differences in a marriage.

أَبْغَضُ الْحَلَالِ إِلَى اللّٰهِ الطَّلَاقُ

"The most hated of permissible things to Allah is divorce."
(Sunan Abi Dawood)

- At the time of signing the contract for Marriage, it is the utmost desire of both man and woman to remain in this wedlock forever.

- They make a strong pact to support and commit to each other through thick and thin.

- However, when it becomes almost impossible for husband and wife to stay together and disagreements reach a level where the marriage has broken down, and there is no way to reconcile, Islam allows the couple to seek divorce (Talaq) and separate.

- The Quran provided a complete guideline on the procedure for Talaq and how to deal with this challenging situation.

- The central verse for this law is this one:

اَلطَّلَاقُ مَرَّتٰنِ فَاِمْسَاكٌ بِمَعْرُوْفٍ اَوْ تَسْرِيْحٌ بِاِحْسَانٍ

The divorce can be pronounced twice (in one relationship), either holding with kindness or leaving with grace. (2:229)

Eela (an innovation in Arab)

- Eela was a practice of the Arab Jahiliyyah society in which a person would swear an oath to sever the physical relationship with his wife without giving her a divorce.

- It would leave the wife in an uncertain state for an indefinite period.

- God advised men practicing Eela to decide within four months whether to continue their marriage (by paying atonement for breaking the marriage oath) or divorce.

- Islam discouraged the practice of Eela, calling it a bad practice. Men were advised to follow the procedure of divorce as suggested in Shariah.

Those who swear to abstain from their wives must wait four months. If they change their mind, Allah is Forgiving and Ever-Merciful; but if they decide to divorce them, [they should know that] He hears all and knows all. (2:226-227)

Zihar (another innovation in the Arab)

اَلَّذِيْنَ يُظٰهِرُوْنَ مِنْكُمْ مِّنْ نِّسَاۤئِهِمْ مَّا هُنَّ أُمَّهٰتِهِمْ ۖ اِنْ أُمَّهٰتُهُمْ اِلَّا الّٰٓئِىْ وَلَدْنَهُمْ ۖ وَ اِنَّهُمْ لَيَقُوْلُوْنَ مُنْكَرًا مِّنَ الْقَوْلِ وَ زُوْرًا ۖ وَ اِنَّ اللّٰهَ لَعَفُوٌّ غَفُوْرٌ   وَ الَّذِيْنَ يُظٰهِرُوْنَ مِنْ نِّسَاۤئِهِمْ ثُمَّ يَعُوْدُوْنَ لِمَا قَالُوْا فَتَحْرِيْرُ رَقَبَةٍ مِّنْ قَبْلِ اَنْ يَّتَمَاۤسَّا ۖ ذٰلِكُمْ تُوْعَظُوْنَ بِهٖ ۖ وَ اللّٰهُ بِمَا تَعْمَلُوْنَ خَبِيْرٌ فَمَنْ لَّمْ يَجِدْ فَصِيَامُ شَهْرَيْنِ مُتَتَابِعَيْنِ مِنْ قَبْلِ اَنْ يَّتَمَاۤسَّا ۖ فَمَنْ لَّمْ يَسْتَطِعْ فَاِطْعَامُ سِتِّيْنَ مِسْكِيْنًا ۖ ذٰلِكَ لِتُؤْمِنُوْا بِاللّٰهِ وَ رَسُوْلِهٖ ۖ وَ تِلْكَ حُدُوْدُ اللّٰهِ ۖ وَ لِلْكٰفِرِيْنَ عَذَابٌ اَلِيْمٌ

Those among you who commit *Zihar* with their wives, they [–these wives–] cannot become their mothers: none can be their mothers except those who gave birth to them. And in fact, such people say something very immoral and false. And truly, Allah is Forgiving and Merciful. And [in this matter, the directive is that] those who do *Zihar* with their wives, then wish to go back on the words they uttered, then a slave should be liberated before they touch each other. Thus, you are admonished to do, and Allah is well-acquainted with all you do. And if a slave is unavailable to a person, he should fast for two months consecutively before touching each other. And if he cannot do this, he should feed sixty indigent ones. This is because you may show your faith in Allah and His Messenger. Those are limits set by Allah; [only the rejecters of Allah and His Messenger cross them]. And there is a grievous punishment for such rejecters. (58:2-4)

- This is another practice from the time of Jahiliyyah in Arab society, which the Quran scolded them for.
- Husband utters words like "If I touch you, it would be as if I touched the back of my own mother"; this was practiced in place of divorce.
- The Quran termed it an evil and indecent practice that must be stopped, and the person should be punished for doing so.
- Atonement for uttering such words:
  - Set free a slave-woman or – man
  - Or fast consequently for 2 months
  - Or feed 60 indigent people
- In a typical patriarchal society, it was very difficult for women to get any relief from such absurd practices.
- This is despite the fact that Talaq was known among Arabs, and they had some traces of the practices from the time of Prophet Ismail.
- The Quran came and fixed it for all.

Shariah of Divorce (Talaq)

- The law of divorce is described in many places in the Quran, but the main verses that outline the law are in Surah Talaq, verses 1-7.

يَا أَيُّهَا النَّبِيُّ إِذَا طَلَّقْتُمُ النِّسَاءَ فَطَلِّقُوهُنَّ لِعِدَّتِهِنَّ وَ أَحْصُوا الْعِدَّةَ ۖ وَ اتَّقُوا اللهَ رَبَّكُمْ ۖ لَا تُخْرِجُوهُنَّ مِنْ بُيُوتِهِنَّ وَ لَا يَخْرُجْنَ إِلَّا أَنْ يَأْتِينَ بِفَاحِشَةٍ مُبَيِّنَةٍ ۚ وَ تِلْكَ حُدُودُ اللهِ ۚ وَ مَنْ يَتَعَدَّ حُدُودَ اللهِ فَقَدْ ظَلَمَ نَفْسَهُ ۚ لَا تَدْرِي لَعَلَّ اللهَ يُحْدِثُ بَعْدَ ذٰلِكَ أَمْرًا

فَإِذَا بَلَغْنَ أَجَلَهُنَّ فَأَمْسِكُوهُنَّ بِمَعْرُوفٍ أَوْ فَارِقُوهُنَّ بِمَعْرُوفٍ وَّ أَشْهِدُوا ذَوَيْ عَدْلٍ مِّنْكُمْ وَ أَقِيمُوا الشَّهَادَةَ لِلهِ ۚ ذٰلِكُمْ يُوعَظُ بِهِ مَنْ كَانَ يُؤْمِنُ بِاللهِ وَ الْيَوْمِ الْآخِرِ ۚ وَ مَنْ يَتَّقِ اللهَ يَجْعَلْ لَّهُ مَخْرَجًا ۙ ﴿٢﴾ وَ يَرْزُقْهُ مِنْ حَيْثُ لَا يَحْتَسِبُ ۚ وَ مَنْ يَتَوَكَّلْ عَلَى اللهِ فَهُوَ حَسْبُهُ ۚ إِنَّ اللهَ بَالِغُ أَمْرِهِ ۚ قَدْ جَعَلَ اللهُ لِكُلِّ شَيْءٍ قَدْرًا

وَ اللَّائِي يَئِسْنَ مِنَ الْمَحِيضِ مِنْ نِّسَائِكُمْ إِنِ ارْتَبْتُمْ فَعِدَّتُهُنَّ ثَلَثَةُ أَشْهُرٍ ۙ وَّ اللَّائِي لَمْ يَحِضْنَ ۚ وَ أُولَاتُ الْأَحْمَالِ أَجَلُهُنَّ أَنْ يَّضَعْنَ حَمْلَهُنَّ ۚ وَ مَنْ يَتَّقِ اللهَ يَجْعَلْ لَّهُ مِنْ أَمْرِهِ يُسْرًا

ذٰلِكَ أَمْرُ اللهِ أَنْزَلَهُ إِلَيْكُمْ ۚ وَ مَنْ يَتَّقِ اللهَ يُكَفِّرْ عَنْهُ سَيِّئَاتِهِ وَ يُعْظِمْ لَهُ أَجْرًا

أَسْكِنُوهُنَّ مِنْ حَيْثُ سَكَنْتُمْ مِّنْ وُّجْدِكُمْ وَ لَا تُضَارُّوهُنَّ لِتُضَيِّقُوا عَلَيْهِنَّ ۚ وَ إِنْ كُنَّ أُولَاتِ حَمْلٍ فَأَنْفِقُوا عَلَيْهِنَّ حَتَّى يَضَعْنَ حَمْلَهُنَّ ۚ فَإِنْ أَرْضَعْنَ لَكُمْ فَآتُوهُنَّ أُجُورَهُنَّ ۚ وَ أْتَمِرُوا بَيْنَكُمْ بِمَعْرُوفٍ ۚ وَ إِنْ تَعَاسَرْتُمْ فَسَتُرْضِعُ لَهُ أُخْرَى

لِيُنْفِقْ ذُو سَعَةٍ مِّنْ سَعَتِهِ ۖ وَ مَنْ قُدِرَ عَلَيْهِ رِزْقُهُ فَلْيُنْفِقْ مِمَّا آتَاهُ اللهُ ۚ لَا يُكَلِّفُ اللهُ نَفْسًا إِلَّا مَا آتَاهَا ۚ سَيَجْعَلُ اللهُ بَعْدَ عُسْرٍ يُسْرًا

Shariah of Divorce (Talaq)

O Prophet! When you and other Muslims divorce your wives, divorce them **according to their waiting periods**, count this waiting period accurately, and fear God, your Lord. [During this waiting period], do not turn them out of their houses, nor should they [themselves] leave, except in case they are guilty of some open lewdness. These are the bounds set by Allah, and [you should know that] those who transgress the bounds of Allah are the ones who wrong their own souls.

You know not that God might thereafter create new circumstances. Thus, when they approach the end of their waiting period, either take them back on equitable terms or part with them on equitable terms. And [whether you want to keep or part with them, in both cases] call to witness two honest people from among you. And [O Witnesses!] Establish this testimony for God. It is this thing to which those who believe in God and the Last Day are exhorted.

And [if] those who fear God [encounter any difficulty], God will find a way out for them and provide them from where they cannot imagine. And for those who trust God, Allah is enough [to help them]. God is sure to bring about His plans. God has set a measure for all things.

And those of your women who have ceased menstruating and also who have not menstruated [despite reaching their age], if you have any doubts about them, then their waiting period is three months. And the waiting period for pregnant women is till they deliver the child. God will ease the hardship of [those among you] who fear Him. Such is the directive of God He has revealed to you.

He who fears God, God shall brush away his sins and shall richly reward him. [During the waiting period], lodge these women in your homes according to your means. And do not harass them to make their lives intolerable. And if they are pregnant, spend on them until they deliver the child. And if they suckle your [child], give them their remuneration and decide this matter according to the custom after mutual consultation. And if you find yourselves in difficulty, another woman can suckle [the child]. Let the man of means spend according to his means, and he whose resources are restricted spend according to what God has given him. God does not burden a person with more than He has given him. [Rest assured], God will soon grant relief after some difficulty. (65:1-7)

Instructions given in the verses

- The divorce process should start with the exact number of days of the waiting period (called Iddah) to be counted. E.g., if the waiting period is 90 days (3 months), then the exact 90 days should be calculated from that day for the waiting period to be completed.
- During the waiting period, the wife stays in the house (recommended, if she is willing).
- When the waiting period is about to end, decide amicably whether to continue the marriage or let her go with grace and honor.
- If you choose to part ways, call two honest witnesses and pronounce a divorce in front of them.
- The waiting period for the following women is three months:
  - Those who have passed the age of menstruation cycles.
  - Those who have reached puberty but still have not had any cycles for some reason.
- The waiting period for pregnant women lasts until the baby is delivered.
- The waiting period for all other women is 3 menstrual cycles.
- If the husband decides that his wife should suckle his child, he should give her compensation for it.

> *Iddah* or waiting period is the period during which a divorced or widowed woman cannot marry another person to ascertain if the woman is pregnant by her previous husband or not.

Before Divorce

وَ اِنۡ خِفۡتُمۡ شِقَاقَ بَیۡنِهِمَا فَابۡعَثُوۡا حَکَمًا مِّنۡ اَهۡلِهٖ وَ حَکَمًا مِّنۡ اَهۡلِهَا ۚ اِنۡ یُّرِیۡدَاۤ اِصۡلَاحًا
یُّوَفِّقِ اللّٰهُ بَیۡنَهُمَا ۚ اِنَّ اللّٰهَ کَانَ عَلِیۡمًا خَبِیۡرًا

And if you fear a dissent between the two, appoint arbitrators, one from his family, and the other from hers; if [the husband and wife] wish to reconcile, Allah will create harmony between them: for Allah has full knowledge, and is acquainted with all things. (4:35)

1. God wants the couple to make a last-ditch effort, meaning their relatives, clan or tribe, and other well-wishers should come forward and use their influence to try to reconcile them and save the marriage.
2. One arbitrator from each side should be appointed for advice and counsel.
3. If both parties intend to reconcile and are ready to let go of the past, God has promised them a fruitful outcome from this effort.

The Right to Divorce

1. From various verses of the Quran, it can be concluded that God granted the husband the right to initiate divorce.
2. The reason is apparent. The husband has been made in charge of the house and family, and given the responsibility to earn and provide for them.
3. Given the nature of his responsibilities and status in the household, he has been granted the authority to initiate the divorce.
4. Entrusting two people with different responsibilities but granting them equal rights to establish or dismantle an organization cannot keep that institution functioning – a person with more responsibilities should have greater rights within that organization.
5. When a woman seeks a separation from her husband, she must ask her husband to grant her a divorce. God made it mandatory for the husband to comply with the demand after looking at his financial situation.
6. If the husband does not comply with the wife's demand, the wife can seek assistance from his family, his tribe, or the court of law.

The wife of Thabit ibn Qais once came to the Prophet and said: "O Messenger of Allah! I do not have any complaints regarding his character and person; however, I fear losing my faith." When the Prophet heard this complaint, he said: "Would you return his orchard?" She showed her consent. At this, the Prophet directed Thabit to accept the orchard and separate her by pronouncing a divorce. (Sahih Al-Bukhari 5273, 5277)

The Procedure for Divorce – Initiation (Step 1)

1. Divorce should be initiated (uttering words like "I divorce you" one time or in writing) only after the woman has completed her monthly menstrual cycle, in the period of cleanliness in which her husband did not have any sexual relations with her.
2. The number of days starting from the initiation of the divorce until the end of the waiting period must be carefully counted.
3. During this time, the woman would stay in her husband's house, and the husband would be responsible for providing for her (she may stay elsewhere if they both agree).

$$ وَ بُعُوْلَتُهُنَّ اَحَقُّ بِرَدِّهِنَّ فِیْ ذٰلِکَ اِنْ اَرَادُوْٓا اِصْلَاحًا ۚ وَ لَهُنَّ مِثْلُ الَّذِیْ عَلَیْهِنَّ بِالْمَعْرُوْفِ ۪ وَ لِلرِّجَالِ عَلَیْهِنَّ دَرَجَةٌ ؕ وَ اللّٰهُ عَزِیْزٌ حَكِیْمٌ $$

And if their husbands wish to reform affairs, they have more right to take them (wives) back [in this waiting period] should they desire reconciliation. And just as according to [society's] norms, these women have obligations [towards their husbands], they also have rights, although men [as husbands] have a status above women in this marriage. [This is the directive of Allah], and Allah is Mighty and Wise. (2:228)

The Procedure for Divorce – Separation (option 1)

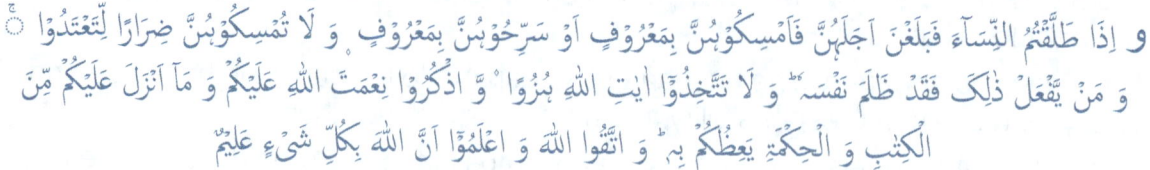

و إِذَا طَلَّقْتُمُ النِّسَاءَ فَبَلَغْنَ أَجَلَهُنَّ فَأَمْسِكُوهُنَّ بِمَعْرُوفٍ أَوْ سَرِّحُوهُنَّ بِمَعْرُوفٍ ۚ وَ لَا تُمْسِكُوهُنَّ ضِرَارًا لِّتَعْتَدُوا ۚ
وَ مَنْ يَفْعَلْ ذَٰلِكَ فَقَدْ ظَلَمَ نَفْسَهُ ۚ وَ لَا تَتَّخِذُوا آيَتِ اللهِ هُزُوًا ۚ وَّ اذْكُرُوا نِعْمَتَ اللهِ عَلَيْكُمْ وَ مَآ أَنْزَلَ عَلَيْكُمْ مِّنَ
الْكِتٰبِ وَ الْحِكْمَةِ يَعِظُكُمْ بِهِ ۚ وَ اتَّقُوا اللهَ وَ اعْلَمُوا أَنَّ اللهَ بِكُلِّ شَيْءٍ عَلِيمٌ

And when you have divorced your wives, and they have reached the end of their waiting period, either retain them with kindness or let them go with kindness. But do not retain them with the intention of harm so that you commit excesses against them. And [you should know that] whoever does this wrongs his own soul. And do not mock Allah's commandments. Remember the favors He has bestowed upon you and the Law and the wisdom which He has revealed, of which He instructs you. And keep fearing Allah and know that He has knowledge of all things. (2:231)

4. Once the waiting period expires and the husband decides not to take back his decision, the relationship of wedlock between husband and wife ceases at that moment.

5. God has cautioned the husband that if he decides to revoke his decision, then it should not be to hurt or harass her – God called this act equal to making a mockery of God's commandments, which is a severe crime in the sight of God.

6. If the husband has initiated the divorce, he should not take back any gifts of wealth, jewelry, property, clothing, or other items given to the wife. Two exceptions: a) if the wife asked for the divorce and the husband hesitates to divorce due to financial loss, and both agreed that the wife should return something, and b) the wife has committed adultery.

7. The husband is not responsible for giving the dower at the time of divorce if no physical relationship was established with the wife. However, if the dower had already been agreed upon, he should pay half of the agreed amount (2:236-237).

8. In every verse in which God allowed the husband to enjoy a financial benefit at the time of the divorce due to the situation, He urged the husband to be generous, to relinquish his rights, and to give more than what is due as a sign of piety.

9. At the time of separation, God asked the husband to provide financial support to the departing wife so she could sustain herself before she remarried (2:241, 2:236).

10. This completes one divorce between the husband and the wife.

11. Both can remarry each other or with anyone they want.

12. If both decide to remarry, all conditions and procedures for a new marriage will be applied.

وَ لَا يَحِلُّ لَكُمْ أَنْ تَأْخُذُوا مِمَّآ اٰتَيْتُمُوهُنَّ شَيْئًا إِلَّآ أَنْ يَّخَافَآ أَلَّا يُقِيْمَا حُدُوْدَ اللّٰهِ ۚ فَإِنْ خِفْتُمْ أَلَّا يُقِيْمَا حُدُوْدَ اللّٰهِ ۙ فَلَا جُنَاحَ عَلَيْهِمَا فِيْمَا افْتَدَتْ بِهٖ ۗ تِلْكَ حُدُوْدُ اللّٰهِ فَلَا تَعْتَدُوْهَا ۚ وَ مَنْ يَّتَعَدَّ حُدُوْدَ اللّٰهِ فَأُولٰٓئِكَ هُمُ الظّٰلِمُوْنَ

And it is unlawful for you [on this occasion] to take back from them anything you have given them unless both husband and wife fear that they may be unable to keep within the bounds set by Allah. Then, if you also feel that they will not be able to remain within the bounds set by Allah, there shall be no offense for either of them [regarding the gifts given by the husband] if the wife seeks divorce [by returning them to him] in ransom. These are the bounds set by Allah, so do not transgress them. And [you should know that] those who transgress the bounds of Allah are wrongdoers. (2:229)

وَ لِلْمُطَلَّقٰتِ مَتَاعٌۢ بِالْمَعْرُوْفِ ۗ حَقًّا عَلَى الْمُتَّقِيْنَ

And Divorced women should also be given some resources according to the norms of society when they are sent off. This is an obligation on those who are fearful of God. (2:241)

The Procedure for Divorce – Revocation

اَلطَّلَاقُ مَرَّتٰنِ ۖ فَإِمْسَاكٌۢ بِمَعْرُوْفٍ أَوْ تَسْرِيْحٌۢ بِإِحْسَانٍ

The divorce can be pronounced twice (in one relationship), then, either holding with kindness or leaving with grace. (2:229)

- According to the Quran, if the husband decides to revoke his decision of divorce before the waiting period is over, he has exercised one of his rights to divorce with the liberty to withdraw it. A husband can only exercise this right twice in one marriage in which he has permission to withdraw it. If he divorces for the third time, he cannot withdraw it.
- If the husband has already exercised his right to divorce twice, then the third time, the only option is separation.
- If the husband and wife want to remarry after the third divorce, the only way it is possible is for the wife to marry another man and then divorce him.

Note: For the wife to marry another man and then divorce him before marrying her first husband is the condition set for remarriage. This is NOT a method described in Shariah to remarry. Those who use this "method" to remarry make a joke of the Shariah of Allah.

A short summary of the divorce procedure

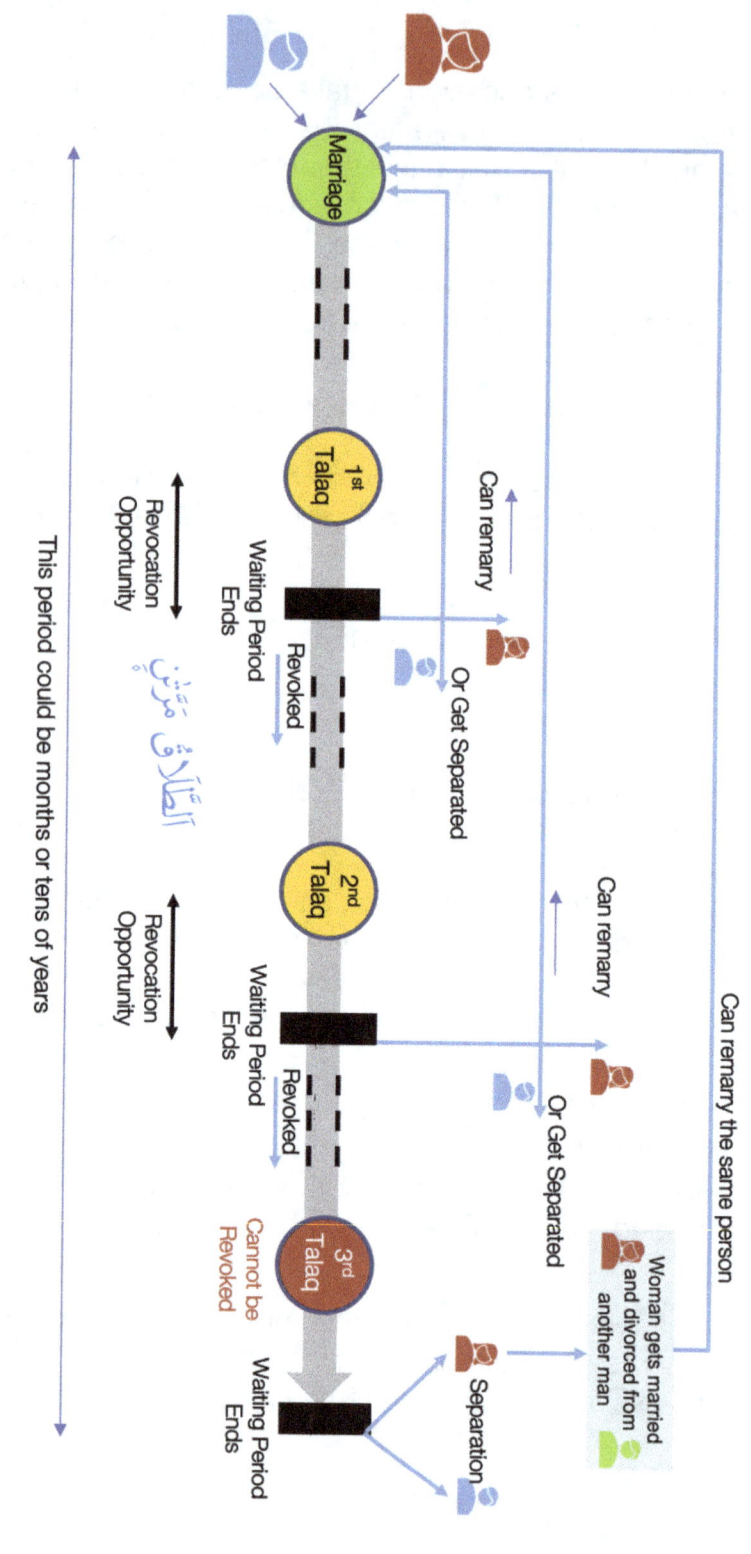

> What wisdom do you see in how divorce is codified in Islam or otherwise?

After the divorce

- In case of young children or the birth of a newborn at the time of divorce, if the mother is willing to suckle the children, then the husband shall pay her for this service, and this remuneration shall be ascertained through mutual consultation and in a befitting manner (he will pay her some money as living expenses until she suckles the child).
- If the father of the child is dead, his heirs will be responsible for her rights during this time.
- Regarding the custody of the children, the Shariah has not provided any directive, as this matter can only be decided with reference to the children's welfare and the parents' circumstances, which vary widely depending on the children's age, the parents' situation, and many other factors. Either the husband and wife should decide, the children should decide, or the court should decide on this matter.

وَ الْوَالِدٰتُ يُرْضِعْنَ اَوْلَادَهُنَّ حَوْلَيْنِ كَامِلَيْنِ لِمَنْ اَرَادَ اَنْ يُّتِمَّ الرَّضَاعَةَ ۚ وَ عَلَى الْمَوْلُوْدِ لَهٗ رِزْقُهُنَّ وَ كِسْوَتُهُنَّ بِالْمَعْرُوْفِ ۚ لَا تُكَلَّفُ نَفْسٌ اِلَّا وُسْعَهَا ۚ لَا تُضَآرَّ وَالِدَةٌ بِوَلَدِهَا وَ لَا مَوْلُوْدٌ لَّهٗ بِوَلَدِهٖ ۗ وَ عَلَى الْوَارِثِ مِثْلُ ذٰلِكَ ۚ فَاِنْ اَرَادَا فِصَالًا عَنْ تَرَاضٍ مِّنْهُمَا وَ تَشَاوُرٍ فَلَا جُنَاحَ عَلَيْهِمَا ۗ وَ اِنْ اَرَدْتُّمْ اَنْ تَسْتَرْضِعُوْۤا اَوْلَادَكُمْ فَلَا جُنَاحَ عَلَيْكُمْ اِذَا سَلَّمْتُمْ مَّاۤ اٰتَيْتُمْ بِالْمَعْرُوْفِ ۗ وَ اتَّقُوا اللّٰهَ وَ اعْلَمُوْۤا اَنَّ اللّٰهَ بِمَا تَعْمَلُوْنَ بَصِيْرٌ

And [after divorce also] mothers shall suckle their offspring for two whole years for those who desire to complete the term. And the child's father [in such a case] shall have to bear the cost of their food and clothing according to the norms. No one should be burdened beyond their capacity. Neither shall the mother be treated unfairly because of her child, nor the father on account of his child – and his heir shall be accountable in the same way – But if they both decide on weaning by mutual consent and after due consultation, there is no blame on them. And if you decide to engage someone else to suckle your offspring, there is no blame on you, provided you pay [the mother] in accordance with the norms [of the society] what you promised. And fear Allah and know that Allah sees well what you do. (2:233)

Chapter 12

Social Shariah

Other Social Instructions

This chapter discusses some other social instructions given by God.

Directives related to parents

- Islam (including Judaism and Christianity) instructs man to show kindness to parents.
- Kindness should be manifested in the form of:
  - Good manners and a well-behaved attitude.
  - Respect.
  - Help, support, and listen to their advice (without compromising the inclination toward the truth).
- The hardships a mother faces in giving birth and raising a child are highlighted to show why we should be kind to her.
- The verse by no means undermines the care and affection shown by the father.
- Even with the status that Islam confers upon parents, we are asked not to be obedient to them if they insist on associating partners with God or going against the good that society accepts in general.

وَ وَصَّيْنَا الْإِنْسَانَ بِوَالِدَيْهِ ۚ حَمَلَتْهُ أُمُّهُ وَهْنًا عَلَى وَهْنٍ وَّ فِصَالُهُ فِى عَامَيْنِ اَنِ اشْكُرْ لِىْ وَ لِوَالِدَيْكَ ۚ اِلَىَّ الْمَصِيْرُ
وَ اِنْ جَاهَدٰكَ عَلٰى اَنْ تُشْرِكَ بِىْ مَا لَيْسَ لَكَ بِهٖ عِلْمٌ ۙ فَلَا تُطِعْهُمَا وَ صَاحِبْهُمَا فِى الدُّنْيَا مَعْرُوْفًا ۙ وَّ اتَّبِعْ سَبِيْلَ مَنْ اَنَابَ اِلَىَّ ۚ ثُمَّ اِلَىَّ مَرْجِعُكُمْ فَاُنَبِّئُكُمْ بِمَا كُنْتُمْ تَعْمَلُوْنَ

And We enjoined man to show kindness to his parents – with much pain, his mother bores him, and he is not weaned before he is two years of age – [We said:] "Be grateful to your parents and Me. To Me shall all things return. But if they insist on you serving besides Me, for which you have no knowledge, do not obey them. (But still) remain kind to them in this world and turn to Me with all devotion. To Me, you shall all return, and I will declare to you everything you have done." (31:14-15)

وَ قَضٰى رَبُّكَ اَلَّا تَعْبُدُوْا اِلَّا اِيَّاهُ وَ بِالْوَالِدَيْنِ اِحْسَانًا ۚ اِمَّا يَبْلُغَنَّ عِنْدَكَ الْكِبَرَ اَحَدُهُمَا اَوْ كِلَاهُمَا فَلَا تَقُلْ لَّهُمَا اُفٍّ
وَّ لَا تَنْهَرْهُمَا وَ قُلْ لَّهُمَا قَوْلًا كَرِيْمًا وَ اخْفِضْ لَهُمَا جَنَاحَ الذُّلِّ مِنَ الرَّحْمَةِ وَ قُلْ رَّبِّ ارْحَمْهُمَا كَمَا رَبَّيٰنِىْ صَغِيْرًا
رَبُّكُمْ اَعْلَمُ بِمَا فِىْ نُفُوْسِكُمْ ۚ اِنْ تَكُوْنُوْا صٰلِحِيْنَ فَاِنَّهٗ كَانَ لِلْاَوَّابِيْنَ غَفُوْرًا

And your Lord has enjoined you to worship none but Him, and to show great kindness to your parents; if either or both of them attain old age in your presence, show them no sign of impatience, nor rebuke them; but speak to them kind words. Treat them with humility and tenderness and say: "Lord, be merciful to them the way they nurtured me when I was young." Your Lord best knows what is in your hearts. If you remain obedient, He will forgive those who turn to Him. (17:23-25)

A man came to the Messenger and said, "Who is more entitled to my best companionship?" The Prophet said, "Your mother." The man said. "After that?" The Prophet said, "Your mother." The man said, "After that?" The Prophet said, "Your mother." He asked for the fourth time, "After that?" The Prophet said, "Your father." (Sahih Al-Bukhari #5971)

- Kindness towards parents should emerge from the sense of gratitude towards them, which must not be expressed merely by the tongue.
- Even if the person is annoyed (due to their behavior in old age), they are asked to be soft, sympathetic, loving, and affectionate toward them and to continue making dua for them.
- The directive not to associate partners with God can also be extended to other situations. Any calls to evade the commandments of the Almighty must not receive a positive response, even if the caller is a parent.
- Regardless of the situation, children have been asked to continue to treat them in a befitting manner.
- Regarding this relationship, both parents and children are warned to watch their attitude, as one day we will return to our Lord and be held accountable for our deeds.

Ahadith on the rights of parents

- Prophet said: "Disgrace is for that person. Disgrace is for that person. Disgrace is for that person." People asked: "For whom, O Prophet?" He replied: "A person whose parents or any of them reached old age in his presence, and still he could not enter Paradise. (Sahih Muslim #6510)
- Once, a person asked the Prophet (saws) for permission to participate in jihad (when no active Jihad was happening). At this, the Prophet (sws) inquired: "Are your parents alive?" The person replied in the affirmative. The Prophet (sws) then remarked, "Keep serving them. This is jihad. (Sahih Bukhari #3004)
- Abu Bakr reported that the Prophet said, "There is no wrong action more likely to bring punishment in this world in addition to what is stored up in the next world than oppression and severing ties of kinship." (Adab Al-Mufrad #29)

Directives relating to orphans

وَ اٰتُوا الْيَتٰمٰى اَمْوَالَهُمْ وَ لَا تَتَبَدَّلُوا الْخَبِيثَ بِالطَّيِّبِ ۖ وَ لَا تَأْكُلُوا اَمْوَالَهُمْ اِلٰى اَمْوَالِكُمْ ۚ اِنَّهُ كَانَ حُوبًا كَبِيرًا

وَ اِنْ خِفْتُمْ اَلَّا تُقْسِطُوا فِي الْيَتٰمٰى فَانْكِحُوا مَا طَابَ لَكُمْ مِّنَ النِّسَاءِ مَثْنٰى وَ ثُلٰثَ وَ رُبٰعَ ۚ فَاِنْ خِفْتُمْ اَلَّا تَعْدِلُوا فَوَاحِدَةً اَوْ
مَا مَلَكَتْ اَيْمَانُكُمْ ۚ ذٰلِكَ اَدْنٰى اَلَّا تَعُولُوا ۚ وَ اٰتُوا النِّسَاءَ صَدُقٰتِهِنَّ نِحْلَةً ۚ فَاِنْ طِبْنَ لَكُمْ عَنْ شَيْءٍ مِّنْهُ نَفْسًا فَكُلُوهُ هَنِيئًا مَّرِيئًا

وَ لَا تُؤْتُوا السُّفَهَاءَ اَمْوَالَكُمُ الَّتِي جَعَلَ اللّٰهُ لَكُمْ قِيٰمًا وَّ ارْزُقُوهُمْ فِيهَا وَ اكْسُوهُمْ وَ قُولُوا لَهُمْ قَوْلًا مَّعْرُوفًا

وَ ابْتَلُوا الْيَتٰمٰى حَتّٰى اِذَا بَلَغُوا النِّكَاحَ ۚ فَاِنْ اٰنَسْتُمْ مِّنْهُمْ رُشْدًا فَادْفَعُوا اِلَيْهِمْ اَمْوَالَهُمْ ۚ وَ لَا تَأْكُلُوهَا اِسْرَافًا وَّ
بِدَارًا اَنْ يَّكْبَرُوا ۚ وَ مَنْ كَانَ غَنِيًّا فَلْيَسْتَعْفِفْ ۖ وَ مَنْ كَانَ فَقِيرًا فَلْيَأْكُلْ بِالْمَعْرُوفِ ۚ فَاِذَا دَفَعْتُمْ اِلَيْهِمْ اَمْوَالَهُمْ
فَاَشْهِدُوا عَلَيْهِمْ ۚ وَ كَفٰى بِاللّٰهِ حَسِيبًا

لِلرِّجَالِ نَصِيبٌ مِّمَّا تَرَكَ الْوَالِدٰنِ وَ الْاَقْرَبُونَ ۖ وَ لِلنِّسَاءِ نَصِيبٌ مِّمَّا تَرَكَ الْوَالِدٰنِ وَ الْاَقْرَبُونَ مِمَّا قَلَّ
مِنْهُ اَوْ كَثُرَ ۚ نَصِيبًا مَّفْرُوضًا وَ اِذَا حَضَرَ الْقِسْمَةَ اُولُوا الْقُرْبٰى وَ الْيَتٰمٰى وَ الْمَسٰكِينُ فَارْزُقُوهُمْ مِّنْهُ وَ قُولُوا لَهُمْ قَوْلًا مَّعْرُوفًا

وَ لْيَخْشَ الَّذِينَ لَوْ تَرَكُوا مِنْ خَلْفِهِمْ ذُرِّيَّةً ضِعٰفًا خَافُوا عَلَيْهِمْ ۖ فَلْيَتَّقُوا اللّٰهَ وَ لْيَقُولُوا قَوْلًا سَدِيدًا

اِنَّ الَّذِينَ يَأْكُلُونَ اَمْوَالَ الْيَتٰمٰى ظُلْمًا اِنَّمَا يَأْكُلُونَ فِي بُطُونِهِمْ نَارًا ۖ وَ سَيَصْلَوْنَ سَعِيرًا

And give the orphans the wealth that is theirs. Neither exchange their valuables for your worthless ones nor devour their wealth by mixing it with yours. Indeed, this is a great sin.

And if you fear that you cannot treat orphans equitably, then you may marry [their mothers] who are lawful to you: two, three, or four of them. But if you fear that you cannot maintain equality [among them], marry only one or any slave-girls you may own. This will make it easier for you to avoid injustice. And give these women their dower the way it is given, but if they give you a part of it, you may consume it willingly.

And [if the orphan is naive and immature as yet], do not give to these immatures the wealth with which Allah has entrusted you for their sustenance and support; but feed and clothe them with its proceeds, and say words of kindness to them. And keep judging these orphans until they reach a marriageable age. Then, if you find them capable of sound judgment, hand over their wealth to them, and do not devour it by squandering it and consuming it hastily, fearing that they would soon come of age.

And let the [guardian of the orphan] who is rich abstain [from his wealth] and [the guardian] who is poor eat [from] it [in lieu of his service] according to the norms [of society]. Then, when you hand over their wealth to them, call in some witnesses, and Allah alone suffices to take account of all your actions.

Men shall have a share in what their parents and kinsmen leave, and women shall have a share in what their parents and kinsmen leave, whether this legacy is little or much, as an ascertained amount. However, if relatives, orphans, or the needy come by at the division of an inheritance, give them a share of it and speak to them with kind words. And those people should fear that if they themselves had left their young children after their own death, they would have been very anxious. For this reason, fear Allah and speak for justice [in every matter]. Undoubtedly, those who unjustly devour the wealth of orphans swallow fire into their bellies, and soon they shall burn in the flames of Hell. (4:2-10)

- The Quran has emphasized the welfare of orphans and the kind treatment they deserve at various places.
- Guardians of the orphans and their wealth should return their wealth to them and should not think of devouring it unjustly.
- They should know that unjustly consuming the wealth of orphans is like filling one's belly with fire.
- If it becomes difficult to fulfill these responsibilities alone, and people think that ease and facility can be created by involving the mothers of the orphans, then they can marry the lawful among them (max 4).
- The guardians should not hastily consume the orphans' wealth, for fear of losing access to it when the orphans reach maturity.
- If a guardian is well-off, he should not take anything from the orphans in return for his service; if he is poor, he may take his due in accordance with societal norms.
- When the time comes to hand over an orphan's wealth, some trustworthy and reliable people should be made witnesses to avoid any misconceived notions and dissensions.
- Although the shares of the heirs to a deceased are fixed, if at the time of distribution of inheritance, some close relatives, orphans, or poor people happen to come by, then even though they may not have any legal right in the inheritance, they should be given something and be spoken to in a befitting manner at their departure.

Slavery

Commonly Asked Question

Is there slavery in Islam?

Answer: Wrong Question!

> Slavery existed in the earliest civilizations (such as Sumer in Mesopotamia, dating back to 3500 BC). Slavery is featured in the Mesopotamian Code of Hammurabi (c. 1860 BCE), which refers to it as an established institution. (Wikipedia)

- The source of slavery was warfare in which the prisoners of war were turned into slaves and sold in the marketplaces, which then contributed to the economic engine of the society.
- At the time of the revelation of the Quran, the institution of slavery was as essential to the economic and social needs of society as interest is in present-day societies.
- In markets, slave men and slave women were bought and sold, and affluent houses had slave men and slave women of all ages.
- In such circumstances, a sudden directive for their emancipation would have resulted in many evils: for livelihood, men would have been forced to resort to beggary and women to prostitution.
- The Quran adopted a gradual way to eradicate this evil from society, and after many gradual measures of eradication, a final provision was given for slaves to sign a contract of freedom with their masters.

History of slavery in the US

- The United States represents a unique, particularly harsh chapter in this history, often termed "chattel slavery," where humans were treated strictly as property.
- Unlike many historical forms of slavery, American slavery became exclusively racialized, targeting people of African descent. It was "chattel" slavery, meaning enslaved people were legally considered property, not humans, and this status was hereditary—children born to enslaved mothers were automatically enslaved for life.
- Slavery was deeply ingrained in the American economy, particularly in the South, where enslaved labor was used to produce massive quantities of cash crops like cotton, tobacco, and rice, which fueled the nation's economic growth.
- Millions of Africans were forcibly transported across the Atlantic Ocean in brutal conditions, a traumatic journey known as the Middle Passage, which resulted in high mortality rates.

Islam's unique approach

- As a religion, Islam is the only religion that has actually taken concrete steps in eradicating slavery over a period of time.
- However, it is unfortunate that later Muslim leaders and rulers did not follow the instructions of the Quran and were influenced by the prevalent behavior towards it around them.

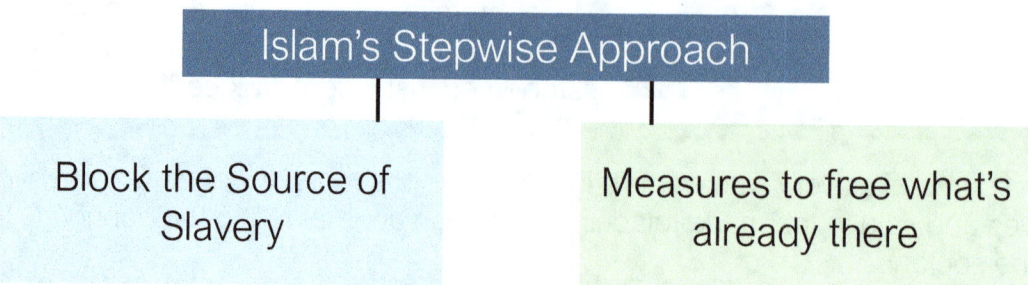

Block the source

- First, Islam blocked the source of slavery, which is through capturing men and women as prisoners of war and then selling them as slaves.
- God declared in Surah Muhammad that from now on, Muslims have only two options for the prisoners of war:
  - Set them free as a favor
  - In exchange for a ransom
- This means Muslims cannot make prisoners of war slaves anymore.
- That was a huge shift from the prevailing practices of Arabs at that time.

فَإِذَا لَقِيتُمُ الَّذِينَ كَفَرُوا فَضَرْبَ الرِّقَابِ ۖ حَتَّىٰ إِذَآ أَثْخَنْتُمُوهُمْ فَشُدُّوا الْوَثَاقَ ۚ فَإِمَّا مَنًّا بَعْدُ وَ إِمَّا فِدَآءً حَتَّىٰ تَضَعَ الْحَرْبُ أَوْزَارَهَا

So, when you encounter the disbelievers in a battle, smite at their necks until you overpower them, then take them as captives when they are defeated. <u>Then you may set them free as a favor to them, or in exchange for a ransom,</u> when the battle lays its arms (Surah Muhammad: 4)

Method Islam adopted to eradicate slavery

1. At the beginning of its revelation, the Quran regarded the emancipation of slaves as one of the greatest virtues and urged people to do as much as they could afford.
2. The term "release the neck" is used explicitly in the Quran in many places for the virtue of emancipation of the slaves.
3. People were urged that if they were not in a position to free their slaves, then they should treat them with kindness, and no one should in any way violate the rights they possess as human beings.
4. In cases of unintentional murder, Zihar, and other similar offenses against people and God, liberating a slave was set as their atonement and Sadaqah.
5. It was directed to marry off slave men and slave women who were capable of marriage so that they could become equivalent in status, both morally and socially, to other members of the society. (Quran 24: 32-33)

فَلَا اقْتَحَمَ الْعَقَبَةَ وَ مَآ اَدْرٰىکَ مَا الْعَقَبَةُ فَكُّ رَقَبَةٍ

But he did not climb the uphill path. And how would you know what this uphill path is? Releasing the necks (90:11-13)

"Whoever liberated a Muslim slave, the Almighty, in return for every limb of that slave, would shield every limb of that person from Hell". (Sahih Al-Bukhari #2517)

6. People who did not have the means to marry free women were encouraged to marry Muslim slave women with the permission of their masters, who were kept chaste.
7. Under the heads of Zakah distribution, a specific head was kept for freeing slaves paid by the state.
8. People were reminded that they are all slaves of God, so instead, they should call their slave boy/man or girl/woman so that the psyche of the society evolves from the mentality of ownership.
9. Prisoners of war were the primary source of slavery. God prohibited Muslims from taking any more prisoners in the verses of Surah Muhammad. Muslims were asked to either accept a ransom for the prisoners or free them as a favor.
10. According to the Quran, a slave can make a contract with his/her master under which he/she would be required to pay a certain sum of money within a specific time period or to perform a specific service for the master; after that, he/she would be liberated.

11. In this new method, all slaves who could become financially independent were encouraged, and masters were asked to enter into such contracts with them. It is further stated that a Muslim government should spend money from the public treasury to help such slaves.

12. This verse was the final directive regarding the gradual eradication of slavery.

وَمَنْ لَّمْ يَسْتَطِعْ مِنْكُمْ طَوْلًا اَنْ يَّنْكِحَ الْمُحْصَنٰتِ الْمُؤْمِنٰتِ فَمِنْ مَّا مَلَكَتْ اَيْمَانُكُمْ مِّنْ فَتَيٰتِكُمُ الْمُؤْمِنٰتِ ۚ وَ اللهُ اَعْلَمُ بِاِيْمَانِكُمْ ۚ بَعْضُكُمْ مِّنْ بَعْضٍ ۚ فَانْكِحُوْهُنَّ بِاِذْنِ اَهْلِهِنَّ وَ اٰتُوْهُنَّ اُجُوْرَهُنَّ بِالْمَعْرُوْفِ مُحْصَنٰتٍ غَيْرَ مُسٰفِحٰتٍ وَّ لَا مُتَّخِذٰتِ اَخْدَانٍ ۚ فَاِذَآ اُحْصِنَّ فَاِنْ اَتَيْنَ بِفَاحِشَةٍ فَعَلَيْهِنَّ نِصْفُ مَا عَلَى الْمُحْصَنٰتِ مِنَ الْعَذَابِ ۚ ذٰلِكَ لِمَنْ خَشِيَ الْعَنَتَ مِنْكُمْ ۚ وَ اَنْ تَصْبِرُوْا خَيْرٌ لَّكُمْ ۚ وَ اللهُ غَفُوْرٌ رَّحِيْمٌ

And if any of you do not have the means to wed free believing women, he may wed believing girls from among those whom you own, and Allah has full knowledge about your faith. You are all one in humanity: so, wed them with the permission of their owners, and give them their dowers, according to the norms, with the condition that they should be kept chaste, neither being lustful nor taking paramours; and when they are taken in marriage, then if they are guilty of open indecency, they shall be punished with half the punishment which is (inflicted) upon free women. This permission is for those who fear sin, but it is better for you to practice self-restraint. And Allah is Ever-Forgiving, Most Merciful. (4:25)

وَ الَّذِيْنَ يَبْتَغُوْنَ الْكِتٰبَ مِمَّا مَلَكَتْ اَيْمَانُكُمْ فَكَاتِبُوْهُمْ اِنْ عَلِمْتُمْ فِيْهِمْ خَيْرًا ۖ وَّ اٰتُوْهُمْ مِّنْ مَّالِ اللهِ الَّذِيْۤ اٰتٰىكُمْ

And if any of your slaves ask for *Mukatabat*, give it to them if you know any good in them and [for this] give them out of the wealth Allah has given you. (24:33)

Treatment of slaves

Abu Hurairah narrated from the Prophet: "A slave has a right to food and clothing, and he shall not be asked to carry out an errand that is beyond him or her." (Sahih Muslim #4316)

Abu Dharr al-Ghifari narrated from the Prophet: "They are your brothers. The Almighty has made them subservient to you. So, whatever you eat, feed them with it, whatever you wear, clothe them with it, and never ask them to do something which is beyond them, and if there is such a task, then help them out with it (Sahih Al-Bukhari #6050)

Ibn Umar narrated from the Prophet: "Whoever slapped a slave or beat him up should atone this sin by liberating him." (Sahih Muslim 4298)

Quick Recap

- Islam (including Judaism and Christianity) instructs man to show kindness to parents.
- Kindness towards parents should emerge from the sense of gratitude towards them, which must not be expressed merely by the tongue.
- Any calls to evade the commandments of the Almighty must not receive a positive response, even if the caller is a parent.
- Guardians of the orphans are warned that unjustly consuming the wealth of orphans is like filling one's belly with fire.
- Islam did not start slavery, nor did it condone it. It did not abolish it immediately in the Arab society, as slaves were the primary vehicle for economic activity in that society.
- The Quran adopted a gradual way to eradicate this evil from society, and after many gradual measures of eradication, a final provision was given for slaves to sign a contract of freedom with their masters.

1. Why did Islam allow the owning of slaves and having sexual relations with slave girls?
2. Why did the Quran's scheme to end slavery not work, and why did slavery not end?

Chapter 13

Political Shariah

Guidance of politics and government

This chapter discusses an important topic: the kind of guidance God has provided regarding politics and the formation and running of a government.

Political Shariah (state and government)

Why do we need a state?

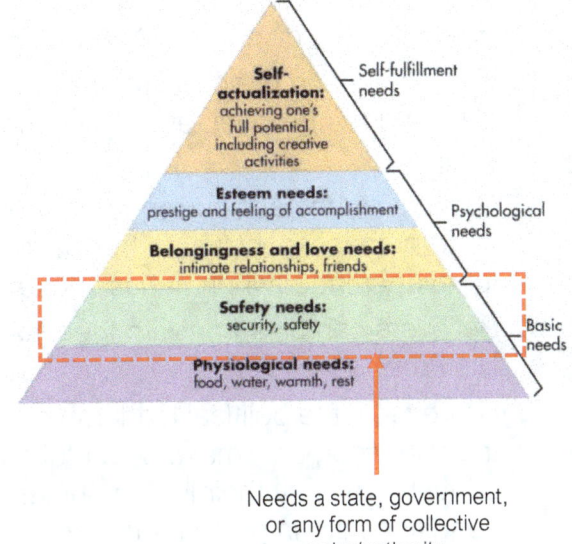

Maslow's Hierarchy of Human Needs

Needs a state, government, or any form of collective order/authority.

- A collective social setup, in the form of a state or collective order, is an essential requirement of the nature in which God created human beings.
- We are given free will by God, and in any social setup, some members are prone to misuse it.
- To protect other members from this misuse, a political authority with the collective power to restrain its impact on society is required.
- The sole purpose of this collective order is to cleanse the system from evils, protect its members, and develop it in the right direction that benefits all its members.
- Human intellect swings between extremes and cannot decisively resolve certain basic issues in this regard without divine guidance; this is where political shariah helps.

The Basic Principle

يَٰٓأَيُّهَا الَّذِينَ ءَامَنُوٓا أَطِيعُوا اللهَ وَ أَطِيعُوا الرَّسُولَ وَ أُولِى الْأَمْرِ مِنْكُمْ ۖ فَإِنْ تَنَازَعْتُمْ فِى شَىْءٍ فَرُدُّوهُ إِلَى اللهِ وَ الرَّسُولِ إِنْ كُنْتُمْ تُؤْمِنُونَ بِاللهِ وَ الْيَوْمِ الْأَخِرِ ۚ ذَٰلِكَ خَيْرٌ وَّ أَحْسَنُ تَأْوِيلًا

Believers! Obey God and obey the Prophet and those of you who are in authority, and if you disagree among yourselves in any matter, refer it to God and the Prophet if you believe in Allah and the Last Day. This is better and more proper with regard to the consequences. (4:59)

1. The above directive was given when the Prophet was present among the people, and it was quite practical to do so.

2. Today, for matters in which an eternal directive is given, the people in authority must present every dispute to God and His Prophet (i.e., the Quran and Sunnah).

3. The orders and directives of these rulers can be carried out only after obedience to God and His Prophet, and only if they do not overrule or exceed the limits set by Shariah.

4. Muslims (who have surrendered their will to God) cannot enact any law in their country that is contrary to the Quran and Sunnah or without considering the Shariah for every matter where it has spoken.

5. Believers can disagree with their leaders, but they cannot disagree with God and His Prophet.

6. However, if the political leadership does not adhere to the Shariah given by God, then they can only make peaceful efforts to change the situation. They must continue to obey their leaders unless they show clear signs of disbelief and the right conditions are in place for change.

7. Islam does not like political anarchy. In times of political anarchy and chaos, the Prophet has directed Muslims not only to refrain from participating in any activity against the state but also to obey state authority with complete faithfulness and sincerity.

Hold firm to the state authority

- From the following narrations, it is clear that the Prophet is adamant that people obey their state authorities as much as possible.

مَنْ رَأَى مِنْ أَمِيرِه شَيْئًا يَكْرَهُهُ فَلْيَصْبِرْ عَلَيْه فَإِنَّهُ مَنْ فَارَقَ الْجَمَاعَةَ شِبْرًا فَمَاتَ إِلَّا مَاتَ مِيتَةً جَاهِلِيَّةً

He who sees something despicable in his ruler should bear it, for he who even slightly disassociates himself from the state authority and dies in this condition shall die the death of Jahiliyyah (Sahih Al-Bukhari #7054)

تَلْزُمُ جَمَاعَةَ الْمُسْلِمِينَ وَ اِمَامَهُمْ

Prophet advised Hudhaifa once: [in such a state of chaos], you should remain attached to the state authority and the ruler of the Muslims. (Sahih Al-Bukhari #3606)

اسْمَعُوا وَأَطِيعُوا وَإِنْ اسْتُعْمِلَ عَلَيْكُمْ عَبْدٌ حَبَشِيٌّ كَأَنَّ رَأْسَهُ زَبِيبَةٌ

Listen and obey even if an Abyssinian slave, whose head is like a raisin, is made your ruler (Sahih Al-Bukhari #7412)

عَلَى الْمَرْءِ الْمُسْلِمِ السَّمْعُ وَالطَّاعَةُ فِيمَا أَحَبَّ وَكَرِهَ إِلَّا أَنْ يُؤْمَرَ بِمَعْصِيَةٍ فَإِنْ أُمِرَ بِمَعْصِيَةٍ فَلَا سَمْعَ وَلَا طَاعَةَ

Whether they like it or not, it is mandatory for a Muslim to listen and obey his rulers except when he is ordered **to commit a sin**. If he is ordered to do so, he should neither listen nor obey (Sahih Muslim #4763)

دَعَانَا النَّبِيُّ صَلَّى الله عَلَيْهِ و سَلَّمَ فَبَايَعْنَاهُ فَقَالَ فِيمَا أَخَذَ عَلَيْنَا أَنْ بَايَعَنَا عَلَى السَّمْعِ وَالطَّاعَةِ فِي مَنْشَطِنَا وَمَكْرَهِنَا وَعُسْرِنَا وَيُسْرِنَا وَأَثَرَةٍ عَلَيْنَا وَأَنْ لَا نُنَازِعَ الْأَمْرَ أَهْلَهُ إِلَّا أَنْ تَرَوْا كُفْرًا بَوَاحًا عِنْدَكُمْ مِنْ اللَّهِ فِيهِ بُرْهَانٌ

The Prophet called us to pledge allegiance to him, which we did. [A narrator said:] among the things on which we had been asked to pledge were the following: "We shall listen and obey whether willingly or unwillingly, whether we are in difficulty or at ease, and even when we do not receive what our right is, and that we shall not contest the authority of our rulers. You can only contest their authority if you witness **outright disbelief** in any matter from them, in which you have clear evidence from God." (Sahih Al-Bukhari #7056)

شَرَارُ أَئِمَّتِكُمُ الَّذِينَ تُبْغِضُونَهُمْ وَيُبْغِضُونَكُمْ وَتَلْعَنُونَهُمْ وَيَلْعَنُونَكُمْ قِيلَ يَا رَسُولَ اللَّهِ أَفَلَا نُنَابِذُهُمْ بِالسَّيْفِ فَقَالَ لَا مَا أَقَامُوا فِيكُمْ الصَّلَاةَ

The worst of your rulers are those whom you hate and who hate you; you curse them, and they curse you. It was asked: "O Prophet of Allah! Should we not put them to the sword?" The Prophet (sws) replied: "No, as long as they are diligent in the prayer among you." (Sahih Muslim #4804)

مَنْ أَتَاكُمْ وَأَمْرُكُمْ جَمِيعٌ عَلَى رَجُلٍ وَاحِدٍ يُرِيدُ أَنْ يَشُقَّ عَصَاكُمْ أَوْ يُفَرِّقَ جَمَاعَتَكُمْ فَاقْتُلُوهُ

When you are organized under the rule of a person, and someone tries to break your collectivity apart or disrupt your government, kill him. (Sahih Muslim #4798)

Contrary to general perception and practice in many Muslim countries, the Prophet has directed Muslims not only to refrain from participating in any activity against the state but also to obey the state authority with complete faithfulness and sincerity. In other words, Muslims should be law-abiding citizens of their country.

Rights and Responsibilities

The Real Responsibility of a Muslim State

إِنَّ اللهَ يَأْمُرُكُمْ أَنْ تُؤَدُّوا الْأَمَانَاتِ إِلَى أَهْلِهَا ۞ وَ إِذَا حَكَمْتُمْ بَيْنَ النَّاسِ أَنْ تَحْكُمُوا بِالْعَدْلِ ۚ إِنَّ اللهَ نِعِمَّا يَعِظُكُمْ بِهِ ۗ إِنَّ اللهَ كَانَ سَمِيعًا بَصِيرًا

God commands you to hand over the trusts to their rightful owners, and when you judge between men, pass this judgment with fairness. Indeed, this is an excellent admonition from God. Indeed, God is He who hears and sees all things. (4:58)

- The real responsibility of a state based on this principle of obedience to God and His Prophet is to entrust the trust of the nation based on merit to people and to strive to establish justice and fairness in its ultimate form in every walk of life.
- All positions of authority given to the people must be given on merit, with no favoritism and nepotism in play.
- Justice means that there should be no discrimination in the eyes of the law between various classes of society, such as the rich and the poor or the upper and the lower classes.
- The Prophet, on this very basis, insisted that a person who greedily desires public office should never be considered for it since justice cannot be expected from such a person.
- The Prophet also urged his companions to fear God in such matters and never to seek public office unless they had been given that responsibility.
- To establish justice, those in authority must keep their doors open to public criticism, petitions, and appeals, and view these as a service to the people rather than a privilege.

Prophet's guidance

إِنَّا وَاللهِ لَا نُوَلِّي عَلَى هَذَا الْعَمَلِ أَحَدًا سَأَلَهُ وَلَا أَحَدًا حَرَصَ عَلَيْهِ

By God! We shall not grant any person a position in this system if they ask for it and covet it. (Sahih Muslim #4707)

لَا تَسْأَلِ الْإِمَارَةَ فَإِنَّكَ إِنْ أُوتِيتَهَا عَنْ مَسْأَلَةٍ وُكِلْتَ إِلَيْهَا وَإِنْ أُوتِيتَهَا مِنْ غَيْرِ مَسْأَلَةٍ أُعِنْتَ عَلَيْهَا

Do not seek a post. If it is granted to you because of your desire, you shall [find yourself] being handed over to it (it will consume you), and if it is granted to you without your desire, you shall be helped. (Sahih Al-Bukhari #6622)

Religious Obligations of a Muslim State

اَلَّذِينَ اِنْ مَّكَّنَّٰهُمْ فِى الْأَرْضِ اَقَامُوا الصَّلٰوةَ وَ اٰتَوُا الزَّكٰوةَ وَ اَمَرُوْا بِالْمَعْرُوْفِ وَ نَهَوْا عَنِ الْمُنْكَرِ ۗ وَ لِلّٰهِ عَاقِبَةُ الْأُمُوْرِ

These believers are those who, if We grant them authority in this land, will be diligent in prayer and pay zakah and enjoin what is good and forbid what is evil. (22:41)

- The verse above outlines the religious obligations imposed on the Muslim community once it gains political authority in the country.
- They will facilitate the establishment of Salah in society – by building mosques, making laws that facilitate daily prayers, arranging and attending Friday prayers, and assigning speakers for the Khutbah, etc.
- Collecting Zakah from the people and distributing and disbursing it as stipulated in Shariah.
- Forming an institution as part of the state that should be entrusted with the responsibility of calling people towards good and forbidding them from evil.
- Exhorting people through advice and counsel, in some cases, through the Friday Khutbah.
- In others, implementing the punishments prescribed by the Shariah for various crimes.
- These are just religious obligations. Every state has the responsibility to strive for the welfare and prosperity of its people, to maintain peace, and to defend its borders.

Citizenship and Rights of a Citizen

فَاِنْ تَابُوا وَ اَقَامُوا الصَّلٰوةَ وَ اٰتَوُا الزَّكٰوةَ فَاِخْوَانُكُمْ فِى الدِّيْنِ

فَاِنْ تَابُوا وَ اَقَامُوا الصَّلٰوةَ وَ اٰتَوُا الزَّكٰوةَ فَخَلُّوْا سَبِيلَهُمْ

So, if they repent, are diligent in their prayers, and pay zakah, they are your brethren in religion. (9:11)

So, if they repent, are diligent in their prayers, and pay zakah, then leave them alone. (9:5)

- These two verses were revealed in the context of the final punishment prescribed by God for the addressees of Prophet Muhammad in the hands of the believers. They were given a chance to live if they met three conditions:
  - Repent and believe
  - Offer prayers
  - Pay Zakah

- From these verses, it is evident that if the Muslim citizens of a state meet these conditions, then the following can be concluded about their rights as citizens:
  - They shall be considered as Muslims in the eyes of the law and the state and entitled to all the rights.
  - The mutual relationship between the rulers and the ruled shall be that of brotherhood, and they possess the same legal rights without any discrimination.
  - Due to this brotherly relationship, all responsibilities that reason and intellect endorse shall be imposed on both.
  - The collective system can legally ask its Muslim citizens to fulfill only these three positive requirements and nothing else. All other laws and regulations are for the purpose of protecting people from each other's misuse of free will. E.g., the rulers cannot ask people to fast or go for Hajj.

- In summary, as far as legislation against crimes is concerned, the state has all the authority to do so, but regarding positive requirements of the Shariah, except for the prayer and zakah, it can only urge and exhort, educate, and indoctrinate Muslims to fulfill them. Its jurisdiction ends here in this regard.
- For non-Muslims in a Muslim state, if the circumstances under which the state was created and what various international accords allow, then any agreement can be made with them regarding their rights in the state as citizens of the state.
- Prophet Muhammad (before the punishment for all the disbelievers was announced) made a pact with the Jews of Medinah when he migrated to Medinah and took charge as the leader.
- Once the final punishment was announced against the Jews of Medinah, the pact was called annulled.

إِنَّ وَدِمَاءَكُمْ وَأَمْوَالَكُمْ وَأَعْرَاضَكُمْ بَيْنَكُمْ حَرَامٌ كَحُرْمَةِ يَوْمِكُمْ هَذَا فِي شَهْرِكُمْ هَذَا فِي بَلَدِكُمْ هَذَا

Indeed, your lives, your wealth, and your honor are as sacred and inviolable as this day of [sacrifice of] yours in this city of [Makkah of] yours in this month of [Dhu al-Hajj of] yours. (Al-Bukhari #67)

- When Abu Bakr fought with the rejectors of Zakah, he famously said:

قال الله تعالى: فإن تابوا وأقاموا الصلوة وأتوا الزكوة فخلوا سبيلهم ـ والله لا اسئل فوقهن ولا
اقصر دونــــهن

The Almighty has said: "So, if they repent, are diligent in prayer and pay zakah, spare their lives." By God, I shall neither ask for more nor accept any less. (Ahkam al-Quran)

The System of Governance

وَ أَمْرُهُمْ شُورَىٰ بَيْنَهُمْ.

And their system is based on their (mutual) consultation. (42:38)

- Verse 38 of Surah Shoora provides the cornerstone for all collective affairs Muslims undertake. It is not limited to political affairs. If three people start a new company, God wants them to run its affairs through mutual consultation.
- In the verse, the word "Amr" means their 'system of affairs', which can easily be construed as their political system.
- The way the word شُورَىٰ is used in the verse demands two things:
    - It should not imply that the leader has been appointed by 'someone' and then asked to consult others.
    - It must imply that all decisions are reached with mutual consultation; even the head of a state be appointed through consultation; the system itself be based on consultation; everyone should have an equal right in consultation; whatever is done through consultation should only be undone through consultation; every one that is part of the system should have a say in its affairs, and in the absence of a consensus, the majority opinion should decide the matter.
- As it relates to their system of affairs, all affairs of state like the municipal affairs, national and provincial affairs, political and social directives, rules of legislation, delegation and revocation of powers, dismissal, and appointment of officials, interpretation of Islam for the collective affairs of life – all of them fall under the principle laid down in this verse (which is through mutual consultation).

Guidance from the Prophet

إِنَّ هَذَا الْأَمْرَ فِي قُرَيْشٍ لَا يُعَادِيهِمْ أَحَدٌ إِلَّا كَبَّهُ اللَّهُ فِي النَّارِ عَلَى وَجْهِهِ مَا أَقَامُوا الدِّينَ.

Our political authority shall remain with the Quraysh. In this matter, whoever opposes them as long as they follow Islam, Allah shall cast him face down in Hell. (Sahih al-Bukhari #7139)

النَّاسُ تَبَعٌ لِقُرَيْشٍ فِي هَذَا الشَّأْنِ مُسْلِمُهُمْ تَبَعٌ لِمُسْلِمِهِمْ وَكَافِرُهُمْ تَبَعٌ لِكَافِرِهِمْ

People in this matter follow the Quraysh. The believers of Arabia are the followers of their believers, and the disbelievers of Arabia are the followers of their disbelievers. (Sahih al-Bukhari #3495)

- This instruction was given by the Prophet before his death for the selection of the next Khalifah or ruler.
- He did not mention any names but pointed out that, since there will be two major contenders for the next rulership, i.e., Ansar and Mohajireen, Muslims must choose (through consultation) someone from the Mohajireen, especially from Quraysh, and he gave the reason for that.
- Prophet Muhammad made it very clear that since the majority of the Arab Muslims professed confidence in Quraysh, they were solely entitled to take charge as the rulers of Arabia in the light of the Quranic directive (their system is based on their consultation), and that they would be passed on the political authority not because of any racial precedence or superiority, but only by virtue of this position (confidence of majority).
- Looking at all the elections of later Khalifah until Ali, Muslims selected their next ruler through mutual consultation, which was possible in a tribal society.

1. There was no election process at the time of the Prophet, so how can it be called a political system based on mutual consultation?
2. The history of Islam is full of Kingdoms and Kings, so how does it reconcile with the instructions of God in the Quran?

Addressing Common Misconceptions on Islam and Politics

Misconception #1

Only 'Political Islam' can bring our glory back

- Islam is not a nation but a message; its adherents are called Muslims. The real glory of Islam is in its message (which is still vibrant), not in identifying us as a select group of people.
- From the history of nations and the unalterable law mentioned in the Quran, it is evident that a nation will appear on the face of the earth, establish its rule, witness its glory and peak, and then slowly fade from the face of the earth and disappear before a new nation rises. This is an ongoing phenomenon.
- A nation's glory or downfall depends on its strict adherence to universal moral values and authority in the most up-to-date disciplines of various sciences.
- Muslims cannot gain political authority on the world stage until they are in a position to exert their social and academic dominance. If we look around us, the nations leading on the world stage politically today are ahead in these two areas that Muslims have forsaken.

Actual Reasons for the Lost Glory and Recipe to Get it Back

- Muslims, as a nation, are facing a deteriorating state of universal moral values and backwardness in the required disciplines of various sciences (that are required to lead the world).
- Muslims were entrusted with the final Book of God, which was supposed to be used as a yardstick for settling religious differences, but for many centuries, the Quran has not been the religious authority for Muslims anymore, causing a bitter divide among Muslims.
- Most of the energy of Muslims is spent settling religious differences and fighting with each other on petty issues like whose prayer is right and what is considered Muslim dress.

Misconception #2

The only Political System that Muslims of the World should implement is the Caliphate (Khilafah)

- Caliphate, or Khilafah, is not an Islamic term, and Islam does not promote Caliphate as the only form of political system.
- 'Khalifah' is an Arabic term that is used to describe:
    - A successor
    - A deputy
    - A person of authority
- In the early Islamic era, the term was adopted for the successor of Prophet Muhammad as a political authority.
- Abu Bakr was called "Khalifat ur Rasool" (the successor of the prophet), and Umar was then called "*Khalifatu Khalifat er Rasool*" (the successor of the successor of the prophet). Later, it remained as "Khalifah" or "Ameer ul Momineen" (the leader of the believers).
- Whatever primitive political system was adopted in Muslim lands, the central figure, or ruler, was called the Khalifah, and the system as a whole the Khilafah.
- When God addressed Prophet Dawood about his authority over the children of Israel, he said, "O Dawood, We made you the Khalifah on earth …" (38:26)
- Islam DOES NOT endorse any political system, but it does provide the principles that should govern the political system in a Muslim land.
- The current form of democracy that is adopted in many Western countries is perfectly acceptable to Islam because it is based on mutual consultation through the electoral process and voting.

Misconception #3

Islam is against the democratic system of Government

وَ أَمْرُهُمْ شُوْرَى بَيْنَهُمْ

And their system is based on their consultation. (42:38)

- Contrary to popular belief, the Quran made "mutual consultation" the primary system of government for a state.
- In verse, the word "Amr" means their 'system of affairs', which can easily be construed as their political system.
- As it relates to their system of affairs, all affairs of state like the municipal affairs, national and provincial affairs, political and social directives, rules of legislation, delegation and revocation of powers, dismissal and appointment of officials, interpretation of Islam for the collective affairs of life – all of them fall under the principle laid down in this verse (which is through mutual consultation).
- In every mutual consultation, differences of opinion are natural, and democracy is a system that allows people to resolve disputes raised during such consultations.
- The "mutual consultation" system will be implemented at specific times and places. It will be implemented in a tribal society, very different from the modern society we live in today. The principle of mutual consultation will still be applicable.
- Looking back at the election of the Caliphs Abu Bakr, Omar Farooq, Uthman, and Ali, they were all elected through mutual consultation among the tribal elders of the time, whom people had entrusted with such responsibilities.
- This instruction of mutual consultation covers every aspect of our lives. For example, husbands are made in charge of the household, and they are supposed to consult with their families when making a decision.

Misconception #4

Muslims in non-Muslim countries should struggle for political unity

- Nowhere has Islam directed Muslims living in a non-Muslim country to unite under one leadership; it is not an obligation.

- Muslims may want to do it to serve their interests and socio-political needs within the bounds of the political and legal system imposed in the country where they live.

- This is similar to other religious and ethnic groups that coordinate their affairs to be more influential and effective in society. For example, creating organizations that educate citizens on their political rights, etc.

- Some people try to present this verse (below) to argue that the Quran actually directed Muslims to do so regardless of time and place because God called them "one nation".

- The verse's context suggests something different. In the verses before this one, God enlisted most of the Prophets mentioned in the Quran and then said that all these prophets are one Ummah in the sense that they all brought the same religion from God, and it is the followers of these prophets who introduce innovations, so hold fast to this religion and do not create divisions.

اِنَّ هٰذِهٖٓ اُمَّتُكُمْ اُمَّةً وَّاحِدَةً ۖ وَّ اَنَا رَبُّكُمْ فَاعْبُدُوْنِ

Indeed, this ummah of yours is a single ummah, and I am your Lord and Cherisher. (21:92)

- The demand from God to implement Shariah at the state level is only applicable to Muslims and their authorities when they are in power in a piece of land. But that does not mean they must first struggle to gain that power in order to implement Shariah.

- This is similar to other Shariah directives. For example, Zakah is an obligation for Muslims who have sufficient wealth to give in charity. That does not mean that a Muslim must now work hard to earn enough wealth to give Zakah.

Misconception #5

Muslims are duty-bound to establish an Islamic State (global or within a country)

- Many scholars are of the opinion that if a state with a Muslim majority is not run according to Islamic principles, then every Muslim in that state must strive to establish a state that is run according to the laws of Islam (Islamic Shariah).
- The argument presented is that since Prophet Muhammad did so in the lands of Arabia (by dominating other religions), we are bound to follow his example.
- Looking at the Prophet's life, it is quite evident that the Prophet neither undertook the task of establishing an Islamic state nor was ever directed by God to do so (the Quran is empty of such an instruction).
- It was part of God's plan, and He bestowed Prophet Muhammad and his tribe the supremacy of the lands of Arabia – in other words, it was 'given' by God as part of the Sunnah of God and was not strived for.
- Prophet Muhammad's and his followers' dominance over other religions in the lands of Arabia is part of an established Sunnah of God described in the Quran in many places (for example, 58:20-21).
- The special law of God is called the Law of Conclusive Arguments (*Qanoon e Itmam al Hujjah*), which states that when a Messenger is sent among a nation, he delivers the message with all the proofs necessary to accept the message. When people reject it, they are punished in this life at the hands of people who believed in the Messenger. The believers are handed over the authority of the land. That's exactly what happened in the case of Prophet Muhammad.

هُوَ الَّذِیْ اَرْسَلَ رَسُوْلَهٗ بِالْهُدٰی وَ دِیْنِ الْحَقِّ لِیُظْهِرَهٗ عَلَی الدِّیْنِ کُلِّهٖ وَ لَوْ کَرِهَ الْمُشْرِکُوْنَ

It is He Who has sent His Messenger with Guidance and the Religion of Truth that he may dominate it over all religions, even though the Idolaters may detest it. (61:9)

اِنَّ الَّذِیْنَ یُحَآدُّوْنَ اللهَ وَ رَسُوْلَهٗ اُولٰٓئِکَ فِی الْاَذَلِّیْنَ

کَتَبَ اللهُ لَاَغْلِبَنَّ اَنَا وَ رُسُلِیْ ۭ اِنَّ اللهَ قَوِیٌّ عَزِیْزٌ

Indeed, those who oppose Allah and His Messenger are bound to be humiliated. The Almighty has ordained: "My messengers and I shall always prevail." Indeed, Allah is Mighty and Powerful. (58:20-21)

1. There are many Ahadith that talk about the revival of Khilafah before the end of the world. How should I understand those Ahadith?

2. Why did ISIS claim to be that foretold Khilafah, and why did so many people respond to their call?

Chapter 14

Political Shariah

Shariah of Jihad

This chapter discusses the most controversial topic in Islam: Jihad.
This has been misused by both non-Muslims and Muslims.

Why is Jihad or fighting allowed?

What is Jihad?

- In Arabic, the word Jihad translates to "struggle" or "striving". This struggle can be in any field. Someone struggling to earn money for his family also does Jihad.
- When the context exists, then it is also used for the war prescribed by God and it is also called Qital.

Why is War allowed in Islam?

- Peace and freedom are two essential requirements of a society.
- The way we deal with criminals in a society, we are asked to deal with rogue nations when they commit excesses against people.

- However, as long as diplomacy and negotiations can resolve matters, no one would endorse the use of force to settle affairs.
- War should be used only as a last resort when everything else fails.
- The Quran asserts that if the use of force had not been allowed in such extreme cases, the disruption and disorder caused by rogue nations would have reached the extent that the places of worship would have become deserted and forsaken, let alone society itself.

And had it not been that Allah dislodge one people through another, the monasteries and churches, the synagogues and the mosques, in which His praise is abundantly celebrated, would be utterly destroyed. (22:40)

- Jihad, or Qital, in Islam is permitted for two main reasons, as shown below. What remains until the day of judgment in Islam is now only against injustice and oppression.

1. Against Injustice and Oppression – Use force against people who are using violence to curb the basic rights of human beings. This is an eternal directive in Shariah valid for all times and places.
2. Against the Rejecters of the Truth - This category falls outside of Shariah and pertains to the divine law of *Itmam al-Hujjah*, in which God punished nations for rejecting the truth through the hands of Messengers and their companions.

- The Quran specifically talks about the second type of Jihad in the Quran and why Allah punishes the disbelievers at the hands of believers:

وَ لِكُلِّ أُمَّةٍ رَسُوْلٌ ۚ فَاِذَا جَاءَ رَسُوْلُهُمْ قُضِىَ بَيْنَهُمْ بِالْقِسْطِ وَ هُمْ لَا يُظْلَمُوْنَ

And for each community, there is a Messenger. Then, when their Messenger comes, their fate is decided with justice, and they are not wronged. (10:47)

قَاتِلُوْهُمْ يُعَذِّبْهُمُ اللّٰهُ بِاَيْدِيْكُمْ

Fight with them, God will punish them by your hands. (9:14)

The Permission of Jihad

- Allah did not allow Muslims to fight immediately after Prophet Muhammad announced his prophethood. For the first 13 years in Makkah, Muslims were asked to be patient.

اُذِنَ لِلَّذِيْنَ يُقْتَلُوْنَ بِاَنَّهُمْ ظُلِمُوْا ۚ وَ اِنَّ اللّٰهَ عَلٰى نَصْرِهِمْ لَقَدِيْرٌ
الَّذِيْنَ اُخْرِجُوْا مِنْ دِيَارِهِمْ بِغَيْرِ حَقٍّ اِلَّا اَنْ يَّقُوْلُوْا رَبُّنَا اللّٰهُ

Permission to take up arms is hereby granted to those who are attacked because they have been oppressed, and God indeed has power to help them – those who have been unjustly driven from their homes, only because they said: "Our Lord is Allah." (22:39-40)

- This is the first verse in the Quran that allowed Prophet Muhammad and his companions who migrated from Makkah to Medinah to respond with force.
- "Unjustly driven from their homes only because they said our Lord is Allah" is the charge sheet against the idolaters.
- This right to use force has been given to the Muslims in their collective capacity, not in their individual capacity, similar to the verses that talk about criminal punishments.
- The word "permission" shows that the Almighty allowed the Muslims of those times to fight back against the Quraysh only when Muslims had political authority organized in the form of a state, despite the tremendous oppression let loose upon them.
- This was only possible after Prophet Muhammad and his companions migrated to Medinah, and after Prophet Muhammad was chosen as the leader of the people living there. Muslims were asked to restrain themselves in Makkah due to the lack of political authority.

A Muslim ruler is a shield [of his people]. An armed struggle can only be carried out under him, and people should seek his shelter for themselves [in war]. (Sahih Al-Bukhari #2957)

The Directive of Jihad

- Once permission was granted, a detailed directive on Jihad was revealed in Surah Baqarah, verses 190-194.
- The context of the verses is specific to an incident when Muslims wanted to perform Hajj, and they were expecting resistance from Quraish, but a little deliberation on the verses suggests that the verses have clarified the nature of the responsibility of Muslims and the moral and ethical limits of the undertaking of Jihad, and have provided the following guidelines in this regard.

وَ قَاتِلُوْا فِيْ سَبِيْلِ اللّٰهِ الَّذِيْنَ يُقَاتِلُوْنَكُمْ وَ لَا تَعْتَدُوْا ۚ اِنَّ اللّٰهَ لَا يُحِبُّ الْمُعْتَدِيْنَ

وَ اقْتُلُوْهُمْ حَيْثُ ثَقِفْتُمُوْهُمْ وَ اَخْرِجُوْهُمْ مِّنْ حَيْثُ اَخْرَجُوْكُمْ وَ الْفِتْنَةُ اَشَدُّ مِنَ الْقَتْلِ ۚ وَ لَا تُقٰتِلُوْهُمْ عِنْدَ الْمَسْجِدِ الْحَرَامِ حَتّٰى يُقٰتِلُوْكُمْ فِيْهِ ۚ فَاِنْ قٰتَلُوْكُمْ فَاقْتُلُوْهُمْ ۚ كَذٰلِكَ جَزَآءُ الْكٰفِرِيْنَ ۚ فَاِنِ انْتَهَوْا فَاِنَّ اللّٰهَ غَفُوْرٌ رَّحِيْمٌ

وَ قٰتِلُوْهُمْ حَتّٰى لَا تَكُوْنَ فِتْنَةٌ وَّ يَكُوْنَ الدِّيْنُ لِلّٰهِ ۚ فَاِنِ انْتَهَوْا فَلَا عُدْوَانَ اِلَّا عَلَى الظّٰلِمِيْنَ

اَلشَّهْرُ الْحَرَامُ بِالشَّهْرِ الْحَرَامِ وَ الْحُرُمٰتُ قِصَاصٌ ۚ فَمَنِ اعْتَدٰى عَلَيْكُمْ فَاعْتَدُوْا عَلَيْهِ بِمِثْلِ مَا اعْتَدٰى عَلَيْكُمْ ۚ وَ اتَّقُوا اللّٰهَ وَ اعْلَمُوْا اَنَّ اللّٰهَ مَعَ الْمُتَّقِيْنَ

And fight in the way of Allah with those who fight against you and do not transgress bounds [in this fighting]. Indeed, God does not like the transgressors. And kill them wherever you find them and drive them out [of the place] from which they drove you out, and [remember] persecution is worse than bloodshed. But do not initiate war with them near the Holy Kabah unless they attack you there. But if they attack you, put them to the sword [without any hesitation]. Such disbelievers deserve this very punishment. However, if they desist [from this disbelief], Allah is Forgiving and Merciful. And keep fighting against them until persecution does not remain and [in this land] Allah's religion reigns supreme. But if they mend their ways, then [you should know that] an offensive is only allowed against the evil-doers. A sacred month for a sacred month; [similarly] other sacred things too are subject to retaliation. So, if anyone transgresses against you, you should also pay him back in the same coin. And have a fear of Allah and keep in mind that Allah is with those who remain within the bounds set by Him. (2:190-194)

- The details of the Shariah of Jihad or Qital explained in these verses is covered under four topics:

1	Nature of the Obligation	2	The Driving Force
3	The Ethical Limits	4	The Ultimate Goal

1 – Nature of the Obligation

- Muslims should fight until the persecution perpetrated is uprooted, not just for offering Hajj – the responsibility given to them was much bigger. It could not have been imposed on Muslims without considering their moral and military might.

- In other verses, the Quran promises help in proportion to the moral strength of Muslims (Quran 8:65, 8:66). This moral strength brings 'insight,' which enhances the believer's perseverance and strength.

- Similarly, Jihad never becomes obligatory unless the military might of the Muslims is up to a certain level.

- In the battles of Badr, Uhud, and Tabuk, the responsibility was much greater, and each Muslim was required to present his services as a combatant – a test of their belief.

- When an Islamic state calls for mandatory participation, Muslims are told that if their life, wealth, and kin are dearer to them than fighting, then they should wait for the decision of the Almighty against them, which may be similar to what He has decided for the enemies of Islam.

- In some military campaigns where service was not mandatory, God promised participants a great, extraordinary reward.

- In the Quran, it has unequivocally stated that showing weakness and, as a result, running away from the battlefield is not befitting for believers and is a big sin.

يَا أَيُّهَا الَّذِينَ آمَنُوا إِذَا لَقِيتُمُ الَّذِينَ كَفَرُوا زَحْفًا فَلَا تُوَلُّوهُمُ الْأَدْبَارَ

وَ مَنْ يُوَلِّهِمْ يَوْمَئِذٍ دُبُرَهُ إِلَّا مُتَحَرِّفًا لِقِتَالٍ أَوْ مُتَحَيِّزًا إِلَى فِئَةٍ فَقَدْ بَاءَ بِغَضَبٍ مِّنَ اللهِ وَ مَأْوَاهُ جَهَنَّمُ وَ بِئْسَ الْمَصِيرُ

Believers! When, as an organized army, you meet these disbelievers, never turn your back on them. And [you should know that] whoever turns his back to them on such a day – unless it be a stratagem of war or to retreat to a part of his army – he indeed has drawn upon himself wrath from Allah. And his abode is Hell, and worst indeed is that destination! (8:15-6)

الْآنَ خَفَّفَ اللهُ عَنْكُمْ وَ عَلِمَ أَنَّ فِيكُمْ ضَعْفًا فَإِنْ يَّكُنْ مِّنْكُمْ مِّائَةٌ صَابِرَةٌ يَّغْلِبُوا مِائَتَيْنِ وَ إِنْ يَّكُنْ مِّنْكُمْ أَلْفٌ يَّغْلِبُوا أَلْفَيْنِ بِإِذْنِ اللهِ وَ اللهُ مَعَ الصَّابِرِينَ

Now, God has lightened your burden, for He knows that weakness has come into you: So, if there are a hundred of you, patient and persevering, they will subdue two hundred, and if a thousand, they will subdue two thousand, with the permission of God, and [in reality], God is with those who patiently persevere. (8:66)

لَا يَسْتَوِى الْقَاعِدُونَ مِنَ الْمُؤْمِنِينَ غَيْرُ أُولِى الضَّرَرِ وَ الْمُجَاهِدُونَ فِى سَبِيلِ اللهِ بِأَمْوَالِهِمْ وَ أَنْفُسِهِمْ فَضَّلَ اللهُ الْمُجَاهِدِينَ

بِأَمْوَالِهِمْ وَ أَنْفُسِهِمْ عَلَى الْقَاعِدِينَ دَرَجَةً وَ كُلًّا وَّعَدَ اللهُ الْحُسْنَى وَ فَضَّلَ اللهُ الْمُجَاهِدِينَ عَلَى الْقَاعِدِينَ أَجْرًا عَظِيمًا

Not equal are those of the believers who sit at home without any genuine excuse and those who strive hard and fight for the cause of Allah with their wealth and their lives. Allah has given preference by a degree to those who strive hard and fight with their wealth and their lives above those who sit [at home]. [Truly], for each, Allah has made a good promise, and [truly] Allah has preferred those who strive hard and fight above those who sit [at home] by a huge reward. High status, forgiveness, and mercy from Him. And Allah is Ever-Forgiving, Most-Merciful. (4:95-96)

- Not only should the Muslims consolidate their moral character, but they should also build their military might if they want to wage jihad when the need arises.

وَ أَعِدُّوا لَهُمْ مَّا اسْتَطَعْتُمْ مِّنْ قُوَّةٍ وَّ مِنْ رِّبَاطِ الْخَيْلِ تُرْهِبُونَ بِهِ عَدُوَّ اللهِ وَ عَدُوَّكُمْ وَ اخَرِينَ مِنْ دُونِهِمْ لَا

تَعْلَمُونَهُمْ اللهُ يَعْلَمُهُمْ وَ مَا تُنْفِقُوا مِنْ شَىْءٍ فِى سَبِيلِ اللهِ يُوَفَّ إِلَيْكُمْ وَ أَنْتُمْ لَا تُظْلَمُونَ

And muster against them all the men and cavalry at your disposal so that you can strike terror into the enemies of Allah and of the believers and others beside them who may be unknown to you, [though] Allah knows them. And [remember] whatever you spend for the cause of Allah shall be repaid to you. And you shall not be wronged. (8:60)

2 – The Driving Force

- The Jihad/Qital must neither be undertaken to gratify one's whims nor to obtain wealth or riches, conquer land and territories, nor be called a 'conqueror.'
- It must be undertaken ONLY for God's cause.
- In this war, the believers act as mere agents and instruments for the Will of God to be implemented (oppression is eliminated).
- It is because of this reason and their intention to be pure for the sake of God that God has promised great rewards for the believers.

اَلَّذِينَ امَنُوا يُقَاتِلُونَ فِى سَبِيلِ اللهِ وَ الَّذِينَ كَفَرُوا يُقَاتِلُونَ فِى سَبِيلِ الطَّاغُوتِ فَقَاتِلُوا أَوْلِيَاءَ الشَّيْطَانِ إِنَّ

كَيْدَ الشَّيْطَانِ كَانَ ضَعِيفًا

Those who professed faith fight in the cause of Allah, and those who have rejected faith fight in the cause of Satan. So, fight against the friends of Satan. Ever feeble indeed is the plot of Satan. (4:76)

وَ لَا تَحْسَبَنَّ الَّذِيْنَ قُتِلُوْا فِيْ سَبِيْلِ اللّٰهِ اَمْوَاتًا ۚ بَلْ اَحْيَآءٌ عِنْدَ رَبِّهِمْ يُرْزَقُوْنَ ۙ فَرِحِيْنَ بِمَآ اٰتٰهُمُ اللّٰهُ مِنْ فَضْلِهٖ

And do not consider those who are killed in the way of Allah as dead. Nay, they are alive with their Lord and being provided for. They rejoice in what Allah has bestowed upon them of His bounty (3:169)

Once, a person came to the Prophet and said that some people fight for the spoils of war, some for fame, and some to show off their valor; he then asked the Prophet: "Which one of them fights in the way of Allah?" The Prophet replied: "Only that person fights in the way of Allah who sets foot in the battlefield to raise high the name of Allah." (Sahih Al-Bukhari #2810)

The Prophet said, "The fate of three types of people shall be decided first on the Day of Judgement: A person who was martyred while fighting. The Almighty will remind him of His favors. Once the person remembers them, the Almighty will ask: 'What did you do for me?' He will reply: 'I fought for you until I embraced martyrdom.' The Almighty will say: 'You have told a lie; you fought so that people would acknowledge your bravery, and that has [already] taken place.' The Almighty would then order his punishment, and he would be dragged by his face and thrown into Hell. (Sahih Muslim #4923)

Once, a person came to the Prophet and asked, "Tell me of a deed whose reward is equivalent to that of jihad." The Prophet replied: "There is no such deed." The Prophet then asked that person: "Is it possible for you that once the Mujahidin (warriors) depart for jihad, you go to the mosque and keep standing in prayer without pausing and also keep fasting [simultaneously] without breaking the fast?" The person replied: "How can anyone do this?" (Sahih Al-Bukhari #2785)

The Prophet said: "I swear by the Almighty that a person who is wounded in the way of Allah – and Allah knows full well who is actually wounded in His way – he shall be raised on the Day of Judgement such that his color will be the color of blood with the fragrance of musk around him." (Sahih Al-Bukhari #2803)

3 – The Ethical Limits

- Jihad cannot be waged in the way of God with no regard to ethical limits set by God.
- Islam insists that basic ethics and morality must prevail even in chaotic situations like war.
- Muslims should not initiate proceedings to violate anything that God has declared sacred.
- Muslims can answer any excess committed by the enemy by inflicting equal damage only. They have no right to go beyond this.
- God has made it amply clear to the Muslims that in both forms of Qital, Muslims must not initiate the violation of any treaty contracted with a nation (9:4)
- The contract cannot be violated even if the other nation is committing oppression against Muslims in their land.
- However, if Muslims fear any foul play and breach of contract from the opposite side, they, in the words of the Qur'an, can also terminate the treaty and throw the promise on their faces on equal footing.

اَلشَّهْرُ الْحَرَامُ بِالشَّهْرِ الْحَرَامِ وَ الْحُرُمٰتُ قِصَاصٌ ۚ فَمَنِ اعْتَدٰى عَلَيْكُمْ فَاعْتَدُوْا عَلَيْهِ بِمِثْلِ مَا اعْتَدٰى عَلَيْكُمْ ۚ وَ اتَّقُوا اللهَ وَ اعْلَمُوْۤا اَنَّ اللهَ مَعَ الْمُتَّقِيْنَ

A sacred month for a sacred month; [similarly] other sacred things too are subject to retaliation. Therefore, if anyone transgresses against you, you should also pay back in equal terms. Have fear of Allah and keep in mind that Allah is with those who remain within the bounds [stipulated by religion]. (2:194)

وَ الَّذِيْنَ اٰمَنُوْا وَ لَمْ يُهَاجِرُوْا مَا لَكُمْ مِّنْ وَّلَايَتِهِمْ مِّنْ شَيْءٍ حَتّٰى يُهَاجِرُوْا ۚ وَ اِنِ اسْتَنْصَرُوْكُمْ فِى الدِّيْنِ فَعَلَيْكُمُ النَّصْرُ اِلَّا عَلٰى قَوْمٍ بَيْنَكُمْ وَ بَيْنَهُمْ مِّيْثَاقٌ ۚ وَ اللهُ بِمَا تَعْمَلُوْنَ بَصِيْرٌ

And to those who accepted faith but did not migrate [to Madinah], you owe no duty of protection to them until they migrate; but if they seek your help in religion, it is your duty to help them except against a people with whom you have a treaty of mutual alliance; and Allah sees what you do. (8:72)

وَ اِمَّا تَخَافَنَّ مِنْ قَوْمٍ خِيَانَةً فَانْبِذْ اِلَيْهِمْ عَلٰى سَوَآءٍ ۚ اِنَّ اللهَ لَا يُحِبُّ الْخَآئِنِيْنَ

And if you fear any treachery from a people, throw back their covenant to them on equal terms. Certainly, Allah does not like the treacherous. (8:58)

The Prophet said: "On the Day of Judgement, to proclaim the traitorship of a traitor and the betrayal of a person who betrayed his words, a flag shall be hoisted which would be as high as [the extent of his] traitorship", and then said: "Remember that no traitor or betrayer of promises is greater than the traitor who is the leader and ruler of people." (Sahih Muslim #4538)

The Prophet said: "One who kills a person with whom he has an agreement of peace, will not be able to smell [the fragrance] of Paradise, even though its fragrance can be smelt from a place as far off as forty years from it in distance." (Sahih Al-Bukhari #3166)

Other directives on ethical limits

- A display of pomp and pride should be avoided when an army sets out for a battle. In Surah Anfal, where the Quran has asked the Muslims to spend more time in the remembrance of God when war is at hand, it has also asked them to abstain from show and pomposity, as such vanity and conceit are not befitting for the believers.
- People who want to remain neutral in war should be left alone and not be troubled.
- People who neither take part in a battle nor can take part in it – as per the dictates of custom as well as sense and reason – should not be killed.
- People among the enemy should not be killed by setting them ablaze.
- Plundering and looting should be abstained from.
- Dead bodies should not be mutilated.
- Setting up obstructions and robbing travelers is forbidden.

وَ لَا تَكُونُوا كَالَّذِينَ خَرَجُوا مِنْ دِيَارِهِمْ بَطَرًا وَّ رِئَآءَ النَّاسِ وَ يَصُدُّونَ عَنْ سَبِيلِ اللهِ ۚ وَ اللهُ بِمَا يَعْمَلُونَ مُحِيطٌ

And be not like those who came out of their homes boastfully and displaying their grandeur and those who stopped [people] from the way of Allah, even though Allah fully encompasses what they do. (8:47)

اَوْ جَآءُوكُمْ حَصِرَتْ صُدُورُهُمْ اَنْ يُّقَاتِلُوكُمْ اَوْ يُقَاتِلُوا قَوْمَهُمْ ۚ وَ لَوْ شَآءَ اللهُ لَسَلَّطَهُمْ عَلَيْكُمْ فَلَقَاتَلُوكُمْ ۚ فَاِنِ اعْتَزَلُوكُمْ فَلَمْ يُقَاتِلُوكُمْ وَ اَلْقَوْا اِلَيْكُمُ السَّلَمَ ۙ فَمَا جَعَلَ اللهُ لَكُمْ عَلَيْهِمْ سَبِيلًا

Or those who approach you such that they neither have the courage to fight you nor their own people [and are such that] had Allah willed, indeed He would have given them power over you, and they would have fought you. So, if they withdraw from you, and fight not against you, and offer you peace, then Allah does not give you permission to take any action against them. (4:90)

Once in a battle, when it became known that a woman had been killed, the Prophet emphatically forbade the killing of women and children during the battle. (Sahih Al-Bukhari #4547)

Once, when the Prophet bade the Muslims to set out for a battle (to punish disbelievers), he named two persons and directed the Muslims to burn them if they encountered them. However, when the Muslim army was about to set out, he said: "I had asked you to set two people ablaze; the truth of the matter is that it is only Allah Who can punish someone in this manner; so, if you find these two, just kill them." (Sahih Al-Bukhari #3016)

Once while traveling for jihad, because of great compulsion, some people of the Muslim army snatched some goats to appease their hunger. When the Prophet came to know about this, he overturned all the utensils and remarked: "Plundered [food] is no better than dead meat." (Abu Dawood #2705)

4 – The Ultimate Goal

- The ultimate goal of Jihad is to:
  - Uproot persecution – Eternal Directive
  - Supremacy of Islam in the Arabian Peninsula – For Messengers Only

a) Uprooting Persecution – eternal directive

- The Quran used the term 'persecution' to describe forcing someone to give up their religion or stop them from practicing it freely.
- When the Islamic State was formed in Medina, Muslims were directed to take up arms against people who were responsible for persecuting Muslims.
- This is an eternal directive of the Quran, and believers are asked to help the oppressed if they have the power to do so.
- The other forms of oppression against life and wealth, besides religion, can be included in the definition of persecution today.
- If oppressors are Muslims, then the Quran instructed other Muslims to (49:9-10):
- First, try to reconcile the two groups while remaining neutral.
- Support the right group and fight the oppressors if they persist in their attitude.

وَ مَا لَكُمْ لَا تُقَاتِلُوْنَ فِيْ سَبِيْلِ اللّٰهِ وَ الْمُسْتَضْعَفِيْنَ مِنَ الرِّجَالِ وَ النِّسَآءِ وَ الْوِلْدَانِ الَّذِيْنَ يَقُوْلُوْنَ رَبَّنَآ اَخْرِجْنَا مِنْ
هٰذِهِ الْقَرْيَةِ الظَّالِمِ اَهْلُهَا ۚ وَ اجْعَلْ لَّنَا مِنْ لَّدُنْكَ وَلِيًّا ۙ وَّ اجْعَلْ لَّنَا مِنْ لَّدُنْكَ نَصِيْرًا
اَلَّذِيْنَ اٰمَنُوْا يُقَاتِلُوْنَ فِيْ سَبِيْلِ اللّٰهِ ۚ وَ الَّذِيْنَ كَفَرُوْا يُقَاتِلُوْنَ فِيْ سَبِيْلِ الطَّاغُوْتِ
فَقَاتِلُوْٓا اَوْلِيَآءَ الشَّيْطٰنِ ۚ اِنَّ كَيْدَ الشَّيْطٰنِ كَانَ ضَعِيْفًا

And what has come over you that you fight not in the cause of Allah, and for those weak, ill-treated, and oppressed among men, women, and children whose cry is: "Our Lord! Rescue us from this town of oppressors and raise for us from You one who will protect and raise for us from You one who will help." [You should know that] those who are believers, fight in the cause of Allah, and those who are disbelievers, fight in the cause of Satan. So, fight you against the friends of Satan. Ever feeble indeed is the plot of Satan. (4:75-6)

b) Supremacy of Islam in the Arabian Peninsula – For Messengers only

- For the second objective, the Quran uses the words: "Fight with them until God's religion reigns supreme."

- It is evident from the context of the verses that the word "them" is directed toward the Idolators of Arabia.

- Consequently, these expressions mean that in the land of Arabia, the religion of Islam would reign supreme, which was the main mission of Prophet Muhammad.

- This purpose was achieved in two ways: either the followers of all other man-made religions were put to death (Idolators), or they were subdued and subjugated completely (People of the Book).

- Jews and Christians could live on their religions if they agreed to pay Jizyah and live a life of total subjugation to the Islamic state established in Arabia; the active adversaries among them were put to death or exiled from the land.

- This law (called the Law of Itmam al-Hujjah) is specific to the Messengers and no longer applies, as God directed it with specific instructions given to Prophet Muhammad and his companions.

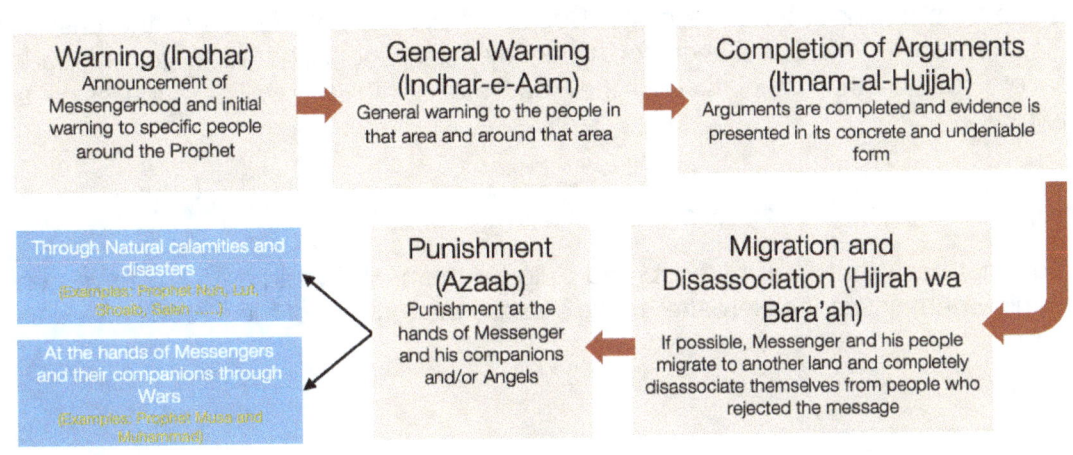

إِنَّ الَّذِينَ يُحَآدُّونَ اللهَ وَ رَسُولَهُ أُولَٰئِكَ فِي الْأَذَلِّينَ   كَتَبَ اللهُ لَأَغْلِبَنَّ أَنَا وَ رُسُلِى ۚ إِنَّ اللهَ قَوِيٌّ عَزِيزٌ

Indeed, those who oppose Allah and His Messenger are bound to be humiliated. The Almighty has ordained: "My messengers and I shall always prevail." Indeed, Allah is Mighty and Powerful. (58:20-21)

بَرَآءَةٌ مِّنَ اللهِ وَ رَسُولِهِ إِلَى الَّذِينَ عَاهَدْتُّمْ مِّنَ الْمُشْرِكِينَ   فَسِيحُوا فِي الْأَرْضِ أَرْبَعَةَ أَشْهُرٍ وَّ اعْلَمُوا أَنَّكُمْ غَيْرُ مُعْجِزِى اللهِ ۙ

وَ أَنَّ اللهَ مُخْزِى الْكَافِرِينَ   وَ أَذَانٌ مِّنَ اللهِ وَ رَسُولِهِ إِلَى النَّاسِ يَوْمَ الْحَجِّ الْأَكْبَرِ أَنَّ اللهَ بَرِىٓءٌ مِّنَ الْمُشْرِكِينَ ۙ وَ رَسُولُهُ ۚ

فَإِنْ تُبْتُمْ فَهُوَ خَيْرٌ لَّكُمْ ۚ وَ إِنْ تَوَلَّيْتُمْ فَاعْلَمُوا أَنَّكُمْ غَيْرُ مُعْجِزِى اللهِ ۗ وَ بَشِّرِ الَّذِينَ كَفَرُوا بِعَذَابٍ أَلِيمٍ

إِلَّا الَّذِينَ عَاهَدْتُّمْ مِّنَ الْمُشْرِكِينَ ثُمَّ لَمْ يَنْقُصُوكُمْ شَيْئًا وَّ لَمْ يُظَاهِرُوا عَلَيْكُمْ أَحَدًا فَأَتِمُّوا إِلَيْهِمْ عَهْدَهُمْ إِلَى مُدَّتِهِمْ ۚ إِنَّ اللهَ

يُحِبُّ الْمُتَّقِينَ   فَإِذَا انْسَلَخَ الْأَشْهُرُ الْحُرُمُ فَاقْتُلُوا الْمُشْرِكِينَ حَيْثُ وَجَدْتُّمُوهُمْ وَ خُذُوهُمْ وَ احْصُرُوهُمْ وَ اقْعُدُوا لَهُمْ كُلَّ

مَرْصَدٍ ۚ فَإِنْ تَابُوا وَ أَقَامُوا الصَّلٰوةَ وَ أَتَوُا الزَّكٰوةَ فَخَلُّوا سَبِيلَهُمْ ۚ إِنَّ اللهَ غَفُورٌ رَّحِيمٌ

And a declaration should be made from Allah and His Messenger to these people on the day of the great hajj that Allah is free from [all] obligations to these Idolaters, and so is His Messenger. So, [O Idolaters!] If you repent, it is better for you; but if you turn away, know that you cannot escape the grasp of Allah. And [O Muhammad (sws)!] Give tidings of a painful torment to these disbelievers. Except those of these Idolaters with whom you have a treaty and who have not shown treachery in it, nor have supported anyone against you. So fulfill their treaty to the end of their term. Indeed, Allah loves those who abide by the limits. Then, when the sacred months [after the hajj] have passed, kill these Idolaters wherever you find them, and capture them and besiege them, and lie in wait for them in each and every ambush. But if they repent, are diligent in their prayers, and give zakah, then leave them alone. Indeed, Allah is Ever-Forgiving, Most-Merciful. (9:3-5)

قَاتِلُوا الَّذِينَ لَا يُؤْمِنُونَ بِاللهِ وَ لَا بِالْيَوْمِ الْأَخِرِ وَ لَا يُحَرِّمُونَ مَا حَرَّمَ اللهُ وَ رَسُولُهُ وَ لَا يَدِينُونَ دِينَ الْحَقِّ مِنَ

الَّذِينَ أُوتُوا الْكِتٰبَ حَتَّى يُعْطُوا الْجِزْيَةَ عَنْ يَّدٍ وَّ هُمْ صَاغِرُونَ

Fight those from among the People of the Book who believe not in Allah or the Last Day, nor hold that forbidden which has been forbidden by Allah and His Messenger, nor adopt the Religion of Truth as their religion, until they pay the Jizyah with willing submission and are subdued. (9:29)

وَ لَوْ لَا أَنْ كَتَبَ اللهُ عَلَيْهِمُ الْجَلَآءَ لَعَذَّبَهُمْ فِي الدُّنْيَا ۖ وَ لَهُمْ فِي الْأَخِرَةِ عَذَابُ النَّارِ

And had it not been that Allah had decreed exile for them, He would certainly have punished them in this world; and in the Hereafter theirs shall be the torment of the Fire. (59:3)

Powerful Nations outside Arabia

- Once Quraysh and the People of the Book were subjugated, the Prophet was asked to present his message to all the nearby nations outside of Arabia.
- The Prophet wrote letters to follow nations, making it clear to them that now Islam alone can guarantee existence for them: Negus of Abyssinia, Maqawqas of Egypt, Khusro Parvez of Persia, Qaysar of Rome, Mundhir ibn Sawi of Bahrain, Hudhah ibn 'Ali of Yamamah, Harith ibn Abi Shamr of Damascus, Jayfar of Amman.
- Just as the truth had been conclusively communicated through the Prophet to the Idolaters and the People of the Book of Arabia, it was also conclusively communicated before his death to these nations.
- In the light of "the law of Itmam al-Hujjah," these nations were also punished in this world. After consolidating their rule in the Arabian Peninsula, the Companions launched attacks against these countries, giving them two options if they wanted to remain alive: accept the faith or pay Jizyah and submit.
- Since none of these nations was an adherent to polytheism in the real sense, most of them were subjugated and ruled over by Muslims.
- These military expeditions were not launched to extend territorial supremacy.

Divine Help

يَٰٓأَيُّهَا النَّبِيُّ حَرِّضِ الْمُؤْمِنِينَ عَلَى الْقِتَالِ ۚ إِن يَكُن مِّنكُمْ عِشْرُونَ صَٰبِرُونَ يَغْلِبُوا مِائَتَيْنِ ۚ وَ إِن يَكُن مِّنكُم مِّائَةٌ يَغْلِبُوٓا أَلْفًا مِّنَ الَّذِينَ كَفَرُوا بِأَنَّهُمْ قَوْمٌ لَّا يَفْقَهُونَ الْـَٰٔنَ خَفَّفَ اللهُ عَنكُمْ وَ عَلِمَ أَنَّ فِيكُمْ ضَعْفًا ۚ فَإِن يَكُن مِّنكُم مِّائَةٌ صَٰبِرَةٌ يَغْلِبُوا مِائَتَيْنِ ۚ وَ إِن يَكُن مِّنكُمْ أَلْفٌ يَغْلِبُوٓا أَلْفَيْنِ بِإِذْنِ اللهِ ۗ وَ اللهُ مَعَ الصَّٰبِرِينَ

O Prophet! Inspire the believers to war. If there are twenty amongst you, patient and persevering, they will subdue two hundred; if a hundred, they will subdue a thousand disbelievers because they are the people without insight. Now, God has lightened your burden, for He knows that there is weakness in you: So, if there are a hundred of you, patient and persevering, they will subdue two hundred, and if a thousand, they will subdue two thousand, with the permission of God and [truly] God is with those who patiently persevere [in His cause]. (8:65-66)

- These and other verses in the Quran highlight the principle by which Divine Help comes to believers in armed conflict.
- The Divine Help is not subject to what we want but only comes under the following conditions:
  - Must have the qualities of patience, perseverance, and resolution.
  - Must be equipped with proper military strength in proportion to what is described above (1:10 or 1:2, depending on the believers' faith and perseverance).

- It is only the force of faith and Divine Help that compensates for any lack of material strength.
- The ratio was high initially because those who entered the fold of Islam were very strong in faith and most sincere in the cause. Later, though Muslims greatly increased in number due to large-scale conversions, the level and extent of faith decreased overall, since the new converts were not as strong in their faith as the pioneers.
- Muslims today can look at this principle and estimate what kind of military strength they need to wage a war.

Captives of War

فَإِذَا لَقِيتُمُ الَّذِينَ كَفَرُوا فَضَرْبَ الرِّقَابِ ۖ حَتَّىٰ إِذَا أَثْخَنْتُمُوهُمْ فَشُدُّوا الْوَثَاقَ ۞ فَإِمَّا مَنًّا بَعْدُ وَ إِمَّا فِدَاءً حَتَّىٰ تَضَعَ الْحَرْبُ أَوْزَارَهَا

So, when you meet [in the battlefield] those who disbelieve, strike off their heads. Then, when you have shed their blood fully, bind them [as captives]. Thereafter, free them as a favor or free them with ransom until war lays down its weapons. (47:4)

- Before this verse was revealed, it was a general practice to take captives of war.
- Muslims were told that when they encounter these enemies of God, the first attempt should be slaying them, as they deserve no leniency.
- For people who are captured, they should now be set free as a favor or after paying a ransom (this was only valid until the final punishment for all was announced).
- This directive was applicable to other expeditions also, and was given to put a cap on the factory that used to generate slaves in those times (as discussed in the section on Slavery in Islam).
- Three types of captives were exceptions to this rule:
  - Brutal adversaries (already identified) about whom the verdict of God was already out were required to be slain.
  - The captives of Banu Qurayzah met a fate decided by an arbitrator appointed by themselves: their men were slain, and their women and children were sold as slaves (as per their Jewish law).
  - Captives who were already slaves prior to their capture, and, in certain instances, were distributed among people as slaves without changing their status.
- All incidents in Seerah suggest that the directives in this verse were followed, except in the cases above.

Spoils of War

- After the very first battle, Muslims had differing opinions about the distribution of the spoils of war.
- The Quran gave its verdict on this matter in these verses.
- First, Muslims were told that they had no claim to the spoils because of the peculiar nature of these wars. They were informed that all these spoils belonged to Allah and His Prophet, and as such, they had discretionary powers as far as their disbursement was concerned.
- Reason: These wars were fought under a specific law of the Almighty, according to which He, through His messengers, punishes people who deliberately deny the truth.
- Later, God reserved 1/5th for collective needs, and the rest was distributed among the soldiers, who began contributing their personal weapons, camels, horses, etc.
- Finally, in military campaigns where personal properties of Muslim soldiers and combatants were not used, spoils were reserved for God's religion, the Prophet and his family, the poor, orphans, and the wayfarers.

يَسْـَٔلُوْنَكَ عَنِ الْاَنْفَالِ ۙ قُلِ الْاَنْفَالُ لِلّٰهِ وَ الرَّسُوْلِ ۚ فَاتَّقُوا اللّٰهَ وَ اَصْلِحُوْا ذَاتَ بَيْنِكُمْ ۖ وَ اَطِيْعُوا اللّٰهَ وَ رَسُوْلَهٗٓ اِنْ كُنْتُمْ مُّؤْمِنِيْنَ

They ask you about the spoils of war. Say: The spoils belong to Allah and the Prophet. Therefore, if you are true believers, fear Allah and reform your personal relationships, and obey Allah and His Prophet. (8:1)

وَ اعْلَمُوْٓا اَنَّمَا غَنِمْتُمْ مِّنْ شَيْءٍ فَاَنَّ لِلّٰهِ خُمُسَهٗ وَ لِلرَّسُوْلِ وَ لِذِى الْقُرْبٰى وَ الْيَتٰمٰى وَ الْمَسٰكِيْنِ وَ ابْنِ السَّبِيْلِ

And you should know that a fifth of the spoils you get hold of are for Allah and the Prophet and his near relatives and the orphans and the needy and the wayfarer. (8:41)

مَآ اَفَآءَ اللّٰهُ عَلٰى رَسُوْلِهٖ مِنْ اَهْلِ الْقُرٰى فَلِلّٰهِ وَ لِلرَّسُوْلِ وَ لِذِى الْقُرْبٰى وَ الْيَتٰمٰى وَ الْمَسٰكِيْنِ وَ ابْنِ السَّبِيْلِ

And whatever the Almighty has bestowed on His Prophet from the people of the cities, it is reserved for Allah and His Prophet and the relatives of the Prophet and the orphans and the needy and the wayfarers. (59:7)

Why has Jihad become such a negative concept in the world?

Chapter 15

Political Shariah

Penal Shariah (Punishments)

This chapter discusses another of the most controversial topics in Islam: Penal Shariah. This has been grossly misrepresented worldwide, especially in the context of the human rights debate.

Punishments in Islam

Why has God prescribed punishments?

قَالُوا اَتَجْعَلُ فِيهَا مَنْ يُّفْسِدُ فِيهَا وَ يَسْفِكُ الدِّمَآءَ

(The Angels) said, (O Allah), Will You create someone who will spread evil on the earth and shed blood? (2:30)

- Free will is a blessing, but at the same time, a source of dishonor for people who misuse it to cause evil and disorder.
- That was the reason angels raised this concern when God told them He was creating Adam and his progeny and that they would be given authority on this Earth.
- In human history, the first such manifestation occurred when Cain killed his brother.
- The most natural (in accordance with the norms of sense and reason) way to shield societies from such evil is to reform the environment through sincere counseling and moral training.
- However, once a person crosses the line and commits a crime, the only solution is to administer punishment to make a point to others and deter them from such evil.
- The history of societies shows that human beings lack a basis for determining the right punishment for a crime, and they have always exhibited extreme behavior in this regard.
- God has given guidance on some of the major crimes committed in a society and left the rest for an Islamic state to make laws for.

Anarchy and Disorder	Murder and Injury	Theft

Fornication	Accusing someone of fornication

كَتَبْنَا عَلَى بَنِيَ اِسْرَآءِيْلَ اَنَّهٗ مَنْ قَتَلَ نَفْسًا بِغَيْرِ نَفْسٍ اَوْ فَسَادٍ فِي الْأَرْضِ فَكَاَنَّمَا قَتَلَ النَّاسَ جَمِيْعًا

We prescribed for the Children of Israel that he who killed a human being without the latter being guilty of killing another or of spreading anarchy in the land should be looked upon as if he had killed all mankind. (5:32)

Some Key Considerations

- The directives in this regard are addressed to Muslims collectively, not to individuals.
- The Surahs that contain these punishments were revealed in Medinah when Muslims had established an authority under the rule of Prophet Muhammad.

- All words used in these verses are addressed to the rulers of the Muslims.
- These are the only crimes for which punishment is divinely ordained. The punishment of other crimes is left to the discretion of those in authority.
- One exception is the death penalty. The punishment of death can only be given to someone:
  - Who has killed someone.
  - Who is guilty of spreading anarchy in society in any possible way.
- All divinely ordained punishments are extreme and must be imposed only when the nature of the crime and the circumstances do not warrant leniency.
- These divinely ordained punishments apply only to Muslim.
- These punishments apply to a Muslim due to breaking the covenant that a Muslim has with their Lord when he/she accepts Islam.

إِنَّمَا جَزَٰٓؤُا۟ ٱلَّذِينَ يُحَارِبُونَ ٱللَّهَ وَ رَسُولَهُ وَ يَسْعَوْنَ فِى ٱلْأَرْضِ فَسَادًا أَن يُقَتَّلُوٓا۟ أَوْ يُصَلَّبُوٓا۟ أَوْ تُقَطَّعَ أَيْدِيهِمْ وَ أَرْجُلُهُم مِّنْ خِلَافٍ أَوْ يُنفَوْا۟ مِنَ ٱلْأَرْضِ ۚ ذَٰلِكَ لَهُمْ خِزْىٌ فِى ٱلدُّنْيَا وَ لَهُمْ فِى ٱلْءَاخِرَةِ عَذَابٌ عَظِيمٌ إِلَّا ٱلَّذِينَ تَابُوا۟ مِن قَبْلِ أَن تَقْدِرُوا۟ عَلَيْهِمْ ۖ فَٱعْلَمُوٓا۟ أَنَّ ٱللَّهَ غَفُورٌ رَّحِيمٌ

The punishments of those who wage war against Allah and His Prophet and strive to spread anarchy in the land are to execute them in an exemplary way, or to crucify them, or to amputate their hands and feet from opposite sides, or to exile them from the land. Such is their disgrace in this world, and in the Hereafter, theirs will be an awful doom except those who repent before you overpower them, then you should know that Allah is Oft-Forgiving, Ever-Merciful. (5:33-34)

A - Anarchy and Disorder (*Muharabah*)

- When a state is ruled by a Messenger of God, anyone who challenges his authority wages war against God (this and similar situations are referred to as *Muharabah* in the verse).
- This punishment deals with people who spread anarchy and disorder in the land, rebel against the law, and attack other people's lives, wealth, honor, and freedom of expression. Murder turns into terrorism; fornication becomes rape; theft becomes an armed robbery; an uprising takes up arms against governments, hijacking.
- All these crimes create anarchy and disorder in the land and are punishable in Islam.
- However, the punishment ranges from severe to light depending on the severity of the crime and the criminal's circumstances.

Most Severe → **Least Severe**

Exemplary capital punishment OR Crucifixion OR Amputating limbs from opposite sides OR Nafi (Exile)

1. Exemplary capital punishment

- Capital punishment is carried out in a manner that would serve as a severe warning to others.
- Stoning to death is one form of Taqtil.
- Other forms that appear severe to observers can be adopted.

2. Crucifixion

- The same form of the word is used for crucifixion, which means that the method adopted must be exemplary for the people who are asked to witness it.
- Any form of Taslib can be adopted.

3. Amputation

- The convicted criminal is allowed to live, but should be made an example for the people.
- The person should be made incapable of doing any evil in the future.

4. Forced Exile

- The convicted criminal should be exiled from his home or country to a foreign land.
- Incarceration or house arrest can also be implemented if exile is impossible due to legal issues.

B - Intentional Murder & Injury (Qisas)

- God has imposed on the state to take retribution (Qisas) for both murder and injury inflicted on behalf of the victim or his/her family.
- Utmost justice should be served. No one should bear the burden of another man/woman.
- The victim or his/her family has two options:
  - Demand life for life, limb for limb, wound for wound.
  - Or forgive the criminal and accept *Diyat* (blood money) from him/her.
- *Diyat* must be given with goodwill and kindness (as best as possible).
- The state must be a party in this deal, and it must ensure that *Diyat* is paid in full and that this forgiveness will not cause unrest in society (influential people can kill and pay money to escape punishment).

- God termed this retribution (Qisas) "Life" because it will guarantee safety and security for everyone in society.
- When a body has an infected limb, at times, only amputation of that limb will secure the body's health.

يَا أَيُّهَا الَّذِينَ اٰمَنُوا كُتِبَ عَلَيْكُمُ الْقِصَاصُ فِى الْقَتْلَى ۖ اَلْحُرُّ بِالْحُرِّ وَ الْعَبْدُ بِالْعَبْدِ وَ الْاُنْثٰى بِالْاُنْثٰى ۚ فَمَنْ عُفِىَ لَهُ مِنْ اَخِيْهِ شَىْءٌ فَاتِّبَاعٌ بِالْمَعْرُوْفِ وَ اَدَآءٌ اِلَيْهِ بِاِحْسَانٍ ۗ ذٰلِكَ تَخْفِيْفٌ مِّنْ رَّبِّكُمْ وَ رَحْمَةٌ ۗ فَمَنِ اعْتَدٰى بَعْدَ ذٰلِكَ فَلَهُ عَذَابٌ اَلِيْمٌ وَ لَكُمْ فِى الْقِصَاصِ حَيٰوةٌ يّاأُولِى الْاَلْبَابِ لَعَلَّكُمْ تَتَّقُوْنَ

Believers! Decreed for you is the *Qisas* of those among you who are killed. If such a murderer is a free man, then this free man should be killed in his place, and if he is a slave, then this slave should be killed in his place, and if the murderer is a woman, then this woman shall be killed in her place. Then, for whom there has been some remission from his brother, [the remission can be accepted; however, it] should be followed according to the norm of the society, and *Diyat* should be paid with kindness. This is a concession and a mercy from your Lord. After this, whoever exceeds the limits shall be afflicted with torment. And there is life for you in *Qisas,* O men of insight, that you may follow the limits set by Allah. (2:178-179)

Directive Given to the Children of Israel

وَ كَتَبْنَا عَلَيْهِمْ فِيْهَآ اَنَّ النَّفْسَ بِالنَّفْسِ وَ الْعَيْنَ بِالْعَيْنِ وَ الْاَنْفَ بِالْاَنْفِ وَ الْاُذُنَ بِالْاُذُنِ وَ السِّنَّ بِالسِّنِّ ۖ وَ الْجُرُوْحَ قِصَاصٌ ۚ فَمَنْ تَصَدَّقَ بِهِ فَهُوَ كَفَّارَةٌ لَّهُ ۚ وَ مَنْ لَّمْ يَحْكُمْ بِمَآ اَنْزَلَ اللهُ فَاُولٰئِكَ هُمُ الظّٰلِمُوْنَ

And We enjoined for them (children of Israel) therein: life for life, eye for eye, nose for nose, ear for ear, tooth for tooth, wound for wound. Then he who forgoes, then this shall be an atonement for his own self. And those who do not judge according to what Allah has revealed are the wrongdoers. (5:45)

> Capital punishment is the **ultimate punishment** when the murderer does not deserve any leniency.

Unintentional Murder & Injury

- For unintentional injury and murder, God gave the following law:

Victim is	If not forgiven, then murderer should
Muslim citizen of a Muslim state.	Pay Diyat + Free a slave + Repent with God, or if you cannot afford to free a slave, then fast for 2 months consecutively.
Muslim citizen from an enemy state.	Free slave only or if cannot afford to free slave then fast for 2 months consecutively.
Non-Muslim citizen from a country with a signed treaty.	Pay Diyat + Free slave + Repent with God, or if you cannot afford to free a slave, then fast for 2 months consecutively.

Note: It can be concluded that the same is true for unintentional injury. The amount of Diyat and fasting required depends on the proportion. E.g., if Diyat for injury is 1/3 of Diyat for Murder, then the fast should also be 1/3.

وَ مَا كَانَ لِمُؤْمِنٍ اَنْ يَّقْتُلَ مُؤْمِنًا اِلَّا خَطَاً ۚ وَ مَنْ قَتَلَ مُؤْمِنًا خَطَأً فَتَحْرِيْرُ رَقَبَةٍ مُّؤْمِنَةٍ وَّ دِيَةٌ مُّسَلَّمَةٌ اِلٰۤى اَهْلِهٖۤ اِلَّاۤ اَنْ يَّصَّدَّقُوْا ۚ فَاِنْ كَانَ مِنْ قَوْمٍ عَدُوٍّ لَّكُمْ وَ هُوَ مُؤْمِنٌ فَتَحْرِيْرُ رَقَبَةٍ مُّؤْمِنَةٍ ۚ وَ اِنْ كَانَ مِنْ قَوْمٍ بَيْنَكُمْ وَ بَيْنَهُمْ مِّيْثَاقٌ فَدِيَةٌ مُّسَلَّمَةٌ اِلٰۤى اَهْلِهٖ وَ تَحْرِيْرُ رَقَبَةٍ مُّؤْمِنَةٍ ۚ فَمَنْ لَّمْ يَجِدْ فَصِيَامُ شَهْرَيْنِ مُتَتَابِعَيْنِ ۫ تَوْبَةً مِّنَ اللّٰهِ ۚ وَ كَانَ اللّٰهُ عَلِيْمًا حَكِيْمًا

And it is unlawful for a believer to kill another believer except if it happens by accident. And he who kills a believer accidentally must free one Muslim slave and pay *diyat* to the victim's heirs, except if they forgive him. If the victim is a Muslim belonging to a people at enmity with you, freeing a Muslim slave is enough. But if the victim belongs to an ally, *diyat* shall be given to his heirs, and a Muslim slave must be set free. He who does not have a slave must fast for two consecutive months. This is from Allah, a way to repent from this sin: and He is Wise, All-Knowing. (4:92)

Regarding Diyat

فَمَنْ عُفِىَ لَهُ مِنْ اَخِيْهِ شَىْءٌ فَاتِّبَاعٌ بِالْمَعْرُوْفِ وَ اَدَآءٌ اِلَيْهِ بِاِحْسَانٍ

Then, for whom there has been some remission from his brother, [the remission] should be followed according to the norms of the society, and diyat should be paid with kindness. (2:178)

وَّ دِيَةٌ مُّسَلَّمَةٌ اِلٰۤى اَهْلِهٖ

A complete Diyat to his/her family.

- The word *diyat* in these verses occurs as a common noun, which means that its meaning is determined by its linguistic and customary usage and by the context in which it is used.
- It means that the family of the murdered person should be given what the general custom and society term as "*diyat*".
- The Quran does not prescribe any amount, nor does it distinguish between the *Diyat* of a man and a woman.
- Prophet Muhammad decided the amount of Diyat according to the customs of that time.
- It was set at many camels in those days, which is not possible in our time, so the state should decide an equivalent based on the culture, norms, and financial situation of society.
- Other forms of community relationships and bonding that have formed must be considered when determining the value of *Diyat* and other penalties.

C - Adultery and Fornication (*Zina*)

Initial Directives

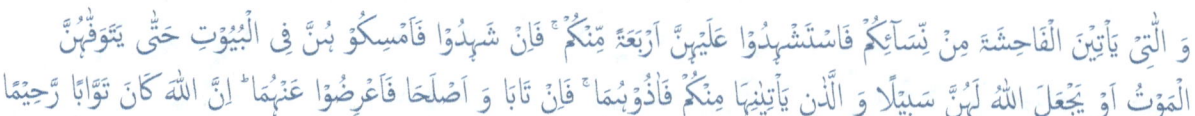

وَ الّٰتِيْ يَأْتِيْنَ الْفَاحِشَةَ مِنْ نِّسَآئِكُمْ فَاسْتَشْهِدُوْا عَلَيْهِنَّ اَرْبَعَةً مِّنْكُمْ ۚ فَاِنْ شَهِدُوْا فَاَمْسِكُوْهُنَّ فِى الْبُيُوْتِ حَتّٰى يَتَوَفّٰهُنَّ الْمَوْتُ اَوْ يَجْعَلَ اللّٰهُ لَهُنَّ سَبِيْلًا وَ الَّذٰنِ يَأْتِيٰنِهَا مِنْكُمْ فَاٰذُوْهُمَا ۚ فَاِنْ تَابَا وَ اَصْلَحَا فَاَعْرِضُوْا عَنْهُمَا ۗ اِنَّ اللّٰهَ كَانَ تَوَّابًا رَّحِيْمًا

And upon those of your women who commit fornication, call in four people among yourselves to testify over them; if they testify [to their ill-ways], confine them to their homes till death overtakes them or God formulates another way for them. And the man and woman among you who commit fornication, chastise them. If they repent and mend their ways, leave them alone. For God is Ever-Forgiving and Most Merciful. (4:15-16)

- The Quran's initial directive regarding this crime appears in Surah Nisa, but no specific punishment is stated there.
- Prophet was asked to deal with some women who, as prostitutes, habitually commit fornication; they should be confined to their homes.
- As for couples who were involved in such a crime, they should be chastised and reprimanded until they repent and mend their ways.
- The chastisement may involve exhorting, scolding, censuring, humiliating, disgracing, or maybe some corporal punishment.
- If someone is accusing a woman or a man of fornication, then they are required to produce four witnesses in front of the authorities before any punishment can be given (please see the punishment for *Qadhaf*).
- Finally, the punishment for fornication is revealed in Surah Nur.

اَلزَّانِيَةُ وَ الزَّانِيْ فَاجْلِدُوْا كُلَّ وَاحِدٍ مِّنْهُمَا مِائَةَ جَلْدَةٍ ۪ وَّ لَا تَأْخُذْكُمْ بِهِمَا رَأْفَةٌ فِيْ دِيْنِ اللّٰهِ اِنْ كُنْتُمْ تُؤْمِنُوْنَ بِاللّٰهِ وَ الْيَوْمِ الْاٰخِرِ ۚ وَ لْيَشْهَدْ عَذَابَهُمَا طَآئِفَةٌ مِّنَ الْمُؤْمِنِيْنَ ٱلزَّانِيْ لَا يَنْكِحُ اِلَّا زَانِيَةً اَوْ مُشْرِكَةً ۫ وَّ الزَّانِيَةُ لَا يَنْكِحُهَآ اِلَّا زَانٍ اَوْ مُشْرِكٌ ۚ وَ حُرِّمَ ذٰلِكَ عَلَى الْمُؤْمِنِيْنَ

The man and the woman guilty of fornication flog each of them with a hundred stripes, and let not compassion move you in their case in the enforcement of the law of God if you truly believe in Allah and the Last Day. And let a party of the believers witness their punishment. The man guilty of fornication may only marry a woman similarly guilty or an idolatress, and the woman guilty of fornication may only marry such a man or an idolater. The believers are forbidden from such marriages. (24:2-3)

Note: The term 'fornication' (Zina) is used for the crime in discussion regardless of whether the person committing it is married or not.

The Punishment for Fornication

- A man and a woman who have committed it shall be flogged a hundred times each.
- Ahadith have described the type of cane/lash to be used for the punishment, as well as the nature of flogging.
  - Cane/Lash should neither be too thick nor too thin.
  - The criminal should not be bare-bodied or tied.
  - Lashing should not be done on just one part of the body.
  - No hitting on the face or private parts.
  - A pregnant woman should be flogged after the delivery, and post-delivery conditions are over
- They should be punished publicly to humiliate and teach a lesson to everyone.
- Ultimate justice should be served with no leniency shown due to a person's status in society.
- Once this punishment is carried out, they are not allowed to marry chaste men/women. They can marry someone who has been convicted of such a crime (this prohibition applies to a person who has been officially convicted by a court).
- The adjectives اَلزَّانِيَةُ وَ الزَّانِیْ imply that these are the people who often commit fornication. Also, this punishment must be imposed when those involved do not deserve leniency, given their circumstances.

When someone is coerced

- Through these two verses, the Quran provides guidance on how to impose punishments for such crimes when society fails to provide the right education, guidance, and environment necessary to curb such inclinations.
- At the time of Prophet Muhammad, masters used to force slave girls to commit such a crime to earn money. The Quran, looking at their situation, prescribed the following for them:
  - If their upbringing did not occur in a good family environment, there should be no punishment for them.
  - If their upbringing occurred in a good family environment, even then their punishment should be half that of free women (50 lashes instead of 100).

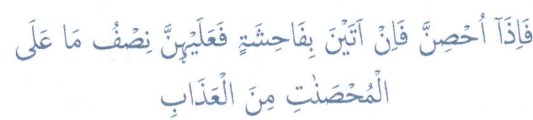

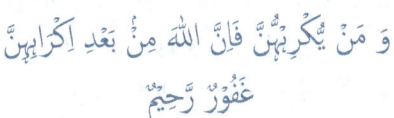

Then when they are kept chaste [in this manner], and they commit fornication, their punishment is half that of free women. (4:25)

And if anyone compels them, Allah will be Forgiving and Merciful to them after their being compelled to it. (24:33)

Islam's perspective on extramarital relationships

قُلْ لِّلْمُؤْمِنِينَ يَغُضُّوا مِنْ أَبْصَارِهِمْ وَ يَحْفَظُوا فُرُوجَهُمْ ۚ ذٰلِكَ أَزْكَىٰ لَهُمْ ۗ
إِنَّ اللهَ خَبِيرٌ بِمَا يَصْنَعُونَ

[O Prophet!] Tell believers to restrain their eyes and guard their private parts (from illicit relationships). That is purer for them. And indeed, Allah is well aware of what they do. (24:30)

- Islam builds its social structure on the bonds of family, with the welfare of children (at different stages of life) as the central focus.
- To preserve this bond, it is necessary to forbid all forms of temporary association between a man and a woman.
- Sex out of wedlock does not allow a healthy family to come into being necessary for the upbringing of the children.
- During one's childhood and old age, a person requires love and affection through relationships (parents, children, brothers, and sisters) that are permanent and can play specific roles in one's life.
- Only the institution of the family can ensure these privileges for him/her. Without this institution, one may have an enjoyable youth, but his/her childhood and old age will likely be spent in misery.
- On the other hand, Islam wants people to purify themselves intellectually, morally, and physically, and marriage is the only institution that can guard their purity and prevent them from being carried away and indulging in unrestricted sexual behavior.

D - *Qadhf*

- God does not want people to take accusing others of fornication/adultery lightly. It's a serious matter.
- This destroys someone's reputation and honor, especially in an Islamic society.
- In Western culture, such an accusation against a married person is still harmful, but it is not something for an unmarried person.
- In Islam, it is encouraged to cover your brothers/sisters if they falter instead of exposing them in public.
- It is recommended that if you know someone is involved in a haram relationship, counsel them privately, but never expose them unless it impacts someone else's life.

وَ الَّذِيْنَ يَرْمُوْنَ الْمُحْصَنٰتِ ثُمَّ لَمْ يَأْتُوْا بِاَرْبَعَةِ شُهَدَآءَ فَاجْلِدُوْهُمْ ثَمٰنِيْنَ جَلْدَةً وَّ لَا تَقْبَلُوْا لَهُمْ شَهَادَةً اَبَدًا ۚ وَ اُولٰٓئِكَ هُمُ
الْفٰسِقُوْنَ ۙ اِلَّا الَّذِيْنَ تَابُوْا مِنْ بَعْدِ ذٰلِكَ وَ اَصْلَحُوْا ۚ فَاِنَّ اللّٰهَ غَفُوْرٌ رَّحِيْمٌ وَ الَّذِيْنَ يَرْمُوْنَ اَزْوَاجَهُمْ وَ لَمْ يَكُنْ لَّهُمْ شُهَدَآءُ
اِلَّاۤ اَنْفُسُهُمْ فَشَهَادَةُ اَحَدِهِمْ اَرْبَعُ شَهٰدٰتٍۭ بِاللّٰهِ ۙ اِنَّهٗ لَمِنَ الصّٰدِقِيْنَ وَ الْخَامِسَةُ اَنَّ لَعْنَتَ اللّٰهِ عَلَيْهِ اِنْ كَانَ مِنَ الْكٰذِبِيْنَ
وَ يَدْرَؤُا عَنْهَا الْعَذَابَ اَنْ تَشْهَدَ اَرْبَعَ شَهٰدٰتٍۭ بِاللّٰهِ ۙ اِنَّهٗ لَمِنَ الْكٰذِبِيْنَ وَ الْخَامِسَةَ اَنَّ غَضَبَ اللّٰهِ عَلَيْهَاۤ
اِنْ كَانَ مِنَ الصّٰدِقِيْنَ

And those who accuse chaste women and bring not four witnesses as evidence [for their accusation] inflict eighty lashes upon them and never accept their testimony in the future. They, indeed, are transgressors. But for those who repent and mend their ways, Allah is Ever-Forgiving and Most-Merciful. And those who accuse their wives but have no witnesses except themselves shall swear four times by Allah that they are telling the truth and the fifth time that the curse of Allah be on them if they are lying. But this shall avert the punishment from the wife if she swears four times by Allah and says that this person is a liar, and the fifth time she says that the curse of Allah be on her if he is telling the truth. (24:4-9)

Explanation of the Verses

• The directives in these verses are explained in the diagram below:

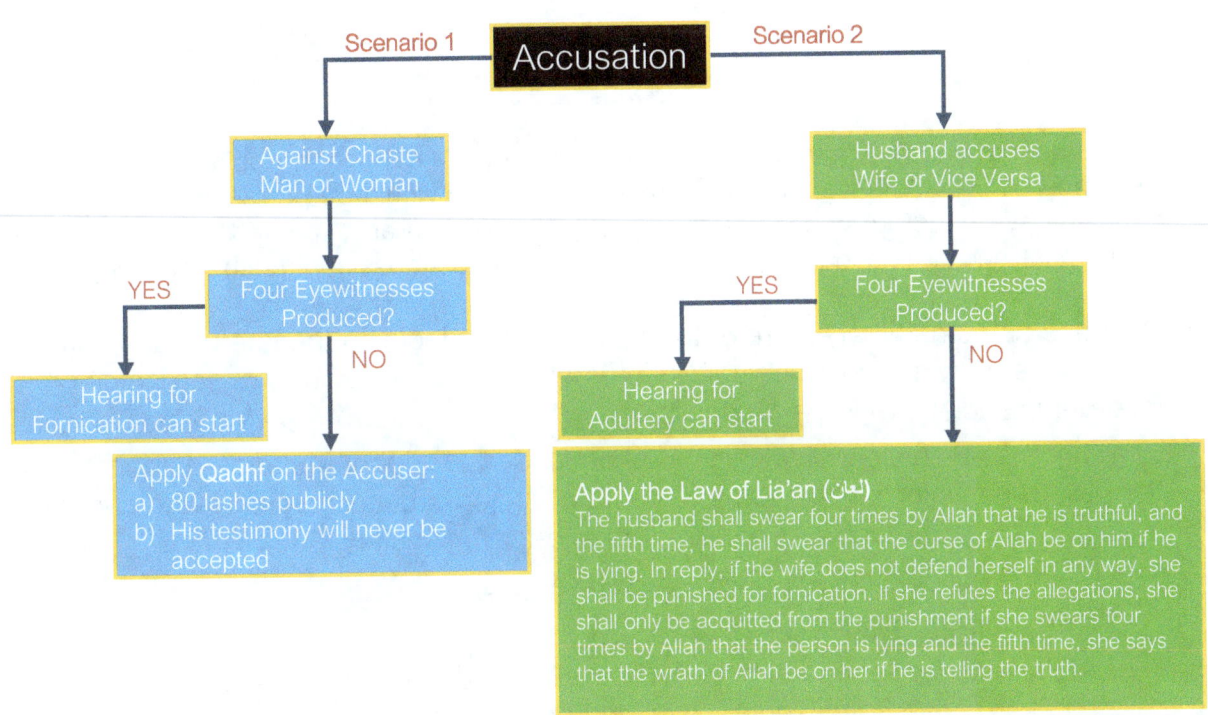

Married vs Unmarried Convicts

The majority of the Islamic Jurists advocate 100 lashes for unmarried convicts and the death penalty for married convicts.

- The Quran does not differentiate between married and unmarried for the punishment of fornication.
- Prophet Muhammad administered the punishment of Muharabah for some of the convicts who were involved in habitual fornication and were presenting a danger to society's moral values.
- Any crime can become a crime of Muharabah if it becomes a clear and present danger to the life, wealth, and honor of people in a society.
- As a judge, Prophet Muhammad, when investigating one such case, inquired, among other things, whether the accused was married to establish that he did not deserve leniency.
- Islamic Jurists erroneously inferred from this inquiry that the marital status of the convict was the basis for administering stoning-to-death (Rajam) (which is the most severe punishment for the crime of Muharabah).
- Consequently, about certain habitual criminals of fornication, the Prophet is reported to have said:

خُذُوا عَنِّي خُذُوا عَنِّي خُذُوا عَنِّي قَدْ جَعَلَ اللّهُ لَهُنَّ سَبِيلًا الْبِكْرُ بِالْبِكْرِ جَلْدُ مائَةٍ وَنَفْيُ سَنَةٍ

وَالثَّيِّبُ بِالثَّيِّبِ جَلْدُ مائَةٍ وَالرَّجْمُ

Acquire it from me, acquire it from me, acquire it from me. The Almighty has revealed a way for these women. In such crimes, unmarried men and women would be punished alike, and their punishment is a hundred stripes and one year of exile. Similarly, married men and women would be punished alike, and their punishment is a hundred stripes and death by stoning.

- Because of the habitual nature of their crime, while deciding the fate of such criminals, he said that they are not merely guilty of fornication but also guilty of spreading disorder in society, which is Muharabah.
- Looking at some historical records, it is evident that Prophet Muhammad combined the punishments for Fornication and Muharabah for habitual criminals who engaged in it as a profession, which was causing moral decay in society.
- Some of the punishments he administered were:
  - 100 lashes plus exile.
  - 100 lashes plus stoning to death (but only the death penalty was administered, as it makes sense from a legal ethics perspective).

E - Theft

- According to linguistic principles, the words Sariq and Sariqah are adjectives and denote thoroughness and completeness in the characteristics of the verb they qualify. Consequently, they can only be used for theft that qualifies as such, and the one who commits it is called a thief (persistence in the act is required for someone to be called a thief).
- Someone stealing some money found on the way, a child stealing a few bucks from his/her father's or mother's wallet, or a hungry man stealing bread from a bakery or plucking fruit from a garden cannot be termed as a thief.
- For this reason, amputating hands is considered the ultimate punishment for the crime when the convict does not deserve any leniency.
- To make the criminal an example in the eyes of others, just as the affinity between the crime and the nature of its punishment requires that his hand be cut, it also requires that his right hand be cut because it is this hand that is actually the instrument of doing things.
- It is also evident that the word "hand," on account of definite linguistic denotation, means that part of the arm that is below the wrist.
- The punishment is not only retribution for the criminal act but also a means of ending many such crimes, as criminals may be deterred by being treated harshly.
- Some new forms of theft prevalent these days should also be considered when deciding punishment for such crimes.

وَ السَّارِقُ وَ السَّارِقَةُ فَاقْطَعُوٓا اَيْدِيَهُمَا جَزَآءً بِمَا كَسَبَا نَكَالًا مِّنَ اللّٰهِ ۗ وَ اللّٰهُ عَزِيزٌ حَكِيمٌ

فَمَنْ تَابَ مِنْ بَعْدِ ظُلْمِهٖ وَ اَصْلَحَ فَاِنَّ اللّٰهَ يَتُوْبُ عَلَيْهِ ۗ اِنَّ اللّٰهَ غَفُوْرٌ رَّحِيمٌ

And as to the thief, male or female, cut off their hands as a reward for their own deeds and as an exemplary punishment from God. For God is Mighty and Wise. But whoever repents and mends his ways after committing this crime shall be pardoned by Allah. Indeed, Allah is Forgiving and Merciful. (5:38-39)

1. Why is there a punishment prescribed by God for the consensual relationship between a man and a woman?
2. In the 21st century, some of these punishments seem pretty violent and may not be acceptable in the societies that we live in. How should we reconcile with the situation?

Quick Recap

- Once a person crosses the line and commits a crime, the only solution is to administer punishment to make a point to others to stay away from such evil.
- The history of societies shows that human beings lack a basis for determining the right punishment for a crime and have always exhibited extreme behavior in this regard.
- God has given guidance on five major crimes committed in a society: Anarchy/disorder, murder/injury, fornication, accusing someone of fornication, and theft.
- The prescribed punishments are extreme and must be administered when the crime is committed in a manner that warrants no leniency.
- For all other crimes not mentioned in the Quran, the state may enact laws to address them. Similarly, in all matters left to societal norms regarding these five crimes, the state may enact laws in accordance with the environment and culture.
- God has prescribed these punishments for a convict as retribution for breaking the pact between him/her and God.
- These punishments are only the payback in this world, and the person should sincerely repent to God for receiving forgiveness from God in the Hereafter.

Chapter 16

Political Shariah

Shariah of Preaching

This chapter discusses the Shariah of preaching the religion to others. We will see that the responsibility is not the same for everyone.

The Shariah of Preaching

Common Misconception

 In Islam, every Muslim is responsible for preaching the religion of Islam to other non-Muslims.

 In Islam, every Muslim is responsible for preaching the religion of Islam to other non-Muslims <u>in their own capacity.</u>

Preaching in Islam

- In Islam, we are asked to make a lifelong effort to urge others to adhere to religion and its teachings.
- For this effort, the terms "dawah" (preaching) and "tabligh" (propagation) are used.
- It is very natural that when we consider something good for us in this world and in the Hereafter, we also want its radiance to reach others.
- Because of its importance in our religion, God has given us a Shariah on preaching, similar to what He has given us in politics, economics, worship, etc.
- However, contrary to the prevalent concept of preaching, God has imposed this responsibility on different people according to their roles in society.

Obligation of Prophets	Obligation of the Rulers	Obligation of the Scholars

Obligation of an Individual	Obligation of Ibrahim's Progeny

- We will discuss all these responsibilities one by one.

Roles and Obligations

Obligation of Prophets

فَبَعَثَ اللهُ النَّبِيّنَ مُبَشِّرِينَ وَ مُنذِرِينَ

Then God sent the Prophets, giving glad tidings and warning (2:213)

يَآأَيُّهَا النَّبِيُّ إِنَّآ أَرْسَلْنٰكَ شَاهِدًا وَّ مُبَشِّرًا وَّ نَذِيرًا
وَّ دَاعِيًا إِلَى اللهِ بِاِذْنِهِ وَ سِرَاجًا مُّنِيرًا

O Prophet! We have sent you forth as a witness, a bearer of good tidings, and a warner and as one who shall call men to God by His leave and as a shining lamp for the guidance [of mankind.] (33:45-46)

- All Prophets of God were sent to:
  - Call people to God.
  - Warn and give glad tidings to them.
- Among them, some were Messengers, and their warnings culminated in Shahadah (Truth is communicated in such clear terms that no excuse remains to deny it).
- The addressees of the Messengers are rewarded or punished in this world, similar to how people will be rewarded/punished on the day of Judgment.
- Before a Messenger reaches that culmination point, he goes through various phases of his preaching mission.

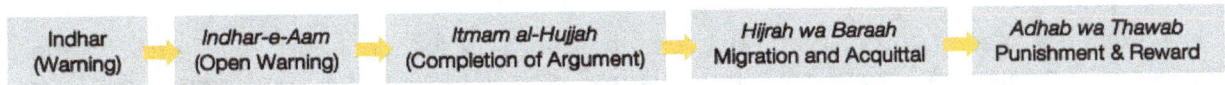

| Indhar (Warning) | Indhar-e-Aam (Open Warning) | Itmam al-Hujjah (Completion of Argument) | Hijrah wa Baraah Migration and Acquittal | Adhab wa Thawab Punishment & Reward |

Phase 1 & 2: *Indhar* and *Indhar-e-Aam*

- In this phase, direct addressees of the Messenger are warned about the punishment of the Hereafter and the punishment in this world.
- People are informed that the Messenger is sent for a specific purpose, and he won't just plead and leave.
- Given the consequences of this warning, people who influence the masses in society are addressed first; if their intellect is convinced of a certain ideology, it becomes a means of convincing their communities and followers.
- For Messenger to attract common people towards him, it is necessary either to convince the influential people (leaders) or intellectually defeat them and uproot their philosophies from their base through sound reasoning, so the common man can break the shackles of their influence.
- In the second phase, God directs the Messenger to deliver an open warning through whatever means he can use and to whatever extent they can.
- This is the toughest phase of preaching for the Messenger, as the reaction is intense.

وَ إِذَا تُتْلَى عَلَيْهِمْ اٰيَاتُنَا بَيِّنٰتٍ ۙ قَالَ الَّذِيْنَ لَا يَرْجُوْنَ لِقَآءَنَا ائْتِ بِقُرْاٰنٍ غَيْرِ هٰذَآ أَوْ بَدِّلْهُ ۚ قُلْ مَا يَكُوْنُ لِيْ أَنْ أُبَدِّلَهُ مِنْ تِلْقَآئِ نَفْسِيْ ۚ اِنْ أَتَّبِعُ إِلَّا مَا يُوْحٰى إِلَيَّ ۚ اِنِّيْ أَخَافُ اِنْ عَصَيْتُ رَبِّيْ عَذَابَ يَوْمٍ عَظِيْمٍ

And when Our clear revelations are recited to them, those who have no hope of meeting Us say [to you]: "Give us a different Quran or change it a little." Tell them: "It is not for me to change it of my own accord. I follow only what is revealed to me, for I fear the punishment of a fateful day if I disobey my Lord." (10:15)

Phase 3: *Itmam al-Hujjah*

- By this phase, the truth becomes so evident to the addressees that they have no excuse except their stubborn refusal to accept it.

- That's why this phase is called the culmination or finality of the arguments.

- In this instance, the Messenger, to a great extent, communicates the fate of the addressees to them if they continue to reject him.

- In Surah Feel and Quraysh, God reminded them of His wrath and His favors upon them, which may soon be withdrawn once the argument phase is over.

اَلَمْ تَرَ كَيْفَ فَعَلَ رَبُّكَ بِاَصْحٰبِ الْفِيْلِ ۚ اَلَمْ يَجْعَلْ كَيْدَهُمْ فِيْ تَضْلِيْلٍ ۙ وَّ اَرْسَلَ عَلَيْهِمْ طَيْرًا اَبَابِيْلَ ۙ تَرْمِيْهِمْ بِحِجَارَةٍ مِّنْ سِجِّيْلٍ ۙ فَجَعَلَهُمْ كَعَصْفٍ مَّأْكُوْلٍ

Have you not seen how your Lord dealt with the people of the elephant? Did He not foil their scheme? And sent down against them swarms of birds? [Such that] you pelted them with stones of baked clay, and He rendered them as straw eaten away. (105:1-5)

لِاِيْلٰفِ قُرَيْشٍ ۙ اٖلٰفِهِمْ رِحْلَةَ الشِّتَآءِ وَ الصَّيْفِ ۚ فَلْيَعْبُدُوْا رَبَّ هٰذَا الْبَيْتِ ۙ الَّذِيْ اَطْعَمَهُمْ مِّنْ جُوْعٍ ۙ وَّ اٰمَنَهُمْ مِّنْ خَوْفٍ

On account of the association of the Quraysh – the association [in the peaceful atmosphere of the Baytullah] they have with the winter and summer travels, they should worship the Lord of this House who [in these barren mountains] fed them in hunger and rendered them secure from fear. (106:1-4)

Phase 4: Hijrah wa Bara'ah

- Once the phase of Itmam al-Hujjah is over, a charge sheet is handed out to the nation's leaders with complete clarity, and they are informed that the time has run out for them.

- On the other hand, the Messenger and his companions are given glad tidings that the time for the promised help is near, and they will be dominant.

- The Messenger and his supporters are asked to cut off all ties with the people whose fate has been decided.

- The Messenger is directed to leave the place with his companions once instructed by God. In this phase, the Messenger cannot exercise his judgment in this regard.
- **Example 1:** When angels came to Prophet Ibrahim to communicate this decision of the Almighty regarding the people of Lot to him, he contended that they had come before their time and argued with the Almighty, as depicted in the Quran (11:74-76)
- **Example 2:** When Prophet Yunus decided to migrate from his people, the Almighty reprimanded him (37:139-148). It became evident from his nation's professing faith once he returned to them that only the Almighty knows when someone can profess faith.
- The Quran cited these examples and cautioned Prophet Muhammad to exercise patience and forbearance as he awaited God's decision.

اِنَّآ اَعْطَيْنٰكَ الْكَوْثَرَ فَصَلِّ لِرَبِّكَ وَ انْحَرْ اِنَّ شَانِئَكَ هُوَ الْاَبْتَرُ

Upon you [O Prophet!] have We bestowed this abundance of good [this House of Ours]. So, pray [now in it] only for your Almighty and offer sacrifice only for Him. Indeed, this enemy of yours is rootless: none of his followers will remain. (108:1-3)

قُلْ يٰٓاَيُّهَا الْكٰفِرُوْنَ لَآ اَعْبُدُ مَا تَعْبُدُوْنَ وَ لَآ اَنْتُمْ عٰبِدُوْنَ مَآ اَعْبُدُ وَ لَآ اَنَا عَابِدٌ مَّا عَبَدْتُّمْ وَ لَآ اَنْتُمْ عٰبِدُوْنَ مَآ اَعْبُدُ

Declare [O Prophet!]: "O Disbelievers! I shall worship not that which you worship. Nor will you ever worship [only] that which I worship. Nor ever before this was I prepared to worship that which you worshipped. Nor were you ever prepared to worship [only] that Whom I have been worshipping. [So now] for you, your religion, and for me, mine." (109:1-6)

اِذَا جَآءَ نَصْرُ اللّٰهِ وَ الْفَتْحُ وَ رَاَيْتَ النَّاسَ يَدْخُلُوْنَ فِيْ دِيْنِ اللّٰهِ اَفْوَاجًا
فَسَبِّحْ بِحَمْدِ رَبِّكَ وَ اسْتَغْفِرْهُ اِنَّهُ كَانَ تَوَّابًا

When the help of God comes and that victory [which We have promised you, O Prophet!], you see men embrace the religion of God in multitudes, exalt His glory while being thankful to Him, and seek His forgiveness. For, indeed, He is ever disposed to mercy. (110:1-3)

Phase 5: Adhab wa Thawab

- In this phase, the divine court of justice is established on earth. Punishment is meted out to the rejecters of the truth, and those who have accepted it are rewarded, and in this way, a Day of Judgement is witnessed on the face of the earth at a smaller scale.
- When God decides the punishment, one of two situations may arise:
  - If the Messenger has only a few companions and there is no place to migrate, then the punishment descends from the Sky through angels.
  - If Messenger's companions are in substantial numbers and there is a place to migrate where their political authority can be established, they subdue their nation by force and punish them.

- In the second situation, while the Messenger and his companions are preparing to punish the nation, the task of communicating the truth continues to the people of the land to which they have migrated.
- At the same time, the Messenger also continues the moral training of his companions to strengthen their faith.
- As a result of this process, the followers and opponents of the Messenger are clearly distinguished from one another to the extent that, as per the established practice of God, each group can be observed distinctly with its complete characteristics.

Categorization of People

A – Opponents

A1 – Antagonists

- They openly and vehemently counter the preaching, viewing it as a direct challenge to their existing system and influence.
- They are motivated by animosity stemming from prejudice and jealousy, and have nationalistic pride.
- They feel that their political & religious authority is endangered and their personal interests are compromised.

A2 – Wait & See Group

- They are the opportunists who understand the veracity of the preaching but want to wait and see which side becomes dominant.
- They sometimes quietly put their weight on the enemies without showing active animosity.
- At times, they may wish good for the Messenger but do not dare to help him actively. They wish to strike a compromise between the two ideologies.

A3 – Ignorant

- Mentally and financially subservient to the prevailing system, they feel safe in following the religious and political pundits of the time.
- They are better than the "wait and see" group in that, when they see their pundits openly challenged and defeated by the weight of the preacher's arguments, they become distrustful of their pundits and start paying attention to the Messenger.
- Slowly, but most of them change over time.

B – Followers

B1 – The Front Runners

- The Quran called them "*As-Sabiqun Al-Awwalun*."
- They take the lead in supporting the Messenger's cause and all that the good society can offer.
- They profess faith in the Messenger in the early days of preaching.
- Possess noble nature, good character, insightful intellect, vibrant heart, and analyze things in the light of sense and reason without prejudice.
- They submit to God and His Messenger with their full heart and are ready to sacrifice anything they have for them.

B2 – The Righteous

- The first group always inspires them to accept the truth and all the goodness it offers.
- Although they do not take the initiative like the first group, once they witness their determination and outstanding behavior, they do not want to fall behind in persevering through difficulties for the cause.
- If others plant doubts in their hearts, the first group's determination allows them to dispel those doubts quickly.
- In the end, they always want to be on the side of the truth.

B3 – Weak & Hypocrites

Weak

- Due to weak will-power, they stumble and recover again and again.
- Every time they stumble, they repent, ask for forgiveness, and continue their journey.
- Their intention is to at least fulfill the minimum requirements and remain on the side of the truth.

Hypocrites

- Hypocrites act like the agents of the enemy in the ranks of the Muslims.
- They plan their association with the Messenger to act as the enemy agent.
- Most Muslims are unaware of their true intent, and God exposed them in the Quran. They are the worst enemies of Islam because they harm it from the inside.
- However, not all hypocrites were alike.

The Punishment

- These groups were punished according to their role, intent, and level of harm to the Muslims.

Antagonists

- They were killed in the battle of Badr.

Wait & See and Ignorant

- Given four months to mend their ways, after which they would be humiliated and disgraced, and would not be able to find a way out in this world, and ultimately would be killed.
- People of the Book were asked to pay Jizyah and live in subjugation to the Muslims. They were further told that if this decision of God and His Prophet Muhammad were not acceptable to them, they would also be killed by the Muslims.

The Reward

The Front Runners and Righteous

- The reins of the political leadership of Arabia and the custodianship of the Baytullah were given to the Muslims who had taken the lead in accepting Islam and ultimately proved righteous.

Hypocrites & Weak

- The Hypocrites were warned that it would be better for them if they repented; otherwise, they would have to encounter the fate destined for the rejecters.
- Those among the followers of the Prophet Muhammad who were sincere but were guilty of some blemishes were forgiven after some punishment, and the weak among these followers were given the glad tidings that if they repented and reformed themselves and remained committed, then hopefully the Almighty would forgive them too

وَعَدَ اللهُ الَّذِيْنَ اٰمَنُوْا مِنْكُمْ وَ عَمِلُوا الصّٰلِحٰتِ لَيَسْتَخْلِفَنَّهُمْ فِى الْأَرْضِ كَمَا اسْتَخْلَفَ الَّذِيْنَ مِنْ قَبْلِهِمْ وَ لَيُمَكِّنَنَّ لَهُمْ دِيْنَهُمُ الَّذِى ارْتَضٰى لَهُمْ وَ لَيُبَدِّلَنَّهُمْ مِّنْ بَعْدِ خَوْفِهِمْ أَمْنًا يَعْبُدُوْنَنِيْ لَا يُشْرِكُوْنَ بِيْ شَيْئًا وَ مَنْ كَفَرَ بَعْدَ ذٰلِكَ فَأُولٰئِكَ هُمُ الْفٰسِقُوْنَ

God has promised those of you who professed belief and did good deeds that He would grant them political authority in the land, the way He granted political authority to those before them, and He would strongly establish the religion He chose for them and replace their fear with peace. They will worship Me and serve none besides Me, and he who again rejects after this will indeed be among the disobedient. (24:55)

Obligation of Ibrahim's Progeny

وَ جَاهِدُوا فِي اللهِ حَقَّ جِهَادِهِ ۚ هُوَ اجْتَبَاكُمْ وَ مَا جَعَلَ عَلَيْكُمْ فِي الدِّينِ مِنْ حَرَجٍ ۚ مِلَّةَ اَبِيكُمْ اِبْرٰهِيمَ ۚ هُوَ سَمّٰكُمُ الْمُسْلِمِينَ ۙ مِنْ قَبْلُ وَ فِي هٰذَا لِيَكُونَ الرَّسُولُ شَهِيدًا عَلَيْكُمْ وَ تَكُونُوا شُهَدَآءَ عَلَى النَّاسِ

And struggle in the path of God in a befitting manner. He has **chosen you** [for this responsibility] and laid on you no burdens in observing your faith. He has chosen for you the way of Abraham, **your father**. He has also named you Muslims earlier, and in this [period of the last Prophet]. [He has chosen you] so that **the Prophet may bear witness against you, and that you may bear witness [to this religion] against other people of this world**. (22:78)

- Just as the Almighty chooses certain great personalities from among the progeny of Adam for Shahadah (bearing witness to the truth), on similar lines, He also chose the progeny of Ibrahim for the responsibility of Shahadah. He directed them to try to fulfill all the requirements of this position.

- After Ibrahim, God also gave the responsibility of 'Messengerhood' to the children of Ishaq (Bani Israel) and Ismail (Bani Ismail) in their collective capacity and ordered them to fulfill this responsibility with or without the Messenger among them.

- Through them, religion would become an established and irrefutable fact before all the world's people to the extent that they are left with no excuse to reject it.

- Because of this special position, they are promised by God that if they adhere to the religion and its teachings, they will be granted prosperity and some dominance over other nations, but if they forsake it, they will struggle and be humiliated in this world at the hands of other nations.

وَ كَذٰلِكَ جَعَلْنٰكُمْ أُمَّةً وَسَطًا لِّتَكُونُوا شُهَدَآءَ عَلَى النَّاسِ وَ يَكُونَ الرَّسُولُ عَلَيْكُمْ شَهِيدًا

And similarly, We have made you a middle community so that you be witnesses [to the truth] before the people, and the Rasul be such a witness before you (2:143)

كُنْتُمْ خَيْرَ أُمَّةٍ أُخْرِجَتْ لِلنَّاسِ تَأْمُرُونَ بِالْمَعْرُوفِ وَ تَنْهَوْنَ عَنِ الْمُنْكَرِ وَ تُؤْمِنُونَ بِاللهِ

You are the noblest community raised up for mankind [to bear witness to the truth before it because] you urge [each other to] good and forbid evil, and you truly believe in God. (3:110)

وَ اَشْرَقَتِ الْاَرْضُ بِنُورِ رَبِّهَا وَ وُضِعَ الْكِتٰبُ وَ جِاْيَءَ بِالنَّبِيّنَ وَ الشُّهَدَآءِ وَ قُضِيَ بَيْنَهُمْ بِالْحَقِّ وَ هُمْ لَا يُظْلَمُونَ

And the earth will shine with the light of her Lord, and the book [in which deeds have been recorded] will be laid open and all the Prophets and all those who were bestowed with the position of Shahadah shall be called in, and all shall be judged with fairness: none shall be wronged. (39:69)

Obligation of the Scholars

وَ مَا كَانَ الْمُؤْمِنُونَ لِيَنْفِرُوا كَافَّةً ۚ فَلَوْ لَا نَفَرَ مِنْ كُلِّ فِرْقَةٍ مِنْهُمْ طَائِفَةٌ لِّيَتَفَقَّهُوا فِى الدِّينِ وَ لِيُنْذِرُوا

قَوْمَهُمْ إِذَا رَجَعُوا إِلَيْهِمْ لَعَلَّهُمْ يَحْذَرُونَ

And it was not possible for all the believers to undertake [this job of deep learning of religion]. So why didn't a few from each of their groups come forward to gain sound knowledge of religion and, after attaining it, return to them and warn the people of their respective nations, so that they might also take heed? (9:122)

This verse outlines the preaching duty for scholars:

- Few Muslims must intend, devote, and develop the capabilities necessary to become scholars of the religion.

- They must gain sound knowledge (deeper) of the religion (Quran, Sunnah, and the examples of Prophet Muhammad) from every aspect, which gives them deeper insight, wisdom, and comprehension necessary to preach to the common masses.

- The responsibility scholars have to discharge is that of Indhar (warning) and only Indhar, which means that people should be warned that one day they would have to give an account of their deeds – similar to what Prophets and Messengers preached.

- The primary audience of a scholar is the nation to which he belongs. Under normal circumstances, they should not go out and preach to other nations. They should focus on their nation regardless of where they are on the planet.

- The objective of the preaching endeavor of the scholars should be to warn people about the displeasure of God.

- With deep concern and empathy, they should continue to warn the people of their nation, as well as those in authority, about their obligations and duties.

- This role of warning their nations must not change if they remain in the position of scholarship. If they want to do something else, for example, politics, they should first leave their position as a scholar and then enter politics.

- That does not mean religiously knowledgeable people cannot enter politics. They can, but their primary role will be that of a politician rather than a scholar of Islam.

Obligation of the Rulers & Individuals

وَلْتَكُنْ مِّنْكُمْ اُمَّةٌ يَّدْعُوْنَ اِلَى الْخَيْرِ وَ يَأْمُرُوْنَ بِالْمَعْرُوْفِ وَ يَنْهَوْنَ عَنِ الْمُنْكَرِ ۖ وَ اُولٰٓئِكَ هُمُ الْمُفْلِحُوْنَ

And there should be some people among you deputed to call towards righteousness, enjoining good, and forbidding evil, and only [those who make this arrangement] shall achieve salvation. (3:104)

اَلَّذِيْنَ اِنْ مَّكَّنّٰهُمْ فِى الْاَرْضِ اَقَامُوا الصَّلٰوةَ وَ اٰتَوُا الزَّكٰوةَ وَ اَمَرُوْا بِالْمَعْرُوْفِ وَ نَهَوْا عَنِ الْمُنْكَرِ ۖ وَ لِلّٰهِ عَاقِبَةُ الْاُمُوْرِ

These [believers] are those who, if We grant them authority in this land, will be diligent in the prayer and pay zakah and enjoin what is virtuous and forbid what is evil. And the end of all deeds is with Allah. (22:41)

- Muslims are addressed here collectively, which refers to their leadership.
- If Muslims are politically dominant on a piece of land, then their rulers should appoint some people from among themselves who should call people towards righteousness, enjoin good, and forbid evil.
- In some cases, the obligation to forbid people from evil shall be discharged by exhorting and urging the Muslims and, in others, through the force of law.
- For exhortation, the Friday sermon is one such opportunity.
- The force of the law should be enforced through the police department (an additional responsibility), which usually protects people from criminal activity.

Obligation of an individual

وَ الْعَصْرِ اِنَّ الْاِنْسَانَ لَفِىْ خُسْرٍ اِلَّا الَّذِيْنَ اٰمَنُوْا وَ عَمِلُوا الصّٰلِحٰتِ وَ تَوَاصَوْا بِالْحَقِّ ۙ وَ تَوَاصَوْا بِالصَّبْرِ

Time bears witness that these people shall definitely be in a state of loss. Yes! Except those who accepted faith, did righteous deeds, exhorted one another to the truth, and exhorted one another to remain steadfast on it. (103:1-3)

وَ الْمُؤْمِنُوْنَ وَ الْمُؤْمِنٰتُ بَعْضُهُمْ اَوْلِيَآءُ بَعْضٍ ۚ يَأْمُرُوْنَ بِالْمَعْرُوْفِ وَ يَنْهَوْنَ عَنِ الْمُنْكَرِ

And believers, both men and women, are friends to one another. They urge one another to do what is good and forbid what is evil. (9:71)

- Muslims are generally directed to urge one another to do good and to advise against evil.
- This is the only responsibility (requirement of faith) that a common Muslim has when it comes to preaching, regardless of his/her residence, ethnicity, financial and social status, education, etc.

- If a believer does righteous deeds and fulfills this faith requirement, the Qur'an has protected him from the punishment of this world and the Hereafter.
- This is mutual counseling in which the preacher and the addressee are at the same level and status.
- A person is counseled and a counselor at the same time.
- When he sees that someone in his close circle has adopted an attitude that is contrary to the truth, he should try to urge him according to his knowledge, capacity, and ability to mend his ways.
- The counseling should start from the nearest circle (whom you have authority over) and go out from there.

يَٰٓأَيُّهَا الَّذِينَ آمَنُوا قُوٓا أَنفُسَكُمْ وَ أَهْلِيكُمْ نَارًا وَّ قُودُبَا النَّاسُ وَ الْحِجَارَةُ عَلَيْهَا مَلَٰٓئِكَةٌ غِلَاظٌ شِدَادٌ لَّا يَعْصُونَ اللهَ مَآ أَمَرَهُمْ وَ يَفْعَلُونَ مَا يُؤْمَرُونَ

Believers! Protect yourselves and your kindred from a Fire fueled with the people and these stones [they worship]. In charge of it will be stern and mighty angels who never disobey God's directive and promptly do what they are told. (66:6)

فَذَكِّرْ ۖ إِنَّمَآ أَنتَ مُذَكِّرٌ ۖ لَّسْتَ عَلَيْهِم بِمُصَيْطِرٍ

(O Prophet) Your duty is only to remind them; you are not a custodian/guardian over them. (88:21-22)

Beware that each of you is a shepherd, and each person will be held accountable for their herd. (Sahih Al-Bukhari #2554)

When any person among you sees an evil [in his circle of authority], he should try to curb it by [the force of] his hands. If he does not have the faith to do it, he should try to curb it by his tongue, and if [even] this is not possible, he should consider it bad in his heart, and this is the lowest level of faith (Sahih Muslim #177)

Strategy of Preaching

اُدْعُ اِلٰى سَبِيْلِ رَبِّكَ بِالْحِكْمَةِ وَ الْمَوْعِظَةِ الْحَسَنَةِ وَ جَادِلْهُمْ بِالَّتِيْ هِيَ اَحْسَنُ ۚ اِنَّ رَبَّكَ هُوَ اَعْلَمُ بِمَنْ ضَلَّ عَنْ سَبِيْلِهٖ وَ هُوَ اَعْلَمُ بِالْمُهْتَدِيْنَ وَ اِنْ عَاقَبْتُمْ فَعَاقِبُوْا بِمِثْلِ مَا عُوْقِبْتُمْ بِهٖ ۚ وَ لَئِنْ صَبَرْتُمْ لَهُوَ خَيْرٌ لِّلصّٰبِرِيْنَ

Call men to the path of your Lord with wisdom and kind exhortation and argue with them in the most befitting manner. Indeed, your Lord best knows those who stray from His path and those who are rightly guided. And if you avenge, let this be commensurate with the wrong that has been inflicted upon you. And if you exercise patience, then this is the best way for the patient. (16:125-126)

- These verses guide the strategy that needs to be adopted for preaching.
- **Wisdom:** Wisdom means that the addressees must be urged through sincere reminders and kindly exhortation, and sound discussion with sound arguments should permeate the tone of this preaching.
- **Responsibility:** The preacher's responsibility is to preach only. The preacher should communicate the truth, elucidate it befittingly, and not show negligence in urging and exhorting people toward it. He should not try to force the truth upon others, nor should he give a verdict about a person's fate in the Hereafter.
- **Reaction:** If the addressee resorts to oppression and inflicting harm on the preacher, the preacher is allowed to avenge it in the same proportion while remaining within moral limits; however, in the eyes of God, a person should bear this oppression without avenging it.

Considerations for preaching

- The message should be presented according to the addressee's intellectual capacity and ability.
- The Prophet taught religion gradually and piecemeal to become deeply rooted in people's hearts and minds and part of their daily actions.
- The addressee's psyche, mental state, and situation must also be considered, just as rain at the wrong time has no effect on the land and sometimes may be detrimental to its yield.
- A preacher should not condemn the beliefs and cherished personalities of his addressees.
- When preaching to leaders or to people who influence the masses, they must be treated with respect.
- Preaching should begin with what is agreed upon and acknowledged to set the stage. Differences should only be discussed gradually once the discussion has already begun.

- A true preacher should always try to present his message in such an effective and natural way (free from any ambiguity) that people who have the slightest potential to understand it can grasp it, and it also becomes evident to those who evade it that they cannot be expected to benefit from it.
- He should present his message in various styles and ways to the extent that his enemies and followers vouch that he has done the utmost in this regard.
- The fervor and enthusiasm displayed by the preacher should be such that his addressees should feel that he is speaking sincerely from his heart.
- A good preacher should adopt all methods of his time and age that are useful and effective for presenting views before people with wisdom and sympathy.

اِنَّكَ لَا تَهْدِىْ مَنْ اَحْبَبْتَ وَ لٰكِنَّ اللهَ يَهْدِىْ مَنْ يَّشَآءُ ۚ وَ هُوَ اَعْلَمُ بِالْمُهْتَدِيْنَ

(O Prophet) You cannot guide whomever you please: it is God who guides [according to His Law] whom He pleases, and He best knows those who are guided. (28:56)

اِنْ تَحْرِصْ عَلٰى هُدٰىهُمْ فَاِنَّ اللهَ لَا يَهْدِىْ مَنْ يُّضِلُّ وَ مَا لَهُمْ مِّنْ نّٰصِرِيْنَ

If you are anxious about their guidance [it should remain clear to you], God does not guide those whom He [according to His law] leads astray, and God does not help such people. (16:37)

فَذَكِّرْ ۫ اِنَّمَآ اَنْتَ مُذَكِّرٌ لَسْتَ عَلَيْهِمْ بِمُصَيْطِرٍ

(O Prophet) Your duty is only to remind them; you are not a custodian/guardian over them. (88:21-22)

فَاِنَّمَا عَلَيْكَ الْبَلٰغُ وَ عَلَيْنَا الْحِسَابُ

So, your responsibility is only to communicate, and it is We who will take their account. (13:40)

وَ مَنْ اَحْسَنُ قَوْلًا مِّمَّنْ دَعَآ اِلَى اللهِ وَ عَمِلَ صَالِحًا وَّ قَالَ اِنَّنِىْ مِنَ الْمُسْلِمِيْنَ

وَ لَا تَسْتَوِى الْحَسَنَةُ وَ لَا السَّيِّئَةُ ؕ اِدْفَعْ بِالَّتِىْ هِىَ اَحْسَنُ فَاِذَا الَّذِىْ بَيْنَكَ وَ بَيْنَهٗ عَدَاوَةٌ كَاَنَّهٗ وَلِىٌّ حَمِيْمٌ

وَ مَا يُلَقّٰىهَآ اِلَّا الَّذِيْنَ صَبَرُوْا ۚ وَ مَا يُلَقّٰىهَآ اِلَّا ذُوْحَظٍّ عَظِيْمٍ

Who is better in calling from the one who calls to Allah and does righteous deeds and says that I have submitted to God. And good and evil are not the same. Repay evil with good, and you will see that he who is your enemy will become your dearest friend. [And remember] none receives this wisdom except those who patiently endure, and none receives it except those who are truly fortunate. (41:33-35)

قُلْ يَآأَهْلَ الْكِتَابِ تَعَالَوْا إِلَى كَلِمَةٍ سَوَاءٍ بَيْنَنَا وَ بَيْنَكُمْ أَلَّا نَعْبُدَ إِلَّا اللّٰهَ وَ لَا نُشْرِكَ بِهِ شَيْئًا وَّ لَا يَتَّخِذَ بَعْضُنَا بَعْضًا أَرْبَابًا مِّنْ دُوْنِ اللّٰهِ ۚ فَإِنْ تَوَلَّوْا فَقُوْلُوا اشْهَدُوْا بِأَنَّا مُسْلِمُوْنَ ۚ يَآأَهْلَ الْكِتَابِ لِمَ تُحَآجُّوْنَ فِيْ إِبْرَاهِيْمَ وَ مَآ أُنْزِلَتِ التَّوْرٰىةُ وَ الْإِنْجِيْلُ إِلَّا مِنْۢ بَعْدِهِ ۚ أَفَلَا تَعْقِلُوْنَ ۗ هَآأَنْتُمْ هٰٓؤُلَآءِ حَاجَجْتُمْ فِيْمَا لَكُمْ بِهِ عِلْمٌ فَلِمَ تُحَآجُّوْنَ فِيْمَا لَيْسَ لَكُمْ بِهِ عِلْمٌ ۚ وَ اللّٰهُ يَعْلَمُ وَ أَنْتُمْ لَا تَعْلَمُوْنَ مَا كَانَ إِبْرَاهِيْمُ يَهُوْدِيًّا وَّ لَا نَصْرَانِيًّا وَّ لٰكِنْ كَانَ حَنِيْفًا مُّسْلِمًا ۗ وَ مَا كَانَ مِنَ الْمُشْرِكِيْنَ

Tell them: "People of the Book, come to what is common among us: that we will worship none but God, that we will associate none with Him, and that none of us shall regard anyone other than God as our Lord." Then, if they turn away, tell them: "Bear witness, then, that we are Muslims." O People of the Book! Why do you argue about Abraham when neither the Torah nor the Gospel was revealed till after him? Don't you think? It is you who has argued about things of which you have some knowledge. Why do you now argue about that of which you have no knowledge at all? [And in reality] God knows, and you know not. Abraham was neither a Jew nor a Christian. He was an upright man, one who submitted to God, and he was not a polytheist. (3:64-67)

Aisha said: The first thing to be revealed in the Quran was a surah from among the *Mufassal,* which mentions Paradise and Hell until when people entered the folds of Islam, then directives regarding prohibition and allowance were revealed and [in reality] if the directive: "Refrain from drinking liquor," had been revealed earlier on, people would have said: "We will never refrain from alcohol," and if the directive: "Do not commit fornication" had been revealed, people would have said: "We will never refrain from fornication." (Sahih Al-Bukhari #4993)

When sending delegations to new tribes, Prophet commanded: You have been sent to create ease, and you have not been sent to create difficulty. (Sahih Al-Bukhari #6128)

Discuss some examples of Surah Asr applying in your life.

Quick Recap

- God has imposed this responsibility on different people according to their societal role.
- The addressees of the Messengers are rewarded or punished in this world, similar to how people will be rewarded/punished on the day of Judgment. This kind of result of preaching is applicable to Messengers only
- Before a Messenger reaches that culmination point, he goes through various phases of his preaching mission guided by God.
- Just as the Almighty chooses certain great personalities from among the progeny of Adam for Shahadah (bearing witness to the truth), on similar lines, He also chose the progeny of Ibrahim for the responsibility of Shahadah and directed them to make an effort to fulfill all the requirements of this position.
- The responsibility scholars have to discharge is that of Indhar and only Indhar, which means that people should be warned about when they will meet their Lord.
- If Muslims are politically dominant on a piece of land, they should depute some people from among themselves who should call people towards righteousness, enjoin good, and forbid evil.
- When an individual Muslim sees that someone in his close circle has adopted an attitude contrary to the truth, he should try to urge him according to his knowledge, capacity, and ability to mend his ways.
- The Quran provides detailed guidance on the strategy the preacher should adopt.

Chapter 17

Food, Customs and Etiquette

Dietary Shariah

In this section, we will learn about food, customs, and etiquette that are made part of Shariah. In this chapter, we will learn about food and drink.

Dietary Shariah

The Principle

وَ يُحِلُّ لَهُمُ الطَّيِّبٰتِ وَ يُحَرِّمُ عَلَيْهِمُ الْخَبٰٓئِثَ وَ يَضَعُ عَنْهُمْ اِصْرَهُمْ وَ الْاَغْلٰلَ الَّتِيْ كَانَتْ عَلَيْهِمْ

And [this Prophet] allows them as lawful what is appropriate for eating and prohibits them from what is inappropriate for eating; he releases them from their heavy burdens and restrictions upon them. (7:157)

- **Reminder:** The objective of Islam is to purify all aspects of human life.
- That aspect of purity is considered even in what we eat and drink.
- The general principle that the Quran has outlined is "all clean/pure food is lawful, and all unclean/impure food is forbidden".
- While inviting the Jews and Christians to profess faith in Prophet Muhammad, the Almighty referred to the extremist attitude they had adopted regarding food and drink. (7:157)
- According to this principle, Shariah has never presented a comprehensive list of what is lawful to eat or drink.
- It is left to human beings and societies, as they generally have ample guidance in this matter from their human nature.
- The Quran provided guidance only on animals about which people may have doubts.

قُلْ لَّاۤ اَجِدُ فِيْ مَاۤ اُوْحِيَ اِلَيَّ مُحَرَّمًا عَلٰى طَاعِمٍ يَّطْعَمُهٗۤ اِلَّاۤ اَنْ يَّكُوْنَ مَيْتَةً اَوْ دَمًا مَّسْفُوْحًا اَوْ لَحْمَ خِنْزِيْرٍ

فَاِنَّهٗ رِجْسٌ اَوْ فِسْقًا اُهِلَّ لِغَيْرِ اللّٰهِ بِهٖ ۚ فَمَنِ اضْطُرَّ غَيْرَ بَاغٍ وَّ لَا عَادٍ فَاِنَّ رَبَّكَ غَفُوْرٌ رَّحِيْمٌ

Say: "I find not in what has been revealed to me through inspiration forbidden to a person who eats things which are edible, unless it be the meat of dead animals, or blood poured forth, or the flesh of swine, because all these are unclean or in disobedience to Allah, animals slaughtered in someone else's name." Then he who is constrained by hunger such that he neither desires to eat nor crosses the limits [incurs no sin]. This is because your Lord is forgiving and merciful. (6:145)

Clarifying a misconception

Q: If human nature guides us related to food, why has Prophet Muhammad explicitly prohibited certain animals from consumption?

When it comes to what humans should eat or drink, the innate guidance found in our nature is enough to lead the way. Several prohibitions attributed to Prophet Muhammad regarding beasts with sharp canine teeth, birds with claws and tentacles on their feet, and tamed donkeys merely delineate this innate guidance. In interpreting this inner guidance, societies will always have minor differences or may become perverted with time. For example, eating a snake may be disgusting in one culture, while in another culture, it is acceptable for some people in that society due to historical reasons.

Prohibitions related to animal meat

حُرِّمَتْ عَلَيْكُمُ الْمَيْتَةُ وَ الدَّمُ وَ لَحْمُ الْخِنْزِيرِ وَ مَآ أُهِلَّ لِغَيْرِ اللهِ بِهِ وَ الْمُنْخَنِقَةُ وَ الْمَوْقُوذَةُ وَ

الْمُتَرَدِّيَةُ وَ النَّطِيحَةُ وَ مَآ أَكَلَ السَّبُعُ إِلَّا مَا ذَكَّيْتُمْ

Forbidden to you [for food] are: meat of dead animals, blood, the flesh of swine, and that on which Allah's Name has not been invoked while slaughtering, and that which has been killed by strangling, or by a violent blow, or by a headlong fall, or by the goring of horns – and that which a wild animal has eaten – unless you can slaughter it [before its death]. (5:3)

- All the animals and related things that are mentioned in this verse are those about which people can have a difference of opinion, and human beings, in general, cannot decide one way or the other.
- For example, the pig is a quadruped beast of the same genus as the goat, sheep, cow, and cattle; however, it consumes meat like other carnivores – this can easily be a doubtful matter.
- With that reason in mind, God gave His verdict in the Quran:
- Whether an animal dies a natural death or is killed by a wild beast, it is considered 'the dead' (*Maytah*), except if it is found alive and then slaughtered in the prescribed way. The word does not apply to a dead sea animal or locust.
- The only method of killing that makes an animal lawful in Islam is *Tadhkiyah*, a Sunnah established by the Prophets of God in which all the animal's blood is drained from the body, and the animal dies because of this reason. The correct methods of *Tadhkiyah* are *Dhibh* (for cows, goats, etc.) and *Nahr* (for camels).
- *Dhibh* means to cut the throat of an animal such that the gullet and the throat are slit open, or to cut the throat and the jugular veins. Nahr means to pierce the animal's throat with a sharp-edged weapon like a spear or knife so that blood bursts out from that wound, and the animal dies because of blood loss. In both cases, the animal should die because of loss of blood.
- The blood drained out is prohibited for eating/drinking, except for what remains with the meat after all the blood has drained out.
- The meat of the pig/swine is also prohibited for eating.
- Also, if the animal is slaughtered properly but by invoking the name of someone other than God, then it is also prohibited.

وَ مَا ذُبِحَ عَلَى النُّصُبِ وَ أَنْ تَسْتَقْسِمُوا بِالْأَزْلَامِ ذٰلِكُمْ فِسْقٌ

And what is slaughtered at the stone altars and [forbidden also] is the division of meat by raffling with arrows. This is [an act of] disobedience. (5:3)

- *Nusub* means the stone altars on which the sacrifices and offerings are made. There were several such altars in Arabia where sacrifices were offered to please numerous deities, demons, and the jinn. These slaughters were also prohibited.
- *Istiqsam* means to look up one's share or to find out about one's fate and future.
- *Azlam* means arrows of divination or gambling. The practice of seeking divination from arrows was in vogue in Arabia, through which people would try to find out fates ordained for them. Similarly, the practice of gambling on arrows was also in vogue in Arabia, through which they would procure pieces of meat or some other thing.
- The Quran condemned all these religious practices and prohibited the meat of animals slaughtered in these places; they called these acts Fisq (defiance and disobedience).

يَسْئَلُوْنَكَ مَاذَآ أُحِلَّ لَهُمْ ۖ قُلْ أُحِلَّ لَكُمُ الطَّيِّبٰتُ ۙ وَ مَا عَلَّمْتُمْ مِّنَ الْجَوَارِحِ مُكَلِّبِيْنَ تُعَلِّمُوْنَهُنَّ مِمَّا عَلَّمَكُمُ اللّٰهُ ۖ فَكُلُوْا مِمَّآ أَمْسَكْنَ عَلَيْكُمْ وَ اذْكُرُوا اسْمَ اللّٰهِ عَلَيْهِ ۖ وَ اتَّقُوا اللّٰهَ ۚ اِنَّ اللّٰهَ سَرِيْعُ الْحِسَابِ

They ask what is lawful to you: "Say all good things are lawful to you as well as [the prey of] the beasts you have taught, training them as Allah has taught you. So, eat of what they catch and hold for you and [before you let loose the beast to catch the prey], pronounce upon it the name of Allah. And fear Allah. Swift is He in taking account." (5:4)

- If a trained animal cuts open a prey, and if such an animal is not found alive, then also it should not be considered dead if the following conditions are met:
- You have said Bismillah before you release the trained animal to catch its prey.
- The animal has not eaten the prey and has kept it for you.

وَ لَا تَأْكُلُوْا مِمَّا لَمْ يُذْكَرِ اسْمُ اللّٰهِ عَلَيْهِ وَ اِنَّهٗ لَفِسْقٌ ۗ وَ اِنَّ الشَّيٰطِيْنَ لَيُوْحُوْنَ اِلٰٓى أَوْلِيٰئِهِمْ لِيُجَادِلُوْكُمْ ۚ وَ اِنْ أَطَعْتُمُوْهُمْ اِنَّكُمْ لَمُشْرِكُوْنَ

And eat not the animal on which Allah's name has not been pronounced [at the time of the slaughtering of the animal], for this is a Fisq. And certainly, the devils do inspire their friends to dispute with you, and [you should know that] if you obey them, then you would indeed be polytheists. (6:121)

- When it comes to taking the name of Allah before slaughtering an animal, the following instructions have been given:
- An animal that is slaughtered in such a way that the name of someone other than Allah is invoked at the time of slaughtering is considered prohibited.

- An animal that is slaughtered in such a way that no name other than Allah is invoked on it, but at the same time, the name of Allah is also not positively invoked while slaughtering, also comes under the category of prohibited meat.
- Any action (especially when taking the life of a living being) that is not initiated in the name of God remains without the blessings of God.
- The sanctity a life possesses requires that even an animal be sacrificed only with the permission of the Almighty, Who is the Creator of life.
- This practice closes the door to polytheism and polytheistic practices.

Slaughter of the People of the Book

اَلْیَوْمَ اُحِلَّ لَکُمُ الطَّیِّبٰتُ ۖ وَ طَعَامُ الَّذِیْنَ اُوْتُوا الْکِتٰبَ حِلٌّ لَّکُمْ ۖ وَ طَعَامُکُمْ حِلٌّ لَّهُمْ

All clean things have this day been made lawful to you, and the food to whom the Book was given is lawful to you and yours to them. (5:5)

- The same prohibition can be extended for slaughter on which, although the name of Allah is taken, the person slaughtering does not believe in God or subscribes to polytheism by associating other deities with God.
- For this reason, the slaughter of the People of the Book is allowed if they take the name of God before slaughtering because they claim to believe in one true God and do not consider their beliefs polytheistic.
- A general principle from this instruction can be understood that if food is cooked or an animal is sacrificed or slaughtered for any other deity but Allah, then it is prohibited for Muslims to eat.

Compelling circumstances

فَمَنِ اضْطُرَّ فِیْ مَخْمَصَةٍ غَیْرَ مُتَجَانِفٍ لِّاِثْمٍ ۙ فَاِنَّ اللہَ غَفُوْرٌ رَّحِیْمٌ

Then he who is constrained by hunger to eat what is forbidden, without showing an inclination to sin, will find Allah Forgiving and Merciful. (5:3)

- Only in the situation of life and death (due to hunger), is one allowed to eat the prohibited meat/food with the condition that the person does not have the intention to cross the boundary set by God.
- All of the items listed above are prohibited as edibles. As for their other uses, they are totally allowed. No believer should have any doubt in this regard, as explained in a hadith as well.

A goat was given in charity to Maymunah's maid. The goat died. [It so happened that] the Prophet (sws) passed by. [Seeing the dead goat], he said: Would that you had taken its hide, tanned it, and then made use of it." People said, "It is a dead animal." The Prophet declared, "Only eating it is forbidden." (Sahih Muslim #806)

The dead of ocean and rivers

- Unlike land animals, there is no specific method for slaughtering catch from the ocean and rivers. They are allowed and can be eaten after the catch. However, it is recommended to say Bismillah when throwing the net.

Its water is pure, and its dead (*Maytah*) is not forbidden. (Sunan Nisai #59)

Other situations

'Adi ibn Hatim says: "O Messenger of Allah! Is it okay to slaughter a prey with a stone or a piece of wood if the prey is at hand and we do not have a knife to slaughter it?" He replied: "Drain out the blood with whatever you have and take the name of Allah on it. (Sunan Abu Daud # 2824)

When you release your dog to catch the prey, take the name of Allah while doing so. If you then see that it has not killed the prey, slaughter it in the prescribed way and take Allah's name while slaughtering it. If it has killed the prey but hasn't taken a bite, you can eat it, since it has preserved it for you. However, if it has eaten from the prey, then such a prey is forbidden for you because the beast of prey has, in this case, preserved it for itself. And if you see other dogs besides yours who have also killed the prey, then do not eat from it, since you do not know which of the dogs has actually killed the prey. (Sunan Nisai #4268)

Prohibition of Alcohol

يَا أَيُّهَا الَّذِينَ آمَنُوا إِنَّمَا الْخَمْرُ وَ الْمَيْسِرُ وَ الْأَنْصَابُ وَ الْأَزْلَامُ رِجْسٌ مِّنْ عَمَلِ الشَّيْطٰنِ فَاجْتَنِبُوهُ لَعَلَّكُمْ تُفْلِحُونَ

Believers! This liquor and gambling and stone altars and these divining arrows are abominations devised by Satan. Avoid them so that you may succeed. (5:90)

- The prohibition of alcohol has also been established in earlier scriptures and has remained so since Adam.
- Any food/drink or other forms of drugs that take away a person's faculty of thinking and intellect, even for a short duration, is prohibited in Islam.
- The terms used by the Quran are quite intense in this regard (abominations devised by Satan) and confirm that it is prohibited in Islamic Shariah.

- The general principle that the Quran has outlined is "all clean/pure food is lawful, and all unclean/impure food is forbidden".
- It is left to human beings and societies, as generally they have ample guidance in this matter from their nature.
- All animals and related things that are mentioned in various verses of the Quran are those about which people can have a difference of opinion, and human beings in general cannot decide one way or the other.
- Following meat/food are specifically prohibited by Islam in the Shariah:
  - A dead animal of the land that could not be slaughtered in the prescribed manner before its death.
  - Flowing blood.
  - Meat of the pig/swine.
  - Meat/food on which the name of any deity other than Allah has been invoked.
  - Meat on which the name of Allah has deliberately not been pronounced at the time of slaughter.
  - Alcohol and similar food/drink/drug that takes away the faculty of thinking and intellect.

- How come some Muslims do eat the meat here in the USA, although it has not been slaughtered as per the prescribed method of Shariah?
- The Quran never used the word prohibited for alcohol, so why is it considered prohibited?

Chapter 18

Food, Customs and Etiquette

Islamic Customs and Etiquette

In this chapter, we will learn about Islamic customs and etiquette that are part of Shariah.

Islamic customs and etiquette

Introduction

Culture   vs   Religion

- Various manifestations of regular, patterned behavior, conduct, and manners within a group of people are called customs and traditions.
- Every human civilization has its own customs and traditions, with no exception.
- Every culture is distinguished from others by its customs.
- Most customs have a long history, and people do not even know when they started.
- The religion revealed to the prophets of Allah directed their respective believers to follow certain customs and etiquette as part of religious guidance and identity.
- The purpose is to remember Allah and purify souls through worship, mutual love, and respect.
- Before Prophet Muhammad, these customs existed in Arabia as practices of the Abrahamic religion, and Prophet Muhammad, except for a few things, made no addition to them (he corrected some of them).
- These customs have been transmitted to us through consensus and the perpetual adherence of the companions of the Prophet and the generations after them.

> Religious customs should not be confused with local/cultural customs.

Eating and Drinking

Eat while taking the name of God and use the right hand. (Sahih Bukhari #5376)

When anyone among you eats, he should eat with the right hand, and when he drinks, he should drink with the right hand. (Sahih Muslim #5265)

- Saying 'Bismillah' before eating or drinking anything – Muslims remember Allah SWT all the time, especially when a blessing is given, and food is the best blessing one can have.
- Eat with your RIGHT hand – Muslims are reminded that on the day of Judgment, people who received good grades will be given their results in their right hand (As'hab-ul-Yameen).
- It is also considered a custom among Muslims to thank Allah SWT after finishing food or drink – Muslims remind themselves that it's only Allah SWT who bestowed these countless blessings on us, and it is our moral obligation to thank Him.

Left-handed people are encouraged to try to develop the habit of eating with their right hand.

Greetings

السلام عليكم ورحمة الله وبركاته وعليكم السلام رحمة الله وبركاته

Peace, Mercy and Blessings of Allah be upon you

The young shall say salam to the old, the one who is walking shall say it to the sitting, and a small group shall say it to a large one. (Hadith)

- When Muslims meet each other (men, women), they say a prayer of peace and well-being for one another in this world and in the Hereafter by saying:

  Assalam O Alaikum Wa Rehmatullah Wa Barakatahu

  Wa Alaikum Assalam Wa Rehmatullah Wa Barakatahu
- Saying the first part is necessary, the rest is recommended.
- The guidance for this greeting is found in the Sunnah and is also mentioned in the Quran.
- Other acts are part of different cultures, like shaking hands, hugging, touching cheeks, etc.

Utterances after sneezing

يهديكم الله ويصلح بالكم يرحمك الله الحمدلله

May Allah guide you and keep your affairs well. May Allah have mercy on you All praises are due to Allah

When any one of you sneezes, he should say "AlhamduLillah," and if his brother or companion hears these words, he should reply by saying "Yarhamukallah". And when he says this, you should say: "May Allah guide you and keep you well." (Sahih Al-Bukhari #6224)

- Sneezing relieves a person from an internal disorder.
- The person who sneezes is required to say *Alhamdulillah*, and the person who hears him/her should say *Yarhamukallah*.
- Since an internal disorder has been restored, we are asked to praise God and be grateful to Him for it.
- The person hearing this is praying for the person sneezing.
- The guidance is given through the Sunnah and is among the oldest traditions, dating back to the time of Adam.
- The existence of the word *Tashmit* for this utterance is evidence that this was already known to the people of Quraish and even the People of the Book.

Circumcision

Five things are from among [the norms of] human nature: circumcision, shaving the pubes, clipping the mustache, paring fingernails, and removing hair under the armpits. (Sahih Bukhari #5891)

- Circumcising a male child is aimed at physical cleanliness and hygiene, and Arabs used to practice it even before the time of Prophet Muhammad.
- The source of this practice lies in our nature, and the Prophets of God have always made it part of religious practice, since religion is given to attain purity. Although we received it through the Abrahamic tradition, it predates that.
- There may be medical benefits to doing so, but Muslims are asked to do so purely for religious purposes to gain the required purification in our bodies.
- It is recommended to be done right after the birth, when doing such a small medical procedure is much easier than later.

Cutting/Cleaning Hair & Fingernails

Five things are from among [the norms of] human nature: circumcision, shaving the pubes, clipping the moustache, paring fingernails, and removing hair under the armpits. (Sahih Bukhari #5891)

The time before which we must trim our moustache, pare our fingernails, shave pubic hair, and remove hair from under the armpits has been fixed as forty days. (Sahih Muslim # 599)

- All these practices also aim at physical cleanliness and hygiene, and Arabs practiced them even before the time of Prophet Muhammad.
- The source of these practices lies in our nature, and the Prophets of God have always made them part of religious practice, since religion is meant to attain purity. Although we received it through the Abrahamic tradition, it predates that.
- Large/hanging mustaches especially give the impression of arrogance and conceit in a person, and contaminate food and drinks when eating.
- Trimming mustaches is important for physical cleanliness and for keeping the heart free of any traces of arrogance.
- Regularly trimming fingernails applies to both men and women. There is no exception for women in this regard. They can always be colored or polished.
- When it comes to hairstyles, there are no recommendations, but they must be combed and kept properly.

Cleaning nostrils, mouth, teeth & after relieving

> Had it not been for the fact that this would burden my ummah, I would have directed them to clean their teeth before every prayer. (Sahih Bukhari #887)

> When the Prophet would go out to relieve himself, I would bring some water in a utensil or a water container. He would clean himself in this water, then rub his hands in the mud to clean them. (Sunan Abu Daud #45)

- Islam's love for cleanliness that it wants to inculcate in a Muslim can be seen from these instructions, which the Prophets of God have made part of religion.
- Historically, these practices are referred to as Sha'air (religious symbols) in Arabia.
- The same instructions are part of Wudu (ablution) also.
- Cleaning the relevant body parts carefully after defecation and urination is also part of the Abrahamic sunnah.
- If water is available, it is the preferred method for cleaning; otherwise, mud or other materials like toilet paper can be used to serve the purpose.

Ceremonial bath after cycles (women)

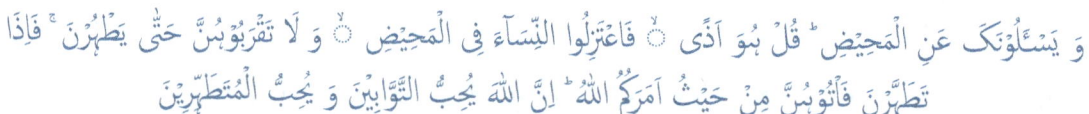

They ask you about women's periods. Tell them: "They are an impurity. So, please keep away from women in their courses and do not approach them until they have cleansed themselves from blood. But when they have purified themselves after taking a bath, approach them as the Almighty has directed you [in your instincts]. Indeed, Allah loves those who constantly repent and keep themselves clean." (2:222)

- For women, when the bleeding ceases in both situations (after the menstrual cycle or puerperal discharge after birth), they must take a bath to enter the state of purity.
- The Quran uses *Tuhur* and *Tatahhurr* to denote complete purity: the former means "the discontinuation of bleeding," and the latter implies "women entering into the state of purity by taking the ceremonial bath." God's intention is that the wife should engage in any sexual activity with her husband after the second purity, even though the real reason for the prohibition of sexual relationships is the flow of blood.

Ceremonial bath after sex (men and women)

يَآ أَيُّهَا الَّذِيْنَ اٰمَنُوْا لَا تَقْرَبُوا الصَّلٰوةَ وَ اَنْتُمْ سُكْرٰى حَتّٰى تَعْلَمُوْا مَا تَقُوْلُوْنَ وَ لَا جُنُبًا اِلَّا عَابِرِىْ سَبِيْلٍ حَتّٰى تَغْتَسِلُوْا

Believers! Approach not the place of the prayer when you are in a drunken state until you can understand what you say, nor when you are in a state of sexual impurity (*Janabah*) till you have taken a bath, except if you only intend to pass through the prayer place. (4:43)

- Again, in the Abrahamic tradition, one must take a ceremonial bath to be out of the state of *Janabah*. (ejaculation).
- Janabah meant the state of impurity that one enters after copulation or after ejaculation, whether copulation has taken place or not.
- How this bath should be taken is transmitted through the practices of the Prophet Muhammad:

  1. Wash your hands and then thoroughly clean the genital area with your left hand.
  2. Make complete Wudu except for the feet.
  3. Soak hair with water by inserting fingers into the roots, or wash hair completely.
  4. For women, it is not necessary to untie their braids, and they can use their fingers to lightly soak the roots.
  5. Pour water over the entire body, then wash the feet.

Aishah reports that when the Prophet would have the ceremonial bath after Janabah, he would first wash both hands. Then, he would clean his genital area with the left hand after pouring water on it with the right one. Then he would do wudu the same way as wudu is done for the prayer. He would then take some water and insert his fingers in his hair until he would pour three handfuls of water on his head when he saw that the water had reached the skin. Then, he would drench his body with water and then wash both feet. (Sahih Muslim #718)

Funeral

A. Bathing the dead body

Bathe this dead body with water and berry leaves three times or five times, or even more if required, and add camphor or [he said] some camphor to the water with which you bathe it. (Sahih Bukhari #1258)

Bathe this dead body an odd number of times: three, five, or seven times, and begin with its right side and from the limbs by which wudu is done. (Sahih Bukhari #1254)

- Bathing a dead body is the first step in the funeral process and is among the practices of the Prophets.
- Just pouring water all over the body should be sufficient, but the spirit of the directive is to clean the dead body with diligence and thoroughness.

B. Enshrouding the dead body

Any one among you who enshrouds your dead brother in a coffin cloth should do it befittingly. (Sahih Muslim #2185)

- Enshrouding the body in coffin cloth is the next step.
- Any single piece of cloth can be used, but it is more befitting to use a new cloth to cover the entire body properly.
- Prophet Muhammad was wrapped in three Yemeni cotton sheets.

C. Burial

- After praying *Janazah* (For more details on *Janazah* prayers, see the chapter on prayers) for the dead, the sunnah of the Prophet of God is to bury the dead in a grave as the final resting place.
- There is no specific procedure for burying the dead, as long as it is properly covered in a suitable ditch.
- The Prophet, however, did not approve of making any building or concrete structure on a grave.
- It is also recommended to make dua for the deceased after the burial.

Eid Al-Fitr and Eid Al-Adha

When the Prophet arrived in Madinah, he found people celebrating two specific days, during which they engaged in play and merriment. He asked them about the nature of these festivities, to which they replied that they were occasions of fun and recreation of the days of *Jahiliyyah*. At this, the Prophet remarked that the Almighty has fixed two days [of festivity] instead of these for you, which are better than these: Eid al-Fitr and Eid al-Adha. (Masnad Ahmad #13210)

- It is evident from the study of the Sunnah that both of these festivals originated with the Prophet Muhammad, as instructed by God.
- Before the time of Prophet Muhammad, there were other days celebrated by both idolaters and the People of the Book, but these two Eids were not among them.
- The two festivals celebrate the two greatest acts of obedience and piety.

Eid Al-Fitr

- Eid al-Fitr is celebrated after Ramadan.
- Zakat al-Fitr must be paid before the Eid prayer on behalf of everyone in the household, including the unborn child in the mother's womb.
- Muslims say *takbiraat* before the Eid prayer.
- Special prayers (2 units) are performed with additional *Takbiraat*. There is no specific number for additional *Takbiraat*. The general practice is to say 6 or 12 additional *Takbiraat*.
- Two short sermons are delivered after the prayer.

Eid Al-Adha

- It commemorates the sacrifice offered by Prophet Ibrahim and coincides with Hajj (10th of Dhul Hijjah).
- Special prayers (2 units) are performed with additional *Takbiraat*. There is no specific number for additional *Takbiraat*. The general practice is to say 6 or 12 additional *Takbiraat*.
- People perform animal sacrifice after the prayers. This is an optional but highly recommended and praised act.
- Muslims call *Takbiraat* after every prayer in the days of *Tashriq (11th, 12th, and 13th of Dhul Hijjah)*.

Chapter 19

Oaths and their Atonement

In this chapter, we will learn about the importance of oaths in Islam and what to do if one is broken.

Oaths and their atonement

Introduction

- Pledging oaths carries great significance in Islam. Keeping one's word is a fundamental part of Islamic ethics.
- When a Muslim swears by the Almighty on an intention or a plan that he wishes to carry out, it is as if he has called the Creator of the heavens and the earth to be a witness over his word.
- In many societies, oaths have long been an important aspect of contracts (written or unwritten) and are usually the main reason for their stability in various social, political, and cultural affairs.
- For this reason, the children of Israel were warned that they must not break their oath with God – something over which they have made the Almighty a witness (verse above).
- Often, it becomes impossible for a person to honor his oath, or he may feel that fulfilling it could infringe on someone's rights, including God's. For the latter, breaking an oath becomes a moral necessity.
- To address such a situation and uphold the importance of oaths, an atonement (*Kaffarah*) has been prescribed when someone breaks a mindful oath for any reason.

وَ اَوْفُوْا بِعَهْدِ اللّٰهِ اِذَا عٰهَدْتُّمْ وَ لَا تَنْقُضُوا الْاَيْمَانَ بَعْدَ تَوْكِيْدِهَا وَ قَدْ جَعَلْتُمُ اللّٰهَ عَلَيْكُمْ كَفِيْلًا ۚ اِنَّ اللّٰهَ يَعْلَمُ مَا تَفْعَلُوْنَ

Fulfill the covenant of Allah when you have entered into it and break not your oaths after you have confirmed them: Indeed, you have made Allah your witness over yourselves. Indeed, Allah knows all that you do. (16:91)

The Shariah

لَا يُؤَاخِذُكُمُ اللّٰهُ بِاللَّغْوِ فِيْ اَيْمَانِكُمْ وَ لٰكِنْ يُّؤَاخِذُكُمْ بِمَا عَقَّدْتُّمُ الْاَيْمَانَ ۚ فَكَفَّارَتُهٗٓ اِطْعَامُ عَشَرَةِ مَسٰكِيْنَ مِنْ اَوْسَطِ مَا تُطْعِمُوْنَ اَهْلِيْكُمْ اَوْ كِسْوَتُهُمْ اَوْ تَحْرِيْرُ رَقَبَةٍ ۚ فَمَنْ لَّمْ يَجِدْ فَصِيَامُ ثَلٰثَةِ اَيَّامٍ ۚ ذٰلِكَ كَفَّارَةُ اَيْمَانِكُمْ اِذَا حَلَفْتُمْ ۚ وَ احْفَظُوْٓا اَيْمَانَكُمْ ۚ كَذٰلِكَ يُبَيِّنُ اللّٰهُ لَكُمْ اٰيٰتِهٖ لَعَلَّكُمْ تَشْكُرُوْنَ

Allah will not hold you accountable for your involuntary oaths, but He will definitely hold you accountable for oaths you swear with solemn intention. So, if such an oath is broken, its atonement is the feeding of ten needy persons of a standard with which you normally feed your own families, or the clothing of ten needy people, or the liberation of one slave. But whosoever cannot afford these should fast for three days. This is the atonement for the oaths when you have sworn. And be true to that which you have sworn. Thus, Allah explains to you His verses that you may be grateful. (5:89)

- God will not hold people accountable for the fulfillment of oaths that are absurd, nonsensical, and meaningless, neither in this world nor in the Hereafter.
- If an oath is pledged with a solemn intent or if some contract has been made on its basis, or it has an effect on the rights and obligations of the parties involved, or it infringes upon the injunctions of the Shariah, the Almighty would hold a person responsible for it.
- If, for some reason, a person is forced to break such an oath, then he must atone for it.
- For this, he is required to feed ten poor people with the standard of food he normally feeds his own family, or give them clothes to wear, or to liberate a slave.
- If he is unable to do either of these, he must fast for three days.

The atonement of a *Nadhr* is the same as that of an oath. (Sahih Muslim #4253)

Note: *Nadhr* is a form of an oath

If you pledge an oath for something and a better alternative comes your way, break the oath and atone for it and do what is better. (Sahih Bukhari #6622)

He who swore by anyone other than Allah has committed an act of polytheism. (Sunan Abu Daud #3251)

Why is taking oaths other than God considered a polytheistic act?

Chapter 20

Course Summary

This chapter summarizes the course that we have covered in this level.
This is an important summary to remember.

Course Summary

1 - The Sources of Islam

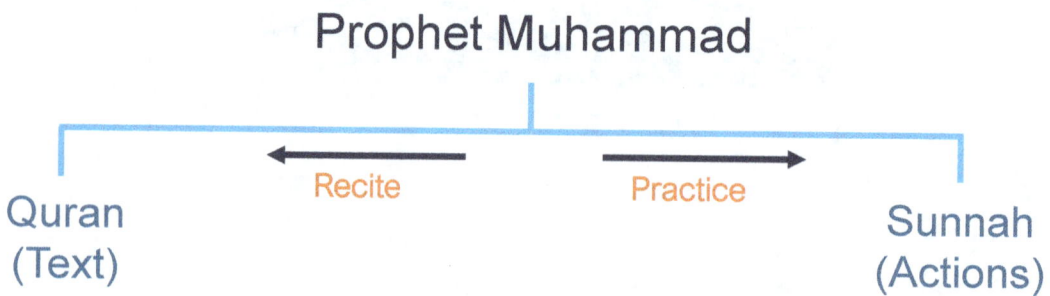

Prophet Muhammad

Quran (Text) ← Recite — Practice → Sunnah (Actions)

Hadith does not add anything to the corpus of Islam and only explains and demonstrates what's already given in the Quran and Sunnah.

2 - Content of Islam

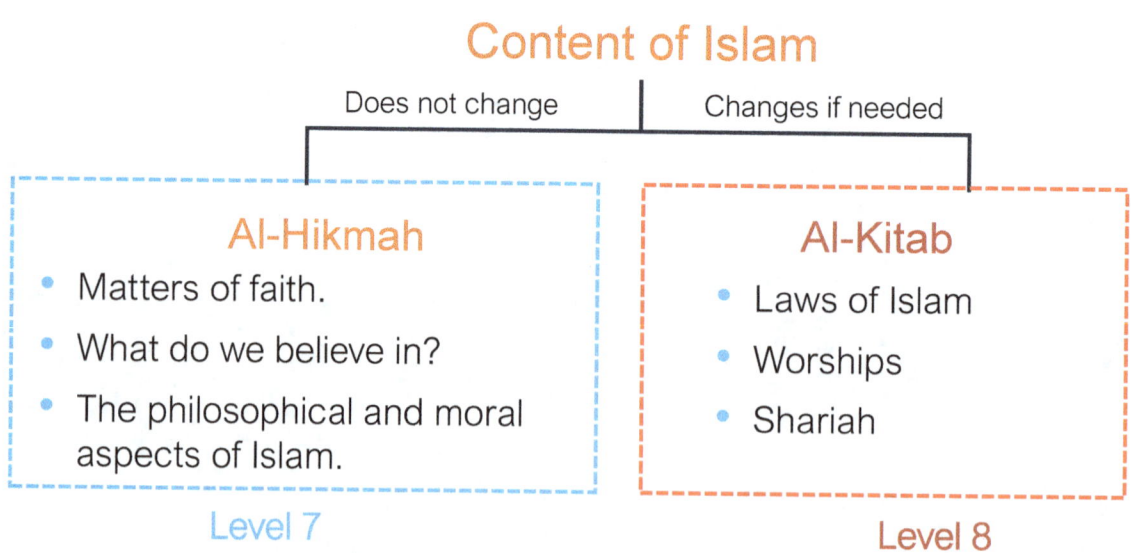

Content of Islam

Does not change — Changes if needed

Al-Hikmah
- Matters of faith.
- What do we believe in?
- The philosophical and moral aspects of Islam.

Level 7

Al-Kitab
- Laws of Islam
- Worships
- Shariah

Level 8

3 – Shariah is a contract with God

We have an unwritten contract with our Creator, and Shariah is given to regulate that contract.

4 – Why is Shariah given?

Allah has given us guiding principles on matters that human beings cannot decide on their own.

5 – The Temperament of Shariah

The principle of relaxation in worship is inconvenience, and in prohibitions is compulsion.

6 – Fiqh and Ijtihad

Fiqh and Ijtihad are human interpretations of and applications of Shariah in real-life situations when details are missing.

7 – The nature of worship and human interactions

In worship, everything is prohibited unless specifically told. In dealings, everything is allowed unless told otherwise.

8 – Prophet Muhammad did not bring a new religion

Prophet Muhammad did not bring a new religion. He simply continued, renewed, and upheld the traditions of Prophet Ibrahim.

9 – Purification, purification, purification .....

Purification is the target of every instruction of Islam.

10 – Parts of Salah

Salah has two parts:
1. Fixed – do as taught
2. Elective – what you prefer from available options

11 – Zakah is a tax prescribed by Allah

Allah has prescribed state taxes (Zakah) as follows:
1. 2.5% on wealth
2. 5, 10, or 20% on production
3. Some portion of cattle

12 – Family is the focus of all social Shariah

In Social Shariah, the family unit is the focus of all instructions. Allah wants to protect the family institution for the children's welfare.

13 – Islam has zero tolerance for Zina

The protection of the family requires zero tolerance for any illicit relationship.

14 – DO NOT go near Zina

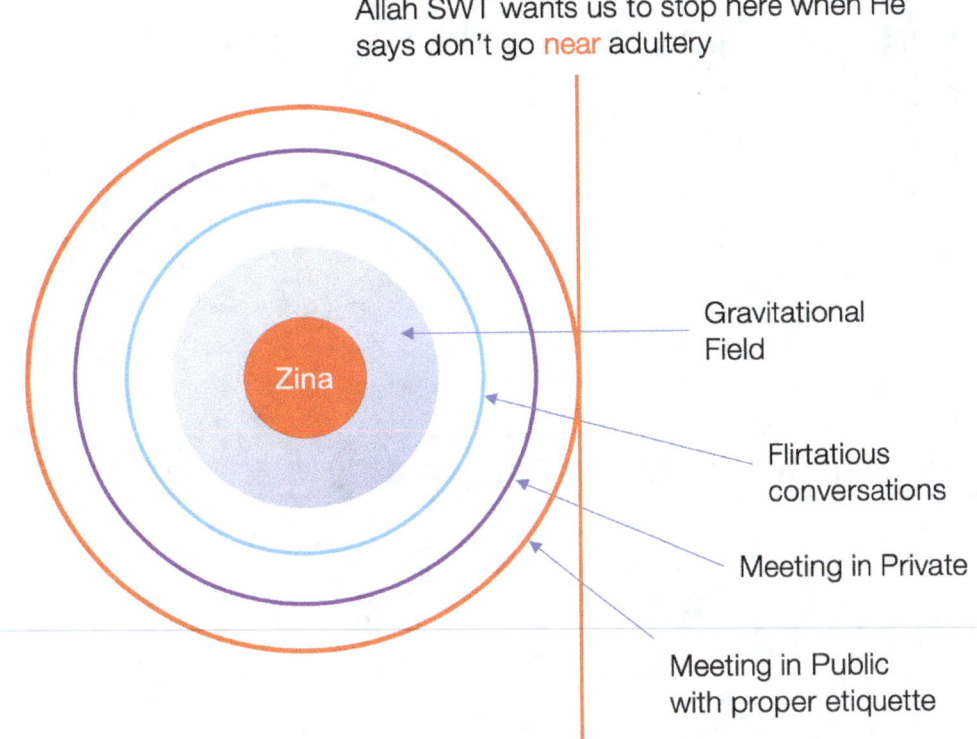

Allah SWT wants us to stop here when He says don't go near adultery

Zina

Gravitational Field

Flirtatious conversations

Meeting in Private

Meeting in Public with proper etiquette

15 – The etiquette of gender interaction

The etiquette of gender interaction is mentioned in Surah Nur Verses 27-31.

16 – Nikah is an OPEN declaration

Nikah (Marriage) is an open declaration of a contract (in writing is preferable) between a man and a woman to live together permanently as husband and wife.

17 – ONE divorce at a time is the Quran's instruction

One divorce at a time, as per the prescribed method by the Shariah.

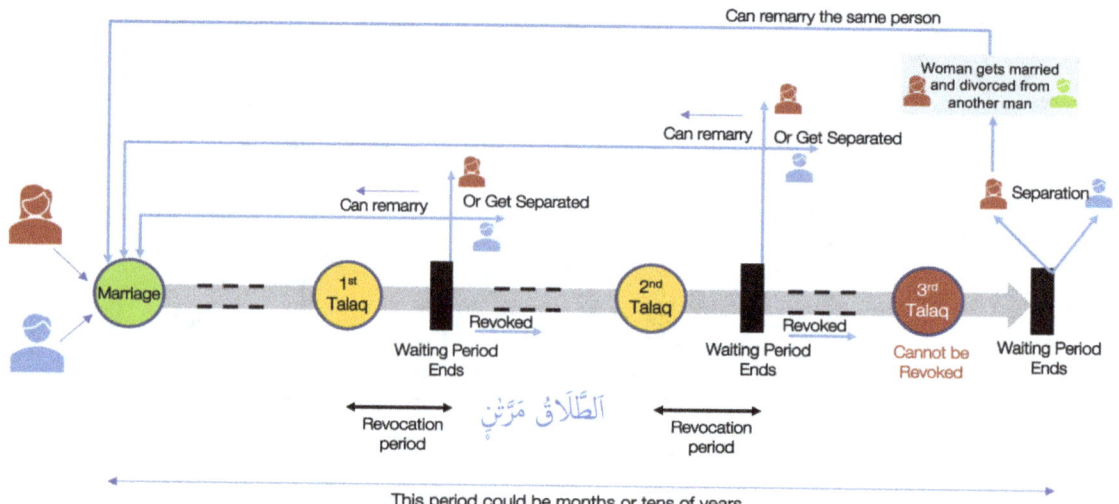

18 – The rights of parents are next to Allah

The rights of parents are next to worship Allah alone. Kindness is required when dealing with them.

19 – Islam does <u>not</u> give any system

Islam has no political system. It allows people to adopt any system based on the principle of mutual consultation. Islam only provides moral guidance for any system.

20 – Jihad can be done only against injustice

Jihad is now <u>only</u> allowed in Islam against injustice and oppression if all the other conditions of Jihad are met by the ruler of Muslims.

21 – Only a government can start Jihad

Jihad is a responsibility given to the state or government. No group or individual can wage Jihad.

22 – Islamic punishments are limited

Allah has prescribed punishments for the following:
1. Anarchy and disorder
2. Murder and Injury
3. Theft
4. Fornication/Adultery
5. Accusation of adultery

23 – Death penalty is very restricted

The death penalty cannot be given for any other crime except for the following:
1. Anarchy and disorder
2. Murder

24 – Preaching responsibility is by capacity

In Islam, every Muslim is responsible for preaching Islam and/or counseling others in their capacity.

25 – Dietary instructions

All pure food that humans eat is allowed. Only 4 items are prohibited in Shariah:
1. Dead Animal
2. Flowing blood
3. Swine/pork
4. Slaughtered in the name of other than Allah

26 – Religious vs Local customs

Religious customs and Sunnah must not be confused with local culture and customs.

Remember,

The Shariah of Islam is to moderate our lives according to the Will of Allah for us to earn the reward of Paradise forever.
It does <u>not</u> benefit Allah.